T0236556

Lecture Notes in Computer Science 13444

Founding Editors

Gerhard Goos
  Karlsruhe Institute of Technology, Karlsruhe, Germany

Juris Hartmanis
  Cornell University, Ithaca, NY, USA

Editorial Board Members

Elisa Bertino
  Purdue University, West Lafayette, IN, USA

Wen Gao
  Peking University, Beijing, China

Bernhard Steffen
  TU Dortmund University, Dortmund, Germany

Moti Yung
  Columbia University, New York, NY, USA

More information about this series at https://link.springer.com/bookseries/558

Ilias Gerostathopoulos · Grace Lewis ·
Thais Batista · Tomáš Bureš (Eds.)

Software Architecture

16th European Conference, ECSA 2022
Prague, Czech Republic, September 19–23, 2022
Proceedings

Springer

Editors
Ilias Gerostathopoulos (iD)
Vrije Universiteit Amsterdam
Amsterdam, The Netherlands

Thais Batista (iD)
Universidade Federal do Rio Grande do Norte
Natal, Rio Grande do Norte, Brazil

Grace Lewis (iD)
Carnegie Mellon Software Engineering
Institute
Pittsburgh, PA, USA

Tomáš Bureš (iD)
Charles University
Prague, Czech Republic

ISSN 0302-9743 ISSN 1611-3349 (electronic)
Lecture Notes in Computer Science
ISBN 978-3-031-16696-9 ISBN 978-3-031-16697-6 (eBook)
https://doi.org/10.1007/978-3-031-16697-6

© The Editor(s) (if applicable) and The Author(s), under exclusive license
to Springer Nature Switzerland AG 2022
This work is subject to copyright. All rights are reserved by the Publisher, whether the whole or part of the
material is concerned, specifically the rights of translation, reprinting, reuse of illustrations, recitation,
broadcasting, reproduction on microfilms or in any other physical way, and transmission or information
storage and retrieval, electronic adaptation, computer software, or by similar or dissimilar methodology now
known or hereafter developed.
The use of general descriptive names, registered names, trademarks, service marks, etc. in this publication
does not imply, even in the absence of a specific statement, that such names are exempt from the relevant
protective laws and regulations and therefore free for general use.
The publisher, the authors, and the editors are safe to assume that the advice and information in this book are
believed to be true and accurate at the date of publication. Neither the publisher nor the authors or the editors
give a warranty, expressed or implied, with respect to the material contained herein or for any errors or
omissions that may have been made. The publisher remains neutral with regard to jurisdictional claims in
published maps and institutional affiliations.

This Springer imprint is published by the registered company Springer Nature Switzerland AG
The registered company address is: Gewerbestrasse 11, 6330 Cham, Switzerland

Preface

The European Conference on Software Architecture (ECSA) is the premier European software architecture conference, providing researchers, practitioners, and educators with a platform to present and discuss the most recent, innovative, and significant findings and experiences in the field of software architecture research and practice.

The special theme for the 16th edition of ECSA 2022 was "Software Architectures and Practices for Emerging Technologies and Applications." We were interested in learning about how software architecture principles and practices are evolving and being applied to address the challenges of emerging technology and applications. This raises questions such as: what are the current research results in developing software architecture principles and practices for systems that include machine learning, quantum computing, blockchain, and other emerging technologies? How is current research dealing with evolving software architecture principles and practices for emerging applications such as collaborative systems, learning systems, autonomous systems, and other emerging applications? What are good examples and case studies of software architecture in the context of emerging technologies and applications? How have software architecture courses changed to accommodate or take advantage of emerging technologies and applications?

Due to the remaining uncertainty concerning COVID-19, this edition of ECSA was held as a hybrid conference during September 19–23, 2022, with the in-person events taking place in the beautiful and historic city of Prague in the Czech Republic. The core technical program included five sessions that blended contributions from the research, industry, and tools & demonstration tracks, plus three keynote talks. Moreover, ECSA 2022 offered a doctoral symposium track with its own keynote. ECSA 2022 also encompassed workshops on diverse topics related to the software architecture discipline, such as architecture erosion and consistency, formal approaches for advanced computing, architecture for automotive systems, and software architecture for machine learning systems.

For the main research track, ECSA 2022 received 47 submissions in the two main categories: full and short research papers. For the first time this year, ECSA followed a double-blind review process. Each paper received three reviews. Based on the recommendations of the Program Committee, we accepted 9 papers as full papers and 6 additional papers as short papers. Hence the acceptance rate for full research papers was 19% for ECSA 2022. The conference attracted papers (co-)authored by researchers, practitioners, and academia from 13 countries (Australia, Austria, Belgium, Chile, Colombia, Denmark, Germany, Italy, Poland, Spain, Sweden, Switzerland, the Netherlands).

The main ECSA program had three keynotes. Patricia Lago from Vrije Universiteit Amsterdam (the Netherlands), leader of the Software and Sustainability (S2) research group in the Computer Science Department, talked about the role of software for sustainability, with special emphasis on software architecture in our highly digitized society. David Garlan from Carnegie Mellon University (USA), recognized as one of the founders of the field of software architecture, and in particular, formal representation and analysis of architectural designs, talked about humanizing software architecture to better exploit human-system synergies that are required by today's increasingly autonomous, self-adaptive, and AI-driven systems. Finally, as the industrial keynote, Jaroslav Gergic (Czech Republic), Director of Engineering in the Cognitive Intelligence Unit of Cisco Security Business Group, talked about software architecture in the age of cloud computing, highlighting the challenges of scalability and the need for a wider variety of skills to deal with all layers of a cloud-based system in a software-as-a-service company.

We are grateful to the members of the Program Committee for their valuable and timely reviews. Their efforts formed the basis for a high-quality technical program for ECSA 2022. We would like to thank the members of the Organizing Committee for successfully organizing the event with several tracks, as well as the workshop organizers, who made significant contributions to this year's successful event.

We thank our sponsor Springer that funded the best paper award of ECSA 2022 and supported us with publishing the proceedings in the Lecture Notes in Computer Science series. Finally, we thank the authors of all the ECSA 2022 submissions and the attendees of the conference for their participation.

The preparation and organization of ECSA 2022 took place during a special time in our history, an ongoing pandemic that has affected us all over the world. We thank the software architecture community for their support in these times, and for continuing to advance the field of software architecture through their scientific submissions to ECSA.

August 2022

Ilias Gerostathopoulos
Grace Lewis
Thais Batista
Tomas Bures

Organization

General Chairs

Thais Batista   Federal University of Rio Grande do Norte, Brazil
Tomas Bures   Charles University, Czech Republic

Steering Committee

Paris Avgeriou   University of Groningen, The Netherlands
Thais Batista   Federal University of Rio Grande do Norte, Brazil
Stefan Biffl   Vienna University of Technology, Austria
Tomas Bures   Charles University, Czech Republic
Rogério de Lemos   University of Kent, UK
Laurence Duchien   CRIStAL, University of Lille, France
Carlos E. Cuesta Rey   Juan Carlos University, Spain
David Garlan   Carnegie Mellon University, USA
Ilias Gerostathopoulos   Vrije Universiteit Amsterdam, The Netherlands
Paola Inverardi   University of L'Aquila, Italy
Patricia Lago   Vrije Universiteit Amsterdam, The Netherlands
Grace Lewis   Carnegie Mellon Software Engineering Institute,
                               USA
Antónia Lopes   University of Lisbon, Portugal
Ivano Malavolta   Vrije Universiteit Amsterdam, The Netherlands
Raffaela Mirandola   Politecnico di Milano, Italy
Henry Muccini   University of L'Aquila, Italy
Elena Navarro   University of Castilla-La Mancha, Spain
Flavio Oquendo (Chair)   IRISA, University of South Brittany, France
Ipek Ozkaya   Carnegie Mellon University, USA
Jennifer Pérez   Technical University of Madrid, Spain
Danny Weyns   KU Leuven, Belgium

Research Track

Program Scientific Co-chairs

Ilias Gerostathopoulos   Vrije Universiteit Amsterdam, The Netherlands
Grace Lewis   Carnegie Mellon Software Engineering Institute,
                               USA

Program Committee

Muhammad Ali Babar	University of Adelaide, Australia
Jesper Andersson	Linnaeus University, Sweden
Pablo Oliveira Antonino	Fraunhofer IESE, Germany
Paolo Arcaini	National Institute of Informatics, Japan
Paris Avgeriou	University of Groningen, The Netherlands
Rami Bahsoon	University of Birmingham, UK
Luciano Baresi	Politecnico di Milano, Italy
Steffen Becker	University of Stuttgart, Germany
Amel Bennaceur	The Open University, UK
Javier Berrocal	University of Extremadura, Spain
Stefan Biffl	Vienna University of Technology, Austria
Justus Bogner	University of Stuttgart, Germany
Barbora Buhnova	Masaryk University, Czech Republic
Javier Cámara	University of York, UK
Rafael Capilla	Universidad Rey Juan Carlos, Spain
Jan Carlson	Malardalen University, Sweden
Vittorio Cortellessa	University of L'Aquila, Italy
Carlos Cuesta	Universidad Rey Juan Carlos, Spain
Eduardo Santana de Almeida	Federal University of Bahia, Brazil
Rogerio De Lemos	University of Kent, UK
Elisabetta Di Nitto	Politecnico di Milano, Italy
Andres Diaz Pace	UNICEN University, Argentina
Khalil Drira	LAAS-CNRS, France
Matthias Galster	University of Canterbury, New Zealand
Joshua Garcia	University of California, Irvine, USA
David Garlan	Carnegie Mellon University, USA
Robert Heinrich	Karlsruhe Institute of Technology, Germany
Petr Hnetynka	Charles University, Czech Republic
Paola Inverardi	University of L'Aquila, Italy
Jasmin Jahic	University of Cambridge, UK
Pooyan Jamshidi	University of South Carolina, USA
Wouter Joosen	Katholieke Universiteit Leuven, Belgium
Anne Koziolek	Karlsruhe Institute of Technology, Germany
Heiko Koziolek	ABB Corporate Research, Germany
Martin Kruliš	Charles University, Czech Republic
Patricia Lago	Vrije Universiteit Amsterdam, The Netherlands
Nuno Laranjerio	University of Coimbra, Portugal
Valentina Lenarduzzi	Tampere University, Finland
Nicole Levy	CNAM, France
Antónia Lopes	University of Lisbon, Portugal
Ivano Malavolta	Vrije Universiteit Amsterdam, The Netherlands

Tomi Männistö	University of Helsinki, Finland
Antonio Martini	University of Oslo, Norway
Nabor das Chagas Mendonça	Universidade de Fortaleza, Brazil
Tommi Mikkonen	University of Helsinki, Finland
Mehdi Mirakhorli	Rochester Institute of Technology, USA
Raffaela Mirandola	Politecnico di Milano, Italy
Marina Mongiello	Politecnico di Bari, Italy
Gabriel Moreno	Carnegie Mellon Software Engineering Institute, USA
Henry Muccini	University of L'Aquila, Italy
Angelika Musil	Technical University of Vienna, Austria
Jürgen Musil	Technical University of Vienna, Austria
Elisa Yumi Nakagawa	University of São Paulo, Brazil
Elena Navarro	University of Castilla-La Mancha, Spain
Flavio Oquendo	Université Bretagne Sud, France
Ipek Ozkaya	Carnegie Mellon Software Engineering Institute, USA
Claus Pahl	Free University of Bozen-Bolzano, Italy
Liliana Pasquale	University College Dublin & LERO, Ireland
Cesare Pautasso	USI Lugano, Switzerland
Patrizio Pelliccione	Chalmers University of Technology, Sweden
Jennifer Perez	Universidad Politécnica de Madrid, Spain
Claudia Raibulet	University of Milano-Bicocca, Italy
Maryam Razavian	Eindhoven University of Technology, The Netherlands
Ralf Reussner	Karlsruhe Institute of Technology, Germany
Matthias Riebisch	University of Hamburg, Germany
Rodrigo Santos	Universidade Federal do Estado do Rio de Janeiro, Brazil
Patrizia Scandurra	University of Begamo, Italy
Bradley Schmerl	Carnegie Mellon University, USA
Lionel Seinturier	University of Lille, France
Romina Spalazzese	Malmö University, Sweden
Girish Suryanarayana	Siemens Corporate Technology, India
Bedir Tekinerdogan	Wageningen University, The Netherlands
Chouki Tibermacine	University of Montpellier, France
Catia Trubiani	Gran Sasso Science Institute, Italy
Dimitri Van Landuyt	Katholieke Universiteit Leuven, Belgium
Roberto Verdecchia	Vrije Universiteit Amsterdam, The Netherlands
Rainer Weinreich	Johannes Kepler University Linz, Austria
Danny Weyns	KU Leuven, Belgium

Xiwei (Sherry) Xu	School of Computer Science and Engineering, Australia
Uwe Zdun	University of Vienna, Austria
Liming Zhu	University of New South Wales, Australia

Organizing Committee

Industrial Track Co-chairs

| Barbora Buhnova | Masaryk University, Czech Republic |
| Stefan Malich | Architectural Change Management, Germany |

Workshops Co-chairs

| Claudia Raibulet | Vrije Universiteit Amsterdam, The Netherlands |
| Henry Muccini | University of L'Aquila, Italy |

Tools and Demos Co-chairs

| Catia Trubiani | Gran Sasso Science Institute, Italy |
| Robert Heinrich | Karlsruhe Institute of Technology, Germany |

DE&I Co-chairs

| Elisa Yumi Nakagawa | University of São Paulo, Brazil |
| Paolo Arcaini | National Institute of Informatics, Japan |

Doctoral Symposium Co-chairs

| Aldeida Aleti | Monash University, Australia |
| Khalil Drira | LAAS-CNRS, France |

Journal First Chair

| Eduardo Santana de Almeida | Federal University of Bahia, Brazil |

Proceedings Chairs

| Martina De Sanctis | Gran Sasso Science Institute, Italy |
| Roberto Verdecchia | Vrije Universiteit Amsterdam, The Netherlands |

Publicity Co-chairs

| Romina Spalazzese | Malmö University, Sweden |
| Rafael Capilla | Universidad Rey Juan Carlos, Spain |

Local Chair

Petr Hnĕtynka   Charles University, Czech Republic

Web Chair

Martin Kruliš   Charles University, Czech Republic

Additional Reviewers

Yuqi Huai
Aaron Matthews
Markus Funke

Abstract of Keynotes

Humanizing Software Architecture

David Garlan

School of Computer Science, Carnegie Mellon University, USA
garlan@cs.cmu.edu

Abstract. The traditional view of software architecture typically places humans outside the system and in the system's environment. In this talk I argue that there are benefits in shifting this view by bringing humans into an architectural design as first-class entities. The resulting architectural designs can then much better exploit human-system synergies that are required by today's increasingly autonomous, self-adaptive, and AI-driven systems. We will illustrate the ideas by examining case studies in which this approach has been used to provide formal human-system architectural models that attempt to maximize the respective strengths of both humans and systems. We also highlight some of the key challenges and potential directions for research in maturing these ideas.

Biography

David Garlan is a Professor of Computer Science and Associate Dean in the School of Computer Science at Carnegie Mellon University. His research interests include software architecture, self-adaptive and autonomous systems, formal methods, and cyber-physical systems. He is recognized as one of the founders of the field of software architecture, and in particular, formal representation and analysis of architectural designs. He has received a Stevens Award Citation for "fundamental contributions to the development and understanding of software architecture as a discipline in software engineering," an Outstanding Research award from ACM SIGSOFT for "significant and lasting software engineering research contributions through the development and promotion of software architecture," an Allen Newell Award for Research Excellence, an IEEE TCSE Distinguished Education Award, and a Nancy Mead Award for Excellence in Software Engineering Education. He is a Fellow of the IEEE and ACM.

Software Architectures in the Age of Cloud Computing

Jaroslav Gergic

Cognitive Intelligence Unit, Cisco, Czech Republic

Abstract. The age of cloud computing presents the software architects with a unique set of opportunities as well as a unique set of challenges. Designing, building, and operating applications at cloud scale has changed the very nature of software architecture discipline to accommodate a much larger set of objectives and skills. Prior to the cloud era, software architecture was primarily about fulfilling functional requirements while maintaining code modularity and meeting a narrow set of nonfunctional requirements, such as performance. The cloud-era architect needs to accommodate not only functional requirements and customer-defined throughput and performance requirements, but also a large set of non-functional requirements related to cyber security, compliance, and most notably also the financial/cost characteristics, which at cloud scale can make or break a software-as-a-service company. The whole discipline of software architecture just became not only wider to accommodate all the above aspects, but also deeper as cloud-scale architecture spans all layers of software all the way down to operating system kernel tuning and in the case of private cloud also requires hardware know-how and hardware assembly design closely aligned with high-level application workload requirements to achieve reasonable performance and economics at cloud scale.

Biography

Jaroslav Gergic is Software as a Service R&D executive with a strong R&D background and years of professional services experience. His focus is on innovation and operational excellence and best practices in project and knowledge management. He has 3+ years of general management practice as a country managing director of a company with 150+ employees. Currently he leads the Cognitive Intelligence unit of Cisco Security Business Group as a Director of Engineering while living in the confluence of cyber-security, machine learning, and cloud computing. Prior to joining Cisco, Jaroslav led R&D and Operations at GoodData and in a more distant past held various positions at Ariba and IBM Research. Besides his full-time job, Jaroslav is actively engaging in local startup communities as a mentor.

Software Sustainability: What it Means for Software Architects and Why Should We Care

Patricia Lago

Vrije Universiteit Amsterdam, The Netherlands
p.lago@vu.nl

Abstract. The need for sustainability is crucial for all aspects of society, as framed by the Sustainable Development Goals (SDGs) of the United Nations, and increasingly prioritized by Governments and Global Organizations. Thanks to digital transformation, most organizations in all sectors are facing incredible challenges to embrace sustainability as related to their software portfolios. Similarly, they struggle in identifying the opportunities that software sustainability can bring. This talk introduces the role of software for sustainability and related research, with special emphasis on software architecture (and architecture design decision making) in our highly digitalized society. Given the pervasive presence of software-intensive systems that are multi-stakeholder and that bring incredible complexities, understanding and managing software architecture design decision making has never been as important as it is nowadays. Examples from collaboration with various industries, sectors, and societal groups are used to illustrate the main takeaways.

Biography

Patricia Lago is a professor at Vrije Universiteit Amsterdam, the Netherlands, where she leads the Software and Sustainability (S2) research group in the Computer Science Department. Her passion in research is to create software engineering knowledge that makes software better, smarter, and more sustainable. Her research focuses on software architecture, software quality assessment, and software sustainability.

She is the initiator of the VU Computer Science Master Track in Software Engineering and Green IT, the director of the Master Information Sciences, and a co-founder of the Green Lab, a place where researchers, students, and companies collaborate to measure the energy footprint of software solutions and the impact on software quality. She has a PhD in Control and Computer Engineering from Politecnico di Torino and a Master in Computer Science from the University of Pisa, both in Italy. She has been awarded an honorary doctorate degree by the Norwegian University of Science and Technology (NTNU).

She is program committee member and reviewer of the major international conferences and journals in her fields of interest; a member of the Steering Committees of IEEE ICSA, ECSA; and currently the Steering Committee Chair of the ICT4S conference series. She is also in the management team of IPN (ICT-research Platform Netherlands). She has published over 200 articles in all major scientific conferences and journals of her field. She is a senior member of ACM and IEEE. More info at: www.pat ricialago.nl.

Contents

Components, APIs and Interface Management

Avoiding Excessive Data Exposure Through Microservice APIs

Patric Genfer[✉] and Uwe Zdun

Research Group Software Architecture, Faculty of Computer Science,
University of Vienna, Vienna, Austria
{patric.genfer,uwe.zdun}@univie.ac.at

Abstract. Data transfer and exchange of information through APIs are essential for each microservice architecture. Since these transfers often include private or sensitive data, potential data leaks, either accidentally or through malicious attacks, provide a high-security risk. While there are different techniques, like using data encryption or authentication protocols to secure the data exchange, only a few strategies are known to reduce the damage when an actual data breach happens. Our work presents a novel approach to identifying the optimal amount of data attributes that need to be exchanged between APIs and minimizes the damage in case of a potential breach. Our method relies only on static source code analysis and easy-to-calculate architectural metrics, making it well suited to be used in continuous integration and deployment processes. We further verified and validated the feasibility of our approach by conducting two case studies on open-source microservice systems.

Keywords: Microservice API · security · data exposure · metrics · source code detectors

1 Introduction

Despite their main principles like autonomy and isolation, microservices often have to cooperate and interchange data to fulfill their tasks [1]. These inter-service communications mainly consist of domain-specific information required to execute particular tasks that might include user-related or other sensitive data [2]. While business-related information can be of high interest for malicious competitors, it is especially the sensitive data that presents a lucrative target for external attackers intent on either stealing or compromising the information [3]. It is therefore not surprising that the exposure of sensitive data is considered an essential security challenge in microservices architectures [4].

Data exchange happens also in monolithic architecture, but here, the attack surface for data-related attacks is much smaller since a large part of the communication takes place inside the process boundaries and is therefore not as easily accessible from the outside [5]. In contrast, microservices communicate via different data transfer technologies [6] by using a variety of data formats [7],

© The Author(s), under exclusive license to Springer Nature Switzerland AG 2022
I. Gerostathopoulos et al. (Eds.): ECSA 2022, LNCS 13444, pp. 3–18, 2022.
https://doi.org/10.1007/978-3-031-16697-6_1

and their endpoints are often accessible through the public cloud, making data attacks much more likely and rewarding [3,5].

To protect the data transfer against leaks or breaches, different security mechanisms have been proposed, such as authentication, authorization, traffic control, and encryption [3,5,8]. However, all these measures come with the price of having a considerable negative impact on other quality properties, such as the system's performance. Yarygina and Bagge [9], for instance, could show that their security framework affects the overall system performance by 11%. In addition, excessive data transfer between services can cause unintended concurrency issues, making it even harder to reason about a system's security aspects [6].

Since data autonomy and isolation are key characteristics of a microservice architecture [10], exchanging data between services is essential and avoiding data transfer at all is not an option for obvious reasons. Dias and Siriwardena [5] refer to data transfer that goes beyond what is strictly necessary, as *excessive data exposure* and further suggest that each API should only provide precisely that part of the information required by its consumers.

Unfortunately, identifying the amount of data mistakenly interchanged between services is not a trivial task: Many APIs were not designed with data parsimony as a primary goal, instead the focus during design is usually on quality goals such as improving maintainability and reducing complexity, resulting in a coarser-grained API structure than sometimes necessary [11]. Beside that, APIs based on underdeveloped or anemic domain models carry the risk of exposing too much and often domain data unrelated to specific use cases [12]. Finally, the polyglot and diverse nature of microservice systems [9] needs to be considered, making optimizing for data parsimony an even more challenging task.

Our work provides a novel approach for tracking the data transferred between microservice APIs and aims to identify any excessive data exposure that happens as part of this transfer[1]. To achieve this, we use our source code detector approach from our previous research [13] to derive a communication and data flow model from the underlying system's code artifacts. Based on this model, we define a set of architectural metrics for guiding architectural design decisions targeting the reduction of excessive data exposure. In this context, we are aiming at answering the following research questions:

RQ1 *How can a communication model for identifying excessive data exposure be derived from a microservice system?* Our goal is to reconstruct such a model only through static code analysis, making our approach exceedingly feasible for continuous development cycles.

RQ2 *How well can the level of data exposure caused by API calls be quantified?* Based on our formal model, we will identify a set of architectural metrics to measure and identify the grade of data exposure through an API.

RQ3 *How can software architects be guided through the process of redesigning microservice APIs to reduce excessive data exposure?* We will investigate

---

[1] For supporting reproducability, we offer the whole source code and data of our study in a data set published on the long term archive Zenodo: https://zenodo.org/record/6700021#.YrRJYHVByA0.

how our metrics can help by restructuring critical architecture elements to reduce the amount of data exposed.

This paper is structured as follows: Sect. 2 gives a short overview of existing research in this area. Section 3 presents some background information regarding the data management in microservice APIs and how it could lead to excessive data exposure. Section 4 describes our communication model and how we constructed it by using our source code detectors. Section 5 introduces the metrics we designed to measure potential data exposure, and in Sect. 6, we assess our metrics on two open-source case studies. The paper concludes with a discussion of our results (Sect. 7), together with an overview of possible threats to validity and a selection of future work tasks (Sects. 8 and 9).

2 Related Work

Microservice security, especially data exposure, is an important research field that has attracted much attention in recent years. Yu et al. [3] investigate security issues in microservice-based fog applications. Similar to our research, they consider inter-service communication a critical security aspect. A more data-centric security approach is pursued by Miller et al. [2], where the authors argue that leaking data can pose an enormous financial risk for companies and accordingly present a security architecture to prevent these data exposures while still enforcing the required business workflows. Shu et al. [14] introduce a method to detect sensitive data exposure in microservice systems by preserving data privacy. For more research in this area, see also Hannousse and Yahiouche [4].

Another essential data security concept is the so-called *taint analysis* that examines how untrusted data – e.g., from user input – can affect the security of a system, be it a web [15] or mobile application [16]. While similar to our approach, taint analysis is a vast research field that focuses on how untrusted data could potentially harm a system. In contrast, our approach is more specific as it aims to minimize the amount of data exposed through microservice APIs.

When it comes to gathering data from microservices through mining source code or other artifacts, Soldani et al. [17] present an approach in which they reconstruct a communication model by parsing Kubernetes configuration files. While their model is similar to ours, they do not analyze the source code directly and therefore have limitations regarding the actual data usage by an API. Fowkes and Sutton [18] introduce an approach for mining API call patterns by creating abstract syntax trees (AST) out of Java programs to reconstruct method invocations. In contrast, our code detector approach is more lightweight and not specific to a particular language.

Studies about architectural metrics related to microservice can be found in [19,20]. Although their metrics are not specific for measuring data exposure, they provide meaningful insights we also used to define our metrics.

3 Excessive Data Exposure in Microservice APIs

To fulfill their tasks, microservices have to manage and process a large amount of data and information, provided by external sources like databases or computed or generated during runtime. A typical pattern here is to provide each microservice with its own database [6], placed inside the internal perimeter of the service boundary. Because of their central role in data-driven architectures, we assume that for each database a data provenance protection exists and they are secured against data breaches [3]. Otherwise, an attacker could target the database directly instead of focusing on the communication channels.

In addition, a microservice API itself can act as a data provider, either by computing derived data from incoming parameters [21] or by transferring data directly from one API to another. To decide whether an API connected to a data source requests its data legitimately, we have to investigate the following cases:

1. *The API processes the incoming data directly.* This would be the case if the API either stores its input in its data store or uses it to derive new information. Consider e.g. an online shop system API that calculates a discount factor based on the customer's shopping history it receives. Since the incoming data is no longer required after being processed, we say the API *consumes* the input data.
2. *The API sends incoming data to another target without modification.* Besides directly consuming incoming information, an API can also leave the input untouched and transfer it directly to another API, acting itself as a data source for its caller. We consider this behavior as *routing*.

If any incoming data is not handled by one of these two mechanisms, we can assume that the API's input is obviously not required and can safely – at least from a security point of view – be omitted. This leads us to the following definition:

Definition 1. *All incoming data received by an API that is neither directly consumed nor routed to another API can be considered* **excessively exposed**.

Figure 1 illustrates this definition: An external client communicates with a microservice system consisting of three APIs, requesting order information by calling the `/order/collect-data` operation. The API itself gathers the required data by calling two other endpoints, `/customer` and `/product`. Both APIs return complex objects containing the required data attributes and additional information not relevant for the current use case (marked with red color). While `/order/collect-data` returns only the required information to the client, it has no use for the remaining data attributes `movementHistory`, `description` and `image`, which, while not used by any endpoints, are still exposed to the network. If the API communication had been compromised by an attacker, they would get access to much more data than one would actually expect based on the underlying use case, making the data breach even more severe.

How could we avoid this unnecessary and excessive exposure of data? First, we have to determine the original source of the data by following the path back from our current API to the one that initially returned the data attributes. Secondly, after investigating our two origin APIs, we recognize that they are not tailored for a specific use case but instead simply return whole data entities, thus exposing too many details [12].

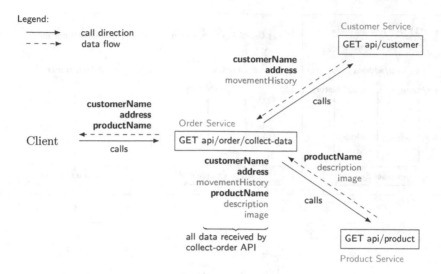

Fig. 1. Example of Excessive Data Exposure: Two APIs are exposing more data than actually required for the use case.

A naive solution would split up the `api/customer` and `api/product` operations into separate APIs for each single data attribute, allowing clients a more fine-grained access to choose each data attribute individually. While this would minimize the risk of a potential data leak, the solution comes with many disadvantages: A single API endpoint per data attribute increases the size of the service interface significantly and also the efforts necessary to implement and maintain the service [19]. Also, a client in need of more than one data attribute at once has to make several network calls to gather all required information, resulting in increased network traffic and poorer system performance.

Somewhere between these two extremes – one endpoint per atomic data attribute vs. one endpoint per domain entity – lies the optimal solution from a data security point of view: Designing the APIs per use case and ensuring that each request receives only the data relevant for the case it implements. In our example, we could design one API `api/customer/order-information` returning the `name` and the `address` attributes and another one returning only the name of the product (see Fig. 2 for an illustration of these three options).

However, even such an optimized solution has drawbacks, as systems with a large number of different use cases would require a corresponding amount of API endpoints, resulting again in increased implementation and maintenance efforts. Furthermore, providing one API per use case creates a strong coupling between the both, reducing the maintainability even further [12]. Choosing the right granularity for a service interface is, therefore, often a decision that depends on many different individual factors [11]. Unfortunately, architects are often left alone in this process and have to rely on their experience or personal preferences to find the optimal API granularity. Our approach presented in the next section closes this gap and supports experts by providing them with additional guidance when redesigning their architectures towards more data security.

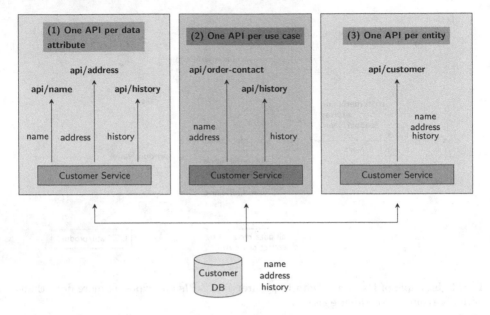

Fig. 2. Different types of API granularity depending on the amount of data exposed per API.

4 Communication Model

4.1 Formal Model Description

The communication model we extract from the underlying microservice artifacts is derived from our previous work [13]. We express inter-service calls within the system as a directed graph $G = (V, E, DA, F)$, where V represents the set of architectural elements essential for the communication flow – like APIs ($V^{API} \in V$) – and $E \subseteq V \times V$ is the set of invocations (each represented by a tuple), both synchronous and asynchronous. We further define DA as the set of all data attributes interchanged and processed by the APIs $v \in V^{API}$ of a Graph G. The last part of our definition specifies F as a set of data-related functions with $F = \{in, out, consume\}$ and $in : V^{API} \to \mathbb{P}(DA)$ (same for out and $consume$). Each of these functions returns the subset of data attributes $\mathbb{P}(DA)$ an API either receives as input or processes.

4.2 Source Code Mining

Code artifacts of a microservice system are often written in various languages and use a large number of different communication and database technologies [6]. Strategies for mining these artifacts with native language parsers would require considerable configuration and maintenance work and are therefore not always practical, or often limited to specific languages (see, for instance [18] or [22]).

Instead, we used a different mining approach adapted from our previous works [13,23]. for mining code artifacts: To identify significant architectural hotspots within a system, it is often sufficient to look only for specific patterns in code that describe a particular communication model or API technology and ignore all other parts that are not relevant in this context. Taking advantage of this fact allows us to implement much more lightweight parsers – we call them detectors – that focus only for detecting specific patterns [23].

In this paper, we substantially extended our detector concept, to enable a more reusable and lightweight detection approach. In particular, we reduced the size of each detector by splitting up responsibilities further through introducing the concept of *Collectors*: While a *Detector* is responsible for identifying an architectural hotspot based on characteristics it finds in an artifact, a Collector's job is to extract relevant information – like an API endpoint or a REST method parameter – from the previously identified artifact. This approach resulted in a multi-phase parsing strategy, where first relevant code artifacts are localized by detectors, and then different collectors run over the artifacts to extract all relevant information.

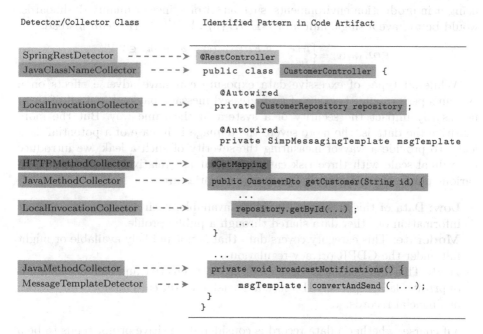

Fig. 3. Source Code Mining through *Detectors* and *Collectors*: Detectors (*Green*) identify relevant architectural hotspots. Language-specific Collectors (*Red*) extract semantic information depending on the language used. Other Collectors (*Blue*) search for specific technology-related patterns. (Color figure online)

Figure 3 illustrates the roles of some example *Detectors* and *Collectors* during processing of a source code file artifact. As seen, a single hotspot can have more than one architectural role. Here, the class `CustomerController` provides different synchronous API endpoints, but also propagates asynchronous messages.

After collecting all hotspots, our algorithm creates the communication model by following local and inter-service invocations and storing the incoming and outgoing API parameters for later processing.

5   Metrics

According to our definition from Sect. 3, an API $v \in V^{API}$ exposes data excessively if not all incoming data attributes are either consumed by or routed to the API's output. On the basis of this observation, we define our main metric $EDE_{API} : V^{API} \to \mathbb{P}(DA)$ (*Excessive Data Exposure*) as the relative complement of the sets of incoming data attributes $in(v)$ versus the set of all processed data attributes ($out(v)$ and $consume(v)$):

$$EDE_{API}(v) = in(v) \setminus \left(out(v) \cup consume(v) \right) \quad with\, v \in V^{API} \tag{1}$$

Since this metric returns a set of data attributes, a more convenient way for using it in production environments, such as CI pipelines or quality dashboards, would be to have a single indicator $isEDE_{API} : V^{API} \to Boolean$ instead:

$$isEDE_{API}(v) = \begin{cases} true, & if\ EDE_{API}(v) \neq \varnothing \quad with\, v \in V^{API} \\ false, & otherwise \end{cases} \tag{2}$$

While all types of excessive data exposure can have adverse effects on a system's performance because of an increased message payload, not all of them necessarily impact the security of a system in the same way. But the more sensitive the data is, the more severe the damage is in case of a potential data leak. To provide a way of measuring the severity of such a leak, we introduce an ordinal scale with three risk categories that are relatively common among various public organizations[2]. The three categories are:

- **Low**: Data of this category is publicly available, such as a person's contact information or other data shared through a public profile.
- **Moderate**: This category covers data that is not publicly available or might fall under the GDPR privacy regulations.
- **High**: This information is considered the most sensitive and includes all kinds of private data, especially IDs such as social or credit card numbers and health or financial records.

Of course, whether a data record is considered sensitive or not tends to be a highly subjective decision, as the privacy of a data attribute often depends on the use case and whether the data-leaking systems are publicly accessible [24]. Since even a single high-risk data leak is a critical incident, a metric to measure the severity of an API's data exposure has to take this into account. To define our *Excessive Data Exposure Severity* $EDES_{API} : V^{API} \to SL$ metric, we, therefore, take the data attribute with the highest severity level to determine the overall severity:

$$EDES_{API}(v) = \max \left(\{ s \in SL : s = severity(d) \wedge d \in EDE_{API}(v) \} \right) \tag{3}$$

---

[2] https://uit.stanford.edu/guide/riskclassifications#risk-classifications.

With $SL = \{Low, Moderate, High\}$ being a set of severity levels and $severity(d) : DA \rightarrow SL$ a function assigning each data attribute one of the three severity values. This mapping has to be done upfront by a domain expert.

The easiest way to reduce data exposure would be to remove all excessively exposed data attributes from the system, but this is only possible if the specific data attribute is not used in another part of the implementation. To identify such 'orphaned' data, we can use the following *Usage Exposure Ratio* metric $UER_{data} : DA \rightarrow \mathbb{R}$ for a given data attribute $d \in DA$:

$$UER_{data}(d) = \frac{|\{v \in V^{API} : d \in consume(v)\}|}{|\{v \in V^{API} : d \in EDE_{API}(v)\}|} \tag{4}$$

Values larger than 0 indicate that at least one API is consuming a data attribute, and therefore removing the attribute from the system is not easily possible. A value between 0 and 1 implies that more APIs receive the attribute unnecessarily than consume it, while a value larger than 1 expresses the opposite situation. Especially the latter can be an indicator that the data attribute plays an essential role in the system. Splitting up its parent data structure – and the APIs returning it – could help reduce the data exposure. It should be noted that calculating this metric makes only sense for exposed data attributes. Hence, we assume that the denominator should never be zero.

6 Case Studies

To validate the explanatory power of our metrics, we evaluated our approach by conducting case studies of two open-source microservice reference implementations. Both projects were chosen because they provide a well-documented architecture and use many current technological standards and best practices. Despite not being real production systems, their maturity makes them a good alternative, also frequently used in other research studies [25–27].

6.1 Case Study 1: Lakeside Mutual

For our first study, we analyzed the excessive data exposure of the service communication within the 2020 Spring-Term edition of the *Lakeside Mutual*[3] project, a mainly Java Spring-based microservice system of a fictional insurance company. While the system consists of seven services, we focused only on the API-exposing functional services, resulting in a subset of five service implementations relevant to our research. Four used a Spring-based Java implementation, with the fifth one written in JavaScript. We also focused on concrete business use cases and ignored simple data reading and manipulation *CRUD* API operations [28] when possible, as they do not provide many insights from an architectural point of view. From a total of 31 analyzed APIs, our approach was able to identify five APIs with a positive *isEDE* value, meaning these APIs expose at least one data attribute unnecessarily. Table 1 summarizes our findings:

---

[3] https://github.com/Microservice-API-Patterns/LakesideMutual/tree/spring-term-2020.

Table 1. Data attributes excessively exposed by *Lakeside Mutual* APIs

Service	API	EDE(v)	EDES(v)
CustomerCore	/changeAddress	firstName, last-Name, birthday, email, phoneNumber	moderate/high (but not relevant)
Policy Management Backend	/getPolicy /getPolicies /getInsuranceQuoteRequest	name id, name name	low low low
Risk Management Server	/handleClientRequest	firstname, last-name, streetAddress, city, email, phoneNumber, additional policy data	moderate/high

The first API in the list, `CustomerCore/changeAddress` can be considered as an edge case, as it calls the DB for changing a customer's address but, in return, receives a complete customer entity as a result. While one could interpret this as an excessive exposure of data from a technical point of view – the API requests more data than it needs – we would not consider this call as a serious problem from a security perspective, since it does not happen between two microservice APIs but instead between a service and its underlying database, which we assume is a secure call within the service boundaries (see Sect. 3). Although reducing the exposure here could positively impact performance because of reduced message payload, we would not rate this exposure as security-critical.

The exposure detected in the following three APIs (from the *PolicyManagementBackend*) service originates mainly from data conversions between different API calls. In these specific cases, the composed `PolicyType` of a `PolicyAggregateRoot` is converted into a flat string representation for simplifying the data transfer. Our algorithm is not yet able to track all of these conversions, thus resulting in a false positive notification here.

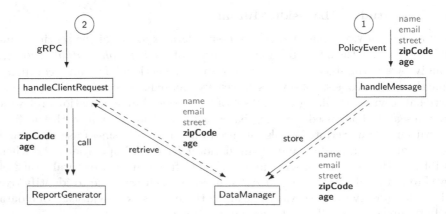

Fig. 4. Data exposure through API calls in the Lakeside Mutual Project. Not all of the incoming data attributes are eventually consumed, resulting in an excessive and unnecessarily exposure of customer information.

The last case is indeed more interesting as it is a two-staged process, illustrated by Fig. 4: First, the *RiskManagementServer* reacts on incoming messages from the *PolicyManagementBackend* (1) and stores the received information in its internal data store. When an incoming gRPC (2) call (from a client application not part of our analysis) triggers the `handleClientRequest` API in the next step, the service starts with the generation of a report by accessing its internal data store. However, generating this report requires only a small subset of the stored data attributes, such as the customer's age or postal code. The remaining customer and policy data attributes the first API call received were stored redundantly and did not serve any purpose. While accessing the datastore from within the same process is again not problematic, here, the store itself acts only as a temporal buffer and the actual exposure already happens at the moment when the first API receives the data through an inter-service call.

Since most of the leaked data represent personal or contact information, we consider the $EDES(v)$ metric value of this exposure at least as *Moderate* or even *High* (see Sect. 5), especially regarding the large number of leaked attributes.

Two different strategies have been determined to avoid the exposure in this concrete case: (1) If other API endpoints do not consume these attributes, they can safely be removed from the API that initially exposed them. (2) If the attributes are instead also consumed elsewhere in the system, splitting up the initial endpoint into several smaller ones – each providing only the data for a specific use case – would be a better solution.

Calculating the $Usage - Exposure - Ratio$ (UER) for each exposed data revealed that despite a few exceptions, most of the exposed contact data (like the customer's phone number or street address) were not processed by any other API included in our analysis. However, skipping these potential redundant attributes from the whole system could be problematic as other client applications, which are not tracked by our approach, might still consume them.

So we suggest that splitting up these data-providing APIs into several, more use-case-specific ones would be the better strategy. In the concrete case, the `/getCustomer` API could therefore be separated into more fine grained endpoints, like, for instance, a `/getCustomerDataForReporting` and a `/getCustomerContactDetails` API.

6.2   Case Study 2: eShopOnContainers

As a second case study, we applied our approach to the *eShopOnContainers* system, Microsoft's reference implementation for a domain-driven-design-based microservice architecture[4]. The project imitates an online shop system consisting of several frontend components and a variety of different backend services, with the backend parts mostly communicating via an asynchronous event bus. For evaluating our method, we focused on the three backend microservices encapsulating the central domain logic and ignored other more infrastructure-related

---

[4] https://github.com/dotnet-architecture/eShopOnContainers, commit 59805331cd2 25fc876b9fc6eef3b0d82fda6bda1.

services like API gateways and authentication components. These three services provide 43 API operations, with the majority being asynchronous event handlers reacting on incoming event-bus messages.

Regarding the system's excessive data exposure, our study revealed the result outlined in Table 2: The first case in the table results from an event-handler that reacts to a `PriceChanged` event. Like the exposure we identified in our previous example, the API retrieves a complete entity from the underlying datastore but changes only a small subset of its attributes, making the requested remaining ones redundant. However, since this communication happens only between the service and its database, we do not consider this data exposure problematic. The second entry results from a false positive match. Here, incoming data is converted into a domain message through different conversion routines, and our detectors could not track the whole conversion process.

Table 2. Data attributes excessively exposed by *eShopOnContainers* APIs

Service	API	$EDE(v)$	$EDES(v)$
Basket	ProductPriceChanged-IntegrationEventHandler	BuyerId, Product-Name, Quantity, PictureUrl	low (not relevant)
Ordering	UserCheckoutAccepted-IntegrationEventHandler	ProductId, ProductName, Quantity, PictureUrl	low (not relevant)
Catalog	UpdateProductAsync	CatalogItem	low
	CreateProductAsync	PictureUri, AvailableStock, RestockThreshold, MaxStockThreshold, OnReorder	moderate

We again had one false positive match regarding the *Catalog Service* due to direct database access from the API operation – instead of reaching out to the database through a repository. Since we had no detector for this kind of data access, our algorithm wrongly assumed that the receiving API did not process any incoming data attributes. The second match, however, indicates an actual case of excessive exposure: The `CreateProductAsync` API receives a new data object but uses only a subset of its attributes to create a new data entity. While these redundant attributes increase the payload of the data transfer, their impact on data security seems limited since none of the fields are processed further by the API. Still, we suggest replacing the current API parameter with a smaller variant containing only the attributes required for the creation process.

6.3 Summary

Our analysis revealed that both architectures are relatively secure regarding the excessive data exposure through their APIs. In most cases where more data was requested than eventually required, the transfer happened between the APIs and their underlying database. Since our research focuses on API-to-API communication, we assume that these connections are sufficiently secured and thus have not included them in our overall review. However, if such a secure database connection is not granted, the severity metric should be reevaluated to better reflect the security impact of these data exposures. We still identified two cases where data exposure between APIs happens and where this could indeed lead to unnecessary exposure of this data in case of a data breach.

7 Discussion

Based on our case studies, we can confirm **RQ1** and show for two non-trivial cases that it is possible to reconstruct a communication model of a microservice system and identify cases of excessive data exposure only by using static source code analysis. The upfront implementation effort for reading different language artifacts was also manageable. However, one limitation we see is that for providing support for dynamic or weakly typed languages we required some heuristics to correctly determine the data type of an API parameter. Our study also showed that our algorithm yielded some false-positive results due to insufficient detection of data conversion routines. Avoiding this would have required more specific detector implementation, which would have increased the implementation effort.

Regarding **RQ2**, we were able to show that our metrics are suitable for identifying data exposures and tracking the origin of these exposed data back to the initial data source. While our boolean or numerical metrics could easily be integrated into a dashboard, the more complex metrics would require a more sophisticated user interface. We think of a graphical representation where expert users could mark a specific data attribute and follow the communication call graph to its origin. As we are not aware at the moment of any visual system like that, it would certainly represent an interesting option for further research.

Considering **RQ3**, our case studies demonstrated how our metrics can guide architects in redesigning a microservice system towards better data security. Based on the findings our metrics provided, we can identify accidentally exposed data and reorganize the API structure to minimize these exposures, thus reducing the damage caused by potential data leaks. However, data security is only one aspect that affects API granularity, and other factors, like maintainability or performance, must also be considered, too [19]. Also, microservice architectures are often based on or interact with older legacy systems, which can constrain their API structure. Balancing out all these aspects is not a trivial task and requires sophisticated domain knowledge. Therefore, although possible, we would advise against a fully automated refactoring process and see our approach more as a supporting tool during the decision process.

8 Threats to Validity

To ensure our case study accounts for potential bias or unintended factors, we tested our approach against commonly used threats that might influence the validity of our findings as suggested in [29].

Construct Validity. While most of our detectors operate directly on the source code, we also applied heuristics at some places to simplify their implementation. To ensure that our model adequately represents the actual system, we added several manual verification steps. Nevertheless, the case studies showed that it is still possible to miss some code artifacts, but we were able to detect and fix these cases manually.

Internal Validity. Although our research focuses on data security, we know that various other factors strongly impact API (re)design. Thus, we present our approach as one possible tool to guide the decision-making process, but other aspects must also be considered for the final decision.

External Validity. Since the data transfer heavily depends on the concrete business domain or use case, finding a reference system across several domains is extremely difficult. Still, we think the projects we chose for our study provide a good compromise. They are actively developed and utilize many best-practices implementations used among other systems. Several authors have also identified data leaks and breaches as a significant problem in microservice architectures (see, for instance, [2,6] or [14]). Therefore, our research provides a significant contribution to reducing the damage caused by these leaks.

9   Conclusions and Future Work

Our paper presents a novel approach for tracking excessive data exposure between microservice APIs. Data is excessively exposed whenever an API receives more data than it actually consumes, causing an unnecessary and avoidable risk for potential data leaks. To make this amount of exposure measurable, we introduced a technique to reconstruct a communication and data flow model from underlying source code artifacts. Based on this model, we defined a set of architectural metrics to identify and evaluate API calls that unnecessarily expose data attributes. We verified our solution on two case studies and, based on our findings, suggested guidance on how the APIs could be restructured to minimize the amount of data being unnecessarily exposed.

While our approach can identify many of the most common matters where data is exposed, some edge cases were not within our scope, e.g., the amount of data leaked through service error handling [5]. Despite data security, other aspects exist that influence the granularity of APIs. Incorporating all these aspects into a more holistic decision model for API granularities would undoubtedly be a promising field for further research.

Acknowledgments. This work was supported by: FWF (Austrian Science Fund) projects API-ACE: I 4268 and IAC^2: I 4731-N. Our work has received funding from the European Union's Horizon 2020 research and innovation programme under grant agreement No 952647 (AssureMOSS project).

References

1. Nadareishvili, I., Mitra, R., McLarty, M., Amundsen, M.: Microservice Architecture: Aligning Principles, Practices, And Culture. O'Reilly Media, Inc., Sebastopol (2016)
2. Miller, L., Mérindol, P., Gallais, A., Pelsser, C.: Towards secure and leak-free workflows using microservice isolation. In: 2021 IEEE 22nd International Conference on High Performance Switching and Routing (HPSR), pp. 1–5. IEEE (2021)
3. Yu, D., Jin, Y., Zhang, Y., Zheng, X.: A survey on security issues in services communication of Microservices-enabled fog applications. Concurr. Comput. Pract. Exp. **31**(22) (2019)
4. Hannousse, A., Yahiouche, S.: Securing microservices and microservice architectures: a systematic mapping study. Comput. Sci. Rev. **41** (2021)
5. Dias, W.K.A.N., Siriwardena, P.: Microservices Security in Action. Simon and Schuster (2020)
6. Laigner, R., Zhou, Y., Salles, M.A.V., Liu, Y., Kalinowski, M.: Data management in microservices: state of the practice, challenges, and research directions. arXiv preprint arXiv:2103.00170 (2021)
7. Sill, A.: The design and architecture of microservices. IEEE Cloud Comput. **3**(5), 76–80 (2016)
8. Newman, S.: Building Microservices. O'Reilly Media, Inc. Sebastopol (2021)
9. Yarygina, T., BaggeA. H.: Overcoming security challenges in Microservice architectures. In: 2018 IEEE Symposium on Service-Oriented System Engineering (SOSE). Bamberg, pp. 11–20. IEEE (2018)
10. Ntentos, E., Zdun, U., Plakidas, K., Schall, D., Li, F., Meixner, S.: Supporting architectural decision making on data management in microservice architectures. In: Bures, T., Duchien, L., Inverardi, P. (eds.) ECSA 2019. LNCS, vol. 11681, pp. 20–36. Springer, Cham (2019). https://doi.org/10.1007/978-3-030-29983-5_2
11. Bogner, J., Fritzsch, J., Wagner, S., Zimmermann, A.: Microservices in industry: insights into technologies, characteristics, and software quality. In: IEEE International Conference on Software Architecture Companion (ICSA-C), pp. 87–195. IEEE (2019)
12. Singjai, A., Zdun, U., Zimmermann, O., Pautasso, C.: Patterns on deriving APIs and their endpoints from domain models. In: 26th European Conference on Pattern Languages of Programs, pp. 1–15 (2021)
13. Genfer, P., Zdun, U.: Identifying domain-based cyclic dependencies in microservice APIs using source code detectors. In: Biffl, S., Navarro, E., Löwe, W., Sirjani, M., Mirandola, R., Weyns, D. (eds.) ECSA 2021. LNCS, vol. 12857, pp. 207–222. Springer, Cham (2021). https://doi.org/10.1007/978-3-030-86044-8_15
14. Shu, X., Yao, D., Bertino, E.: Privacy-preserving detection of sensitive data exposure. IEEE Trans. Inf. Foren. Secur. **10**(5), 1092–1103 (2015)
15. Tripp, O., Pistoia, M., Fink, S.J., Sridharan, M., Weisman, O.: Taj: effective taint analysis of web applications. ACM Sigplan Notices **44**(6), 87–97 (2009)
16. Arzt, S., et al.: Flowdroid: precise context, flow, field, object-sensitive and lifecycle-aware taint analysis for android apps. ACM SIGPLAN Notices **49**(6), 259–269 (2014)
17. Soldani, J., Muntoni, G., Neri, D., Brogi, A.: The μtosca toolchain: mining, analyzing, and refactoring microservice-based architectures. Pract. Exp. Softw. **51** (2021)
18. Fowkes, J., Sutton, C.: Parameter-free probabilistic API mining across GitHUB. In: Proceedings of the 2016 24th ACM SIGSOFT International Symposium on Foundations of Software Engineering, pp. 254–265 (2016)

19. Bogner, J., Wagner, S., Zimmermann, A.: Automatically measuring the maintainability of service-and microservice-based systems: a literature review. In: Proceedings of the 27th International Workshop on Software Measurement and 12th International Conference on Software Process and Product Measurement, pp. 107–115 (2017)
20. Saidani, I., Ouni, A., Mkaouer, M.W., Saied, A.: Towards automated microservices extraction using Muti-objective evolutionary search. In: Yangui, S., Bouassida Rodriguez, I., Drira, K., Tari, Z. (eds.) ICSOC 2019. LNCS, vol. 11895, pp. 58–63. Springer, Cham (2019). https://doi.org/10.1007/978-3-030-33702-5_5
21. Zimmermann, O., Lübke, D., Zdun, U., Pautasso, C., Stocker, M.: Interface responsibility patterns: processing resources and operation responsibilities. In: Proceedings of the European Conference on Pattern Languages of Programs, pp. 1–24 (2020)
22. Walker, A., Das, D., Cerny, T.: Automated code-smell detection in microservices through static analysis: a case study. Appl. Sci. 10(21), 7800 (2020)
23. Ntentos, E., Zdun, U., Plakidas, K., Genfer, P., Geiger, S., Meixner, S., Hasselbring, W.: Detector-based component model abstraction for microservice-based systems. Computing 103(11), 2521–2551 (2021). https://doi.org/10.1007/s00607-021-01002-z
24. Fan, L., Wang, Y., Cheng, X., Jin, S.: Quantitative analysis for privacy leak software with privacy petri net. In: Proceedings of the ACM SIGKDD Workshop on Intelligence and Security Informatics, pp. 1–9 (2012)
25. Rademacher, F., Sachweh, S., Zündorf, A.: A Modeling method for systematic architecture reconstruction of microservice-based software systems. In: Nurcan, S., Reinhartz-Berger, I., Soffer, P., Zdravkovic, J. (eds.) BPMDS/EMMSAD -2020. LNBIP, vol. 387, pp. 311–326. Springer, Cham (2020). https://doi.org/10.1007/978-3-030-49418-6_21
26. Vural, H., Koyuncu, M.: Does domain-driven design lead to finding the optimal modularity of a microservice? IEEE Access 9, 3 2721–3 2733 (2021)
27. El Malki, A., Zdun, U.: Evaluation of API request bundling and its impact on performance of microservice architectures. In: 2021 IEEE International Conference on Services Computing (SCC), pp. 419–424. IEEE (2021)
28. Mashkoor, A., Fernandes, J.M.: Deriving software architectures for crud applications: the FPL tower interface case study. In: International Conference on Software Engineering Advances (ICSEA 2007), pp. 25–25. IEEE (2007)
29. Yin, R.K.: Case Study Research and Applications. Sage, Thousand Oaks (2018)

Documentation-as-Code for Interface Control Document Management in Systems of Systems: A Technical Action Research Study

Héctor Cadavid[1,2](✉) [ID], Vasilios Andrikopoulos[1] [ID], and Paris Avgeriou[1] [ID]

[1] University of Groningen, Groningen, The Netherlands
{h.f.cadavid.rengifo,v.andrikopoulos,p.avgeriou}@rug.nl
[2] Escuela Colombiana de Ingeniería, Bogotá, Colombia

Abstract. The architecting of Systems of Systems (SoS), that is, of systems that emerge from the cooperation of multiple independent constituent systems, is a topic of increasing interest in both industry and academia. However, recent empirical studies revealed what seems to be an overlooked aspect of the architecting of SoS that is linked to major integration and operational issues: the interplay between the various disciplines involved in such an architecting process. This aspect becomes particularly relevant for the management of the interfaces between the SoS constituents, where such disciplines inevitably meet. In this paper, we present the results of the first cycle of a Technical Action Research (TAR) study conducted in cooperation between the authors and a group of practitioners involved in the long-running architecting process of a large-scale radio astronomy SoS project. This TAR is aimed at exploring potential improvements of the document-centered interface management approach currently followed in this project by adopting elements of the *documentation-as-code* philosophy, which is widely adopted in the domain of software systems. As a result, a working proof-of-concept of an ICD (Interface Control Document) management approach was developed by the researchers and evaluated by the practitioners. The results of the study and the corresponding lessons learned are reported in this work.

Keywords: Systems of Systems · Interface Control Documents · Documentation-as-code · Technical Action Research

1 Introduction

The concept of System of Systems (SoS) is used across application domains such as defense, automotive, energy, and health care to describe a family of independent systems that cooperate to provide capabilities that cannot be delivered by the individual systems [14]. The architecting process of this kind of systems is known for being challenging due to the operational and managerial independence of their constituents [21], which arguably explains the significant volume

© The Author(s), under exclusive license to Springer Nature Switzerland AG 2022
I. Gerostathopoulos et al. (Eds.): ECSA 2022, LNCS 13444, pp. 19–37, 2022.
https://doi.org/10.1007/978-3-031-16697-6_2

of work in this area [4]. More recently, a particular aspect of the architecting process of this kind of systems has also been highlighted as posing additional challenges: the interplay between the different engineering disciplines involved in its development, such as systems engineering, software engineering, and electrical engineering, among others [26]. Studying this aspect is particularly important as recent empirical studies suggest that the interaction between those disciplines often leads to major integration and operational issues in SoS when their architecting practices are not harmonized [5,6]. A specific pain point identified by these studies is that of *interface management*.

Interface management in the context of SoS usually involves a formalized description of the interfaces between the constituent systems, i.e., the definition of what must be done to interact with each other, commonly referred to as Interface Control Documents (ICD) or Interface Design Documents (IDD). These documentation artifacts ensure compatibility between the said constituents, prevent integration errors, and improve the quality of the whole system [24]. However, empirical studies in the field [5,6] suggest that the details on these ICDs, defined by one of the involved parties, are often incomplete or not sufficiently clear for the other parties to work with. This, in addition to the domain knowledge gap between these disciplines, seems to be a common cause of *misunderstandings* and *wrong assumptions* in the process [5,26].

Aiming to address this issue, in this paper we present the results of the first cycle of a technical action research (TAR) study [32] designed to investigate an alternative ICD management approach. The study is conducted with a group of engineers from ASTRON[1], the Netherlands Institute for Radio Astronomy. This cooperative work between researchers and practitioners was motivated by the result of a previous exploratory case study on the LOFAR and LOFAR2.0, a long-running large-scale radio-telescope SoS [6], where the aforementioned ICD-management issues emerged. The *documentation-as-code* or *docs-as-code (DaC)* philosophy [10], which encourages the creation and maintenance of technical documentation as rigorously as software, emerged as a common ground idea (between researchers and practitioners) to be explored as an improvement of the existing document-centered ICD management approach. The researchers had already identified that according to a significant amount of gray literature in the area[2], the DaC philosophy has been used successfully to address issues similar to the ICD-management ones discussed above, albeit in the domain of Software Systems. ASTRON practitioners, on the other hand, had already been exploring an ad-hoc DaC approach that involves transcribing parts of the ICDs into a machine-readable documents. These documents would then be used for automating some of the repetitive and error-prone tasks, like artifacts generation, during the development process. Thus, the idea of applying this approach at an ICD level appeared sound for both the practitioners and researchers.

---

[1] https://www.astron.nl/.

[2] A collection of conferences, video Casts and articles from practitioners is available at https://www.writethedocs.org/guide/docs-as-code/.

This study offers as a result four main contributions. First, it characterizes ICD management issues in SoS that are linked to misunderstandings and erroneous assumptions while implementing (parts of) an interface between (sub-)systems. Second, it explores, in collaboration with practitioners, a DaC-inspired solution that is alternative to traditional document-centered ICD management approaches for addressing the aforementioned issues. Third, it proposes a set of tools for implementing DaC pipelines based on the proposed approach. Fourth, it provides evidence of the merit of the proposed approach, together with points for its improvement.

The rest of this paper is structured as follows: Sect. 2 summarizes the background and the works related to this study. Section 3 presents the study design, and Sect. 4 answers the stated research questions. Section 5 elaborates on the lessons learned in the process, while Sect. 6 concludes the study.

2   Background and Related Work

2.1   *DaC*—Documentation-as-Code

In recent years the software engineering community has been steadily shifting from traditional documentation approaches using conventional word processors, wikis, or other collaborative editing system to the DaC philosophy [10]. With DaC, where documentation is managed in the same way as source code in modern software projects, the community has been aiming at improving well-known issues such as outdated or unreliable technical documentation. Consequently, DaC implies the use of lightweight text-based markup languages (instead of proprietary formats and authoring tools) for the documents, so that they can be managed with modern (and proven) source code-oriented version control systems like Git and their related collaboration and automation tools. These automation possibilities mean, in turn, that a DaC documentation pipeline can ensure, to some extent, the quality of the documents by automatically validating or testing critical elements before their publication (e.g., the validity of code snippets within the documents, broken links, etc.) Furthermore, a DaC pipeline can also ensure uniformity and improve maintainability by using vendor-independent text-based specifications (e.g., for diagrams) that can be automatically transformed into visual elements that suit the organization's conventions.

Although the most common target of this documentation philosophy is software artifacts (e.g., APIs), it has also been adopted for higher-level documentation in industrial settings, showing to be useful to improve problems of missing or outdated documentation [27] by reducing the complexity of documentation maintenance [22]. Examples include the documentation of products in government systems [19], architecture documentation in transport systems[3], and product engineering documentation[4]. Moreover, despite this topic having received little attention by researchers [25], it is worth highlighting the large community

---

[3] Deutsche Bahn - DB Systel - https://github.com/docToolchain/docToolchain.
[4] OpenGADES (a work in progress) - https://wiki.eclipse.org/OpenADx.

of technical writers working on it, with the near 2000 members of the DaC-global network in the *Write The Docs*[5] community as a prominent example.

2.2 ICD Management Approaches

In the context of Systems Engineering, an ICD is a formal description of an agreement for the interfacing between two or more systems. There are no conventions nor standards to define these artifacts, as they usually differ from one company to another [24], even within the same application domain [20]. However, when it comes to the approaches to manage these artifacts, it is fair to say that the existing ones fall somewhere between the two ends of the spectrum [13]: from pure model-centric, i.e., following a *model-based systems engineering process* (MBSE), to pure document-centric ones. On the pure model-based end, the overall process is centered on a model of the system, from which documents like the ICDs are generated, when required, as a report. Examples in the context of SoS can be found in industries such as *astronomy* [7,17], *space* [8,29], and *defense* [28]. In these cases, with the exception of the defense industry, which has adopted the *Unified Profile for DoDAF/MODAF* (UPDM), SysML is seemingly the de facto formalism in model-based approaches [15].

On the other extreme, the document-centric one, ICDs are mostly textual documents created with propietary word processing and diagramming tools, which evolve as interfaces are identified, defined, documented, and modified over time [30]. This approach, despite the growing popularity of model-based ones as a response to its limitations, is still widely used in industry [3]. This is evidenced not only by examples in the literature in the *aeronautics* industry [11] and *radio-astronomy* (the LOFAR case) [12], but in the many ICDs publicly available online for other domains[6]. Between these two extremes, there are approaches that neither follow an MBSE process nor use text-based documents for the ICDs. Instead, these make use of computer aided tools to model only the relationships between the parties involved in the described interface (rather than the overall system), so that computations (e.g., evaluating the impact of a change of a parameter) can be performed. Examples in the literature include the use of spreadsheets to model ICDs in *subsea production* [33] and *astronomy* systems [2]; and UML for modelling the interfaces of *cyber-physical systems* [24].

Unlike these approaches, the approach explored in this TAR could be described as one that combines the best of both worlds: the flexibility and expressiveness of text-based documents (something existing modelling languages lack in some cases [34]), with the computability of text-based formalisms, within a workflow that ensures the quality and traceability of the overall documentation.

---

[5] https://www.writethedocs.org.

[6] Particular examples are available in domains like *Healthcare*, *Transport systems*, *Aerospace/robotics*, and *Astronomy*.

3   Research Method

3.1   Problem Formulation and Research Questions

The goal of this study can be described following the *design problem* structure proposed by Wieringa [32]:

> **Improve** the ICD management practices in the context of large-scale SoS such as the ones developed by the ASTRON organization,
> **By** adapting the DaC philosophy to this context,
> **Such that** the managed ICDs lead to fewer erroneous assumptions and misunderstandings while working with them,
> **In order to** reduce potential integration and operational issues caused by these occurrences.

From this problem formulation, the following research questions are derived:

RQ1. What are the issues with ICDs management that cause erroneous assumptions and misunderstandings when working with these documents in SoS?

RQ2. What are the features required for a DaC-based ICD management approach to address such issues?

RQ3. What is the design of an ICD management pipeline that provides such features?

RQ4. To what extent can the designed ICD management pipeline address the identified ICD management-related issues?

3.2   Research Method

This study is based on the Technical Action Research *(TAR)* method [32], as we want to investigate an experimental treatment (a DaC approach for ICDs management), to help a client with previously identified problems (ASTRON) and learn about its effects in practice. A TAR study involves five iterative phases: *diagnosing, action planning, action taking, evaluation,* and *specifying learning.* In this sense, *action* refers to a treatment to address the identified problems. The way each phase contributes to answering the proposed research questions, and the methods used by each are described below. We start by describing the context in which this method was applied.

Context. The research context is characterized by the document-centered management approach followed by ASTRON on the LOFAR and LOFAR2.0 projects over the past 10+ years [6]. Radio telescopes such as LOFAR consist of a large number of omnidirectional antennas concentrated in multiple, geographically distributed stations which, when working together, provide an effective collecting area equivalent to 300,000 square meters [1]. LOFAR2.0, on the other hand, is an ongoing expansion of the scientific and technical capabilities of LOFAR that relies on the lessons learned from its predecessor [16].

Diagnosing. This phase of TAR is focused on exploring and extending the current understanding of ICD documentation problems identified in [6]. Previous to this phase, the general idea of adopting DaC for ICD management was pitched to the potential participants. Subsequently, this phased used a *virtual focus group* with the ASTRON practitioners; a focus groups is a qualitative research method to collect data on a given topic through a group interaction [18]. The discussion points for the focus group were derived from the relevant findings of the afore-mentioned previous study [6]. The actual focus group session was geared toward the collection of more context and details on ICD-management issues experi-enced in the LOFAR/LOFAR2.0 project in order to answer **RQ1**.

Action Planning. This phase is focused on identifying, discussing, and choos-ing solutions to improve the issues experienced by practitioners. As the *DaC* philosophy was defined as a core element up-front in the project formulation, the discussed solutions were oriented towards how to apply such a philosophy in the context of ICD management in a hardware/software-intensive SoS like LOFAR. This phase is comprised of three steps, and its results, that is to say the features required by the DaC pipeline, were used to answer **RQ2**. First, a generic ICD template[7] was distilled from a curated set of existing ICDs, includ-ing those provided by practitioners. This template characterized the common elements included in an ICD, the kind of hardware elements described, and the way these are described in the documents. Second, the template was anno-tated collaboratively by one of the researchers and a group of practitioners (see Table 1) to highlight specific symptoms of the issues identified in the diagnosing phase, e.g., particular elements of a given type of hardware elements that are often missed despite being key. Finally, researchers, in cooperation with one of the practitioners, defined the features that the DaC pipeline should provide in order to address the identified issues, using their particular issue symptoms to gauge their applicability in the process.

Action Taking. Here the solutions selected to improve the identified issues are implemented. Therefore, in this phase the features identified in the previous phase were turned into an actual design that integrates existing DaC tools with any additional custom artifacts required by said features. This design is the answer to **RQ3**, and was implemented as a functional proof-of-concept that practitioners can try out and evaluate.

Evaluation. In this phase, the effects of the action are captured trough different data collection methods [23]. This phase addressed **RQ4** by exploring the efficacy and fitness for purpose of the proposed documentation management approach to address the identified issues during the diagnosing phase. To this end, we chose to perform a single case mechanism experiment [31] with the group of ASTRON engineers described in Table 1. In this experiment[8], practitioners were asked to carry out a number of ICD management activities using an online instance of the functional proof-of-concept created in the action taking phase. In the process, one of the researchers provided help with the process through Slack, so that observations or issues that emerged can also be included in the analysis to

---

[7] Available in the online appendix - https://doi.org/10.6084/m9.figshare.19727671.

[8] Available at https://github.com/search-rug/doc-as-code-single-case-experiment.

Table 1. Practitioners involved in the different phases of the study, and when such phases took place. *P1, P2 ... P8*: practitioners on the ASTRON side. *R1, R2*: external researchers. Phases: *(D)* Diagnosing, *(AP)* Action Planning, *(AT)* Action Taking, *(E)* Evaluation, *(SL)* Specifying Learning

Participant	Role in LOFAR project	D	AP	AT	EV	SL
P1	Researcher	✓				
P2	Software Engineer	✓	✓		✓	
P3	RF Electronics Engineer	✓				
P4	Senior Software Engineer	✓	✓		✓	
P5	Head of Software Development	✓				
P6	Senior Software Engineer				✓	
P7	Software Engineer		✓		✓	
P8	System Engineer		✓	✓	✓	
R1	N/A	✓	✓	✓	✓	✓
R2	N/A	✓			✓	✓
		May 2021- Jun 2021	Aug 2021- Jan 2022	Jan 2022- Mar 2022	Mar 2022- May 2022	Apr 2022- May 2022

answer RQ3 and followed through in the consequent *learning specification phase*. Once the practitioners completed the exercise, they filled up an online survey aimed at measuring the applicability of the proposed features in the identified ICD-management issues.

Specifying Learning. Finally, the lessons learned from this study (which is the first cycle of the action research), and their implications in future iterations of the study and the proposed documentation pipeline, were collected and are reported in the *Discussion* section of the paper.

Participants and Timeline. A total of ten people participated in this TAR study, which took place between May 2021 and the beginning of May 2022: two researchers and eight ASTRON practitioners. One of the researchers actively participated in the design and development activities during the *action planning* and *action taking* phases; both researchers took part in the research activities, designing the research instruments, and drawing lessons from the *action evaluation* phase. The eight participants on the ASTRON side, on the other hand, were free to decide in which phase of the study they will participate. As a result, they participated in different phases of the study, as described in Table 1.

4   Results

4.1   RQ1: What Are the Issues with ICDs Management that Cause Assumptions and Misunderstandings When Working with These Documents in SoS?

A wide variety of interfacing-related issues were identified by the virtual focus group conducted for the *diagnosing* phase of the study, including some not explicitly related to the ICDs management itself, e.g., related to the way the interfaces were designed. As such issues are out of the the scope of this TAR and can be eventually explored in a separate study, the following list only includes the ones that have an actual influence to the *action planning* phase:

Clarity and Cross-Domain Understandability (CLA): an ICD often contains terminology that may be clear for the people involved in its original version, but years later it could be interpreted differently. This is also the case when multiple disciplines are involved in the process (e.g., hardware and software engineering), as in many cases there are similar terms between these disciplines with a different meaning.

Completeness (COM): Some critical details, particularly in the description of the hardware-side of the interfaces, are often omitted in the ICDs. This could lead to risky assumptions, or to error-prone informal information exchange. Additionally, time-behavioral and state-related aspects of the interfaces are rarely included in the ICDs. In particular, scenarios that lead to a failure state are important to include, although it is not always feasible to describe all of them in an ICD.

Uniformity (UNI) : The lack of uniformity between ICDs, in the context of an SoS where many interfaces are usually involved, lead to confusion and misinterpretation.

Timely Update Notifications (UPN): Changes in ICDs are not announced but rather discovered by people while working with them.

Nonduplicated Efforts (NDE): Interfacing-related information is duplicated across ICDs and the artifacts derived from it, e.g. intermediate ad hoc machine-readable formats and other tools created to support the development process. The time and effort required to keep in sync all these information sources is substantial and it could instead be invested in the actual engineering/development activities of the interfaces.

It should be noted that the lack of dynamic behavior details aspect of the completeness issue mentioned above, was not treated at this cycle of the study. As pointed out by the ASTRON part of the team, given the complexity this particular issue carries, addressing it would require a dedicated cycle within the TAR.

4.2   RQ2: What Are the Features Required for a DaC-Based ICD Management Approach to Address Such Issues?

In the *action planning* phase, four features were defined addressing the issues identified in the previous phase:

Documentation-oriented quality gates (QG) enforcing certain minimum quality criteria for the ICDs through centrally-managed rules. This involves automating the publication process of the ICDs through a CI/CD platform, with publication rules (i.e., quality gates) tailored to the context of technical documentation.

Table 2. ICD-management issues, their observed symptoms, and the identified associated features.

Issue	Symptom	DaC feature
(CLA)	Overlapping/colliding abbreviations and terms.	(M) macros to (1) insert references to a centralized glossary, and (2) to generate a glossary section within the document accordingly. (QG) for undefined abbreviations.
	Unclear language.	(QG) number of violations to the writing style rules defined by the organization.
	Broken links.	(QG) Broken links metric.
(COM) (UNI)	Missing details: on specifications for reading/writing from/to a peripheral (e.g., endianness, R/W rights, update rates, etc.).; on atomicity (e.g., which operations are atomic); on timing (e.g., commands timeout, ack signals timeout, etc.)	(F)(M) Support for hardware-oriented formalisms and (QG) to validate the completeness of instances of such formalisms.
	ICDs should be amended when referenced documents are updated.	(DT) Identify and notify when a document has a more recent timestamp than the ones that referenced it.
(UPN)	Changes are discovered rather than announced; outdated documentation.	(F) Support for hardware-oriented formalisms and (M) macros for the generation of software artifacts (e.g., headers) and human-readable sections from the machine-readable formalisms. Based on this, and the (DT) platform, the artifacts' checksum (e.g., headers) previously generated by the documentation pipeline, and currently used in the development environment, could be automatically compared, during the (software) building process, against the most recent one (available online).
(NDE)	Error-prone process of building a command's payload, (e.g., mapping parameter bits within a given index).	(F) Support for hardware-oriented formalisms and (M) macros for the automatic generation of software artifacts (e.g., library headers) and human-readable sections from the machine-readable formalisms.
	Information replicated over multiple ICDs (no need to reiterate what is written elsewhere).	(DT) tracking of the multiple versions of an ICD (sources and published builds) and (M) for referencing versions of other ICDs, reliably, through the centralized document tracking platform, and generating references section automatically.
	Need for the right balance between documentation maintenance efforts and actual engineering/development ones.	(F) Support for hardware-oriented formalisms and (M)macros for the generation of software artifacts (e.g., headers) and human-readable sections from the machine-readable formalisms.

Embedded machine-readable-formalisms (F) integrating existing formalisms for the description of technical elements within ICDs, particularly hardware-oriented ones. Such formalisms, when embedded in an ICD, can be automatically transformed into human-readable content (e.g., sections within the generated documents) and other artifacts (e.g., libraries).

Document macros for automatic content generation (M) providing custom extensions for the selected lightweight markup language used for ICD definition allowing engineers and technical writers to define where and how content will be automatically generated within an ICD.

Centralized document tracking (DT) keeping track of the publication status of the ICDs within the project/organization and of the dependencies between them. As this feature cannot be fully implemented through the version-control system (e.g., Git) itself, it entails creating a custom platform that would work in tandem with/on top of the CI/CD platform.

Table 2 describes particular symptoms of the issues identified in RQ1 and how the proposed features plan to address them. These symptoms indicate the occurrence of the corresponding issues in the context of actual ICDs (as described in Sect. 3).

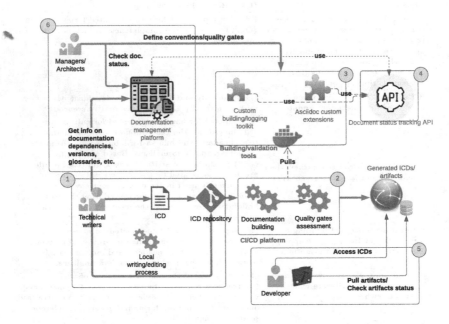

Fig. 1. General overview of the ICD management pipeline

4.3   RQ3: What Is the Design of an ICD Management Pipeline that Provides the Identified Features?

In the *action taking* phase, a solution was implemented as a functional proof of concept of a DaC pipeline instantiating the features identified in the previous phase. The pipeline is depicted in Fig. 1, and is described as follows. First, the writing/editing process of an ICD source document (1) is supported by any text editor since a text-based lightweight markup language is being used. For the proof of concept, Asciidoc was chosen as the lightweight markup language considering (in addition to its extensibility through custom macros) the variety of environments it can be interpreted on[9] and the flexibility this could provide to the solution on this, or follow-up cycles of the study. The collaboration between writers is consequently mediated through a version management system like Git. Once a

---

[9] For example, in front-end or backend, using *Asciidoctor.js* and *AsciidoctorJ* respectively.

new ICD is ready for publication, the authors tag it as an official version. When such a tag is set, a CI/CD platform, linked to the ICD repository (2), launches the publication process using a centrally managed (at the project/organization level) building environment (3) that validates the minimum quality criteria in the process through **Documentation-oriented quality gates (QG)**. This building environment, in turn, includes a number of custom extensions to enable the ICD-related **Document macros (M)** and in particular the ones that deal with the **Embedded machine-readable formalisms (F)**. The events generated by the previous steps are reported to an API (4) as the means to have **Centralized document tracking (DT)** of the overall documentation status, and to provide context information to the building process of other documents (e.g., when dependencies between documents are involved).

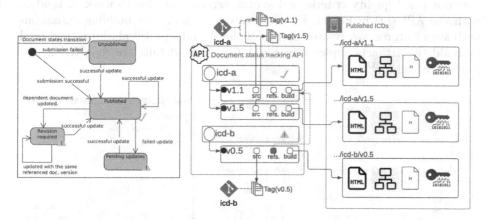

Fig. 2. On the left, the diagram depicts the status transitions of the ICDs indexed in the centralized document tracking API. In the middle, the information indexed for each ICD is shown: (src) sources code, (refs) references to other ICDs, (build) canonical location of each version's generated document. Each published ICD (on the right), contains the generated documents, artifacts, and their corresponding unique checksum. In this particular case, document 'icd-b' has a status of *REVISION-REQUIRED*, as it is based on version 1.1 of 'icd-a', which is no longer the most recent one.

Finally, the documentation and other generated artifacts are kept as the single source of truth for each interface by storing them in a canonical location (i.e., a URL accepted as the official one). With these locations the documentation users (e.g., software developers), besides accessing the latest version of an ICD, can integrate automated checks in their development environment (5) to verify that software artifacts are up-to-date with respect to the documentation they were generated from. The documentation management platform (6), on the other hand, has two purposes in the above process. On the one hand, for engineers or technical writers to have access to easy-to-read information about errors or failed quality gates during the ICD publication process. On the other hand, to serve as a dashboard that provides an overview of the overall documentation status.

In the following, the elements of the ICD-management pipeline that needed custom tools, tailored to suit the features identified in the previous section (RQ2), are described.

Quality-Gates and Markup Language Extensions. There are many tools that can perform a wide variety of quality checks in software source code within a CI/CD platform. However, when it comes to the source code of documentation, that is, markup language documents, quality criteria like the one defined in the *action planning* phase (RQ2) require extending the interpreter of such a markup language so that the criteria are evaluated while the document is being processed. These extensions (e.g., the *custom macros* (M)) need not only to properly report their status during the building process (e.g., distinguishing between failed quality criteria and syntax errors) but also to work in tandem with the API ((4) in Fig. 1). For this reason, a toolkit for building extensions with such features was created on top of the AsciidoctorJ[10] platform, and used to build the artifacts depicted in Fig. 1 (3). More details are reported in the project repository[11].

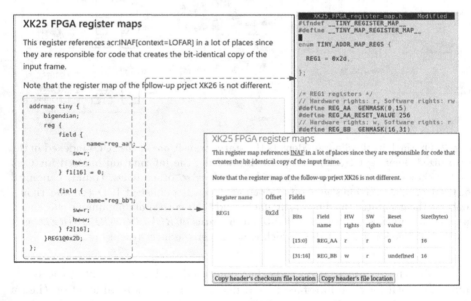

Fig. 3. Excerpt from the source of a document created during an evaluation exercise (left), the generated source code headers (top-right), and the human-readable section expanded in the generated document (bottom-right).

Centralized Document Tracking. For the proposed DaC-based ICD pipeline, the generated documents are expected to become the single source

---

[10] https://docs.asciidoctor.org/asciidoctorj/latest/.
[11] https://github.com/hcadavid/asciidoc-icd-extensions.

of truth for all the development and testing tasks conducted on the interfaces described by it. Therefore, keeping track of the official documents and the sources from which they were generated is key to their proper evolution over time. On top of that, an ICD is often dependent on a specific version of other ICDs it is based on, and hence the validity or consistency of the former could be affected by changes in the latter. Given this, a documentation-status tracking API was implemented for the proposed documentation pipeline. This API, working in tandem with the aforementioned building components, keeps track of the locations of the documents and artifacts generated from each ICD, their dependencies, and their corresponding sources. Furthermore, it updates the status of the documents given the events captured by it as illustrated in Fig. 2, which, in turn, can be accessed through its front-end application ((6) in Fig. 1). More details are reported in the project repository[12].

Macros for Content Generation and Embedded Machine-Readable Formalism. SystemRDL[13], a widely adopted hardware description language was chosen to explore the use of a machine-readable formalism embedded in ICDs to describe hardware elements of interfaces (F). This involved the creation of a SystemRDL macro for Asciidoc that performs validations according to the defined completeness quality-gates, and generates a human-readable representation of the hardware along with base software artifacts (as depicted in Fig. 3). With the automatic generation of check-sums of the said generated artifacts implemented in the extension, developers can check whether their local copy is up to date, as previously described.

Additional content generation extensions, based on the results of the *action planning* phase of the study, include: automatic generation/validation of the document log section (based on Git history), references, and glossary. The source of a sample ICD written in Asciidoc, using the above extensions, and its corresponding output, is included in the online appendix[14].

4.4 RQ4: To What Extent Can the Designed ICD Management Pipeline Improve the Identified ICD Management-Related Issues?

The efficacy and fitness for purpose of the features identified in the *action planning* phase and implemented in the *action taking* phase was evaluated through an online survey filled by the ASTRON practitioners who participated in the *evaluation* phase after conducting the *single-case* mechanism experiment (see Sect. 3.2). Table 3 shows the graded feedback collected by this survey. In the following we elaborate on these results based on the justification given by the participants as answers to open-ended question for their selected choices, and the Slack interaction in the process.

---

[12] https://github.com/hcadavid/documentation-dashboard.
[13] https://www.accellera.org/activities/working-groups/systemrdl.
[14] https://doi.org/10.6084/m9.figshare.19727671.

Table 3. Perceived applicability of the DaC features after using them in the proof-of-concept. Grades: (SA) Strongly Agree, (A) Agree, (N) Neigher agree nor disagree, (D) Disagree, (SD) Strongly disagree

Question	Participants				
	P1	P2	P3	P4	P5
Q1 (QG) I believe that enforcing the expected minimum quality criteria of the texts within the ICDs, by means of automated 'quality gates', would improve their clarity and understandability	A	D	SA	SA	N
Q2 (QG) I believe that enforcing the expected minimum quality criteria of the technical details included on the ICDs (e.g., hardware-level details), by means of automated 'quality gates', would reduce the documentation-related integration/operational issues experienced in the past	A	A	SA	SA	N
Q3 (M) I think that having part of the documentation (e.g., glossaries, hardware description, etc.) and other artifacts (e.g., software components) generated from models embedded in the ICDs would reduce the documentation maintenance efforts when compared with the existing approach	A	N	SA	SA	SA
Q4 (F) I think the automatic generation of human-readable content and software artifacts from formal models embedded in the ICDs (e.g., SystemRDL, ARGS, etc.), would improve the data-transcription-related issues experienced in the past	A	A	A	SA	SA
Q5 (DT) I think that having centrally managed ICDs, with their different versions/dependencies tracked, and status changes reported to relevant roles, would be helpful to mitigate the issues related to outdated documentation experienced in the past	A	A	A	SA	SA
Q6 (DT) I think that integrating the information provided by the centrally-managed ICDs into the software development process, in a realistic setting, would be useful to avoid shipping software based on ICDs that could be outdated or that need to be revisited	A	N	A	SA	A

Documentation-Oriented Quality Gates. The practitioners' perception on enforcing minimum quality criteria by means of quality gates were in general positive, as shown by questions Q1 and Q2 in Table 3. However, the *Disagreement* and *Neutral* responses in Q1, about the enforcement of the style of the ICD elements described in natural language, were justified with doubts about its applicability in a more realistic setting. More specifically, two of the participants pointed out that (1) some text-based descriptions could be very hard to validate, if such validation is at a technical level, and (2) that writing styles are hard to impose and writers could find workarounds to avoid them. The enforcement of technical elements of the ICDs like forgotten keywords and wrong ranges, on the other hand, was seen in general as useful, although some interfacing parameters could be too difficult to validate automatically, especially the ones related to dynamic behavior, time dependencies and performance limitations. Overall, with the ICDs seen as the single source of truth and reference for engineers to work on an interface, the need for these automated quality gates would decrease in the long run, as will the time spent on resolving inconsistencies during development and testing.

Document Macros for Automatic Content Generation. According to the justifications for the grades given in Q3, having macros for content generation would help ICDs to become the single source of truth that can be referenced throughout the process. This would help, in turn, in identifying incorrect assumptions in the early stages of the process. On the other hand, the elements automatically generated through macros tailored for ICDs (content, artifacts, etc.), as long as they are reliable and reproducible, would not only improve their consistency but also free time to work on the content that cannot be automatically generated. However, although the above would improve the overall quality of the documentation, that would not necessarily be the case for its maintainability. In this regard, the analysis of Slack conversations during the evaluation exercise highlighted two areas of improvement. First, as a means to improve the workflow speed, an editing tool tailored to the proposed features, that is to say, that allows technical writers to identify errors or unfulfilled quality criteria before submitting changes to the documentation pipeline was deemed necessary. Second, the pipeline should support allowing locally-defined, document-specific glossary entries, in addition to the ones defined at project/organization level.

Embedded Machine-Readable Formalisms. Question Q4 (see Table 3) and the corresponding open-ended responses also showed an overall positive perception on the applicability of an embedded formalism within the ICDs as a means to remove ambiguity through the uniformity and standardization of the artifacts automatically derived from it. This is seen as a must-have to prevent issues in different engineering groups. Furthermore, this feature was perceived as something that would save a considerable amount of time normally spent writing boilerplate ICD parts, and reduce the human factor that often causes issues when translating from ICD to source code.

Centralized-Documents Tracking. According to the practitioners' views on Q5 and Q6, a centralized platform makes sense if ICDs are expected to be the single source of truth within a project/organization. Moreover, adopting this systematic approach for managing ICDs implies that now it would be necessary to decide, at a higher level within the project/organization, when to go from one version to another across the whole product. Although this would add complexity to the overall process, it would be a positive change. On the other hand, the generation of artifacts with version matching as supported by such a platform would prevent developers from using an outdated version when implementing parts of an interface. However, as pointed out by the participants, to properly close the loop failed version test results should be reported to the central ICD hub so that action can be taken. Furthermore, the tooling should also allow the interfaces to be round-trip converted from source-code back to the model. On top of these observations, practitioners emphasized that although the documentation pipeline tooling itself would prevent small but annoying mistakes, most of the success of the interfacing process would still lie on the communication and cooperation between engineers. Moreover, it would also be important to ensure that engineering and maintenance teams also keep this documentation up-to-date during operations.

5 Discussion/Lessons Learned

The results suggest that the proposed approach, when applied to an actual ICD—making it the *single source of truth* for their related interfacing-related activities—would indeed prevent wrong assumptions early in the process, ensure its uniformity, and improve its overall quality. Similar conclusions have been drawn for related approaches that make use of computer-aided tools (see Sect. 2.2) for this purpose. However, the proposed approach differs from these tools by allowing the specification of interfacing agreements (between the (sub-)systems that will be connected) combining a) the formality of models for describing critical, error-prone elements, with b) the flexibility of using natural language for all the other elements that such models could not describe. The proof-of-concept features related to the latter (i.e. macros and quality gates for glossaries and writing style rules) were seen as nice to have in order to improve clarity and avoid misinterpretations. However, some practitioners' views suggest the need for further research on the applicability of writing style rules outside of the experimental evaluation setting. As a result, in future work we foresee replacing the generic writing rules currently used by the PoC with more tailored, domain-specific ones elicited from existing documentation and practitioners' input.

The evaluation results also highlighted the importance of good user experience (UX), something that needs to be improved in the PoC, as the extra time imposed by the complexity of the proposed approach (when compared to a regular word processor) could exceed the time saved by its features (e.g., content generation). This includes the need for proper authoring tools and glossaries management that allows consistently combining and merging local glossaries with organization-level ones. As part of the work on the latter, collaboration with the *shareable glossaries* project[15] is envisioned in this direction.

The centralized-document tracking feature seems to enable the centralized management of dependencies between ICDs, which is an important element of the engineering process of SoS like LOFAR; such dependencies have neither been considered by previous ICD management approaches, nor supported by regular DaC tools. The results of the evaluation show that this feature makes sense as a means to ensure consistency and traceability between the said documents and the artifacts derived by them. In particular, the version matching mechanism that this feature enables, would ensure consistency by issuing warnings within the development environment. Moreover, closing the loop of this feature (as suggested after its evaluation), that is, reporting the failed version matches back to the central hub, would allow the organization to know when outdated references are being used and take timely actions. Overall, the proposed features would likely help the organization to decide when to move from one interface version to another, which (according to the practitioners) is a positive development.

Finally, it is worth highlighting, as pointed out by practitioners, that the proposed documentation management approach will not (and should not) remove the need for proper communication and collaboration while working on interfaces. Previous studies [5,9] have confirmed that regardless of the tools or methodologies, proper collaboration and communication are still a key element of an engineering project success. However, by freeing the tension between the

---

[15] https://thegooddocsproject.dev/docs/glossaries/.

need to be flexible in terms of writing specifications and the need to create consistent and verifiable documentation, this approach has the potential to not only deliver high-quality ICDs over time, but also provide a solid foundation for such a collaboration.

6   Conclusion

In this paper we report the results of the first cycle of a *technical action research* study in which the authors and a group of ASTRON engineers explored *documentation-as-code*, a philosophy of documentation management with a growing community of practice in software systems, to address ICD management issues identified in large-scale SoS. In doing so, a functional proof-of-concept of a documentation pipeline, with features tailored to particular symptoms of such issues in LOFAR, a long-running radio-astronomy SoS, was designed and implemented. A single-case experiment on ICD management scenarios exercised in said proof-of-concept, also with ASTRON practitioners, was used for validation. According to the results, it is fair to say that this ICD management approach, which to our knowledge has not been explored before in this context, is promising to address some of the recurring issues with SoS of this type. Some areas for improvement are planned to be addressed in the following cycles of the TAR.

References

1. Beck, R.: Future observations of cosmic magnetic fields with LOFAR, SKA and its precursors. In: Lazarian, A., de Gouveia Dal Pino, E.M., Melioli, C. (eds.) Magnetic Fields in Diffuse Media. ASSL, vol. 407, pp. 3–17. Springer, Heidelberg (2015). https://doi.org/10.1007/978-3-662-44625-6_1
2. Borrowman, A.J., Taylor, P.: Can your software engineer program your PLC? In: Software and Cyberinfrastructure for Astronomy IV. vol. 9913, p. 99131S. International Society for Optics and Photonics, July 2016
3. Broy, M., Böhm, W., Rumpe, B.: Advanced systems engineering. In: Model-Based Engineering of Collaborative Embedded Systems, pp. 353–364. Springer, Cham (2021). https://doi.org/10.1007/978-3-030-62136-0_19
4. Cadavid, H., Andrikopoulos, V., Avgeriou, P.: Architecting systems of systems: a tertiary study. Inf. Softw. Technol. **118**, 106202 (2020)
5. Cadavid, H., Andrikopoulos, V., Avgeriou, P., Klein, J.: A survey on the interplay between software engineering and systems engineering during SOS architecting. In: Proceedings of the 14th ACM/IEEE International Symposium on Empirical Software Engineering and Measurement (ESEM). ESEM 2020, Association for Computing Machinery, New York, NY, USA (2020)
6. Cadavid, H., Andrikopoulos, V., Avgeriou, P., Broekema, P.C.: System- and software-level architecting harmonization practices for systems-of-systems : an exploratory case study on a long-running large-scale scientific instrument. In: 2021 IEEE 18th International Conference on Software Architecture (ICSA), pp. 13–24 (2021)

7. Chiozzi, G., Andolfato, L., Kiekebusch, M.J., Kornweibel, N., Schilling, M., Zamparelli, M.: Designing and managing software interfaces for the ELT. In: Guzman, J.C., Ibsen, J. (eds.) Software and Cyberinfrastructure for Astronomy V, p. 78. SPIE, Austin, United States, July 2018

8. Di Maio, M., et al.: Interface Management with Closed-Loop Systems Engineering (CLOSE). In: 2018 IEEE International Systems Engineering Symposium (ISSE), pp. 1–8 (Oct 2018)

9. Fairley, R.E.: Systems Engineering of Software-enabled Systems. Wiley Online Library (2019)

10. Gentle, A.: Docs Like Code. Lulu Press, Inc., Morrisville (2017)

11. Guo, D., Zhang, X., Zhang, J., Li, H.: An interface management approach for civil aircraft design. In: Jing, Z., Zhan, X. (eds.) ICASSE 2020. LNEE, vol. 680, pp. 435–446. Springer, Singapore (2021). https://doi.org/10.1007/978-981-33-6060-0_30

12. van Haarlem, M.P., et al.: LOFAR: the low-frequency array. Astron. Astrophys. **556**, A2 (2013)

13. Harvey, D., Waite, M., Logan, P., Liddy, T.: Document the model, don't model the document. In: Proceedings of Systems Engineering/Test and Evaluation Conference and 6th Asia Pacific Conference on Systems Engineering (2012)

14. Draft bs ISO/IEC 21839 information technology - systems and software engineering - system of systems (SOS) considerations in life cycle stages of a system. Standard, International Organization for Standardization, Geneva, CH, March 2018

15. Japs, S., Anacker, H., Dumitrescu, R.: Save: security & safety by model-based systems engineering on the example of automotive industry. Proc. CIRP **100**, 187–192 (2021)

16. Juerges, T., et al.: LOFAR2.0: Station control upgrade (2021)

17. Karban, R., Troy, M., Brack, G.L., Dekens, F.G., Michaels, S.B., Herzig, S.: Verifying interfaces and generating interface control documents for the alignment and phasing subsystem of the thirty meter telescope from a system model in SysML. In: Angeli, G.Z., Dierickx, P. (eds.) Modeling, Systems Engineering, and Project Management for Astronomy VIII, p. 29. SPIE, Austin, United States, July 2018. https://doi.org/10.1117/12.2310184

18. Kontio, J., Bragge, J., Lehtola, L.: The focus group method as an empirical tool in software engineering. In: Shull, F., Singer, J., Sjoberg, D.I.K. (eds) Guide to Advanced Empirical Software Engineering, pp. 93–116. Springer, London (2008). https://doi.org/10.1007/978-1-84800-044-5_4

19. Lambourne, J.: Why we use a 'docs as code' approach for technical documentation, August 2017. https://technology.blog.gov.uk/2017/08/25/why-we-use-a-docs-as-code-approach-for-technical-documentation/

20. Louadah, H., Champagne, R., Labiche, Y.: Towards automating Interface Control Documents elaboration and management, vol. 1250, pp. 26–33 (2014)

21. Maier, M.W.: Architecting principles for systems-of-systems. Syst. Eng. J. Int. Council Syst. Eng. **1**(4), 267–284 (1998)

22. Ozerova, M.I., Zhigalov, I.E., Vershinin, V.V.: Comparison of document generation algorithms using the docs-as-code approach and using a text editor. In: Silhavy, R., Silhavy, P., Prokopova, Z. (eds.) CoMeSySo 2020. AISC, vol. 1294, pp. 315–326. Springer, Cham (2020). https://doi.org/10.1007/978-3-030-63322-6_25

23. Petersen, K., Gencel, C., Asghari, N., Baca, D., Betz, S.: Action research as a model for industry-academia collaboration in the software engineering context. In: Proceedings of the 2014 International Workshop on Long-term Industrial Collaboration on Software Engineering, pp. 55–62 (2014)

24. Rahmani, K., Thomson, V.: Managing subsystem interfaces of complex products. Int. J. Prod. Lifecycle Manage. **5**(1), 73 (2011). https://doi.org/10.1504/IJPLM. 2011.038103
25. Rong, G., Jin, Z., Zhang, H., Zhang, Y., Ye, W., Shao, D.: DevDocOps: enabling continuous documentation in alignment with DevOps. Softw. Pract. Exp. **50**(3), 210–226 (2020)
26. Sheard, S., Creel, R., Cadigan, J., Marvin, J., Chim, L., Pafford, M.E.: Incose working group addresses system and software interfaces. INSIGHT **21**(3), 62–71 (2018)
27. Thomchick, R.: Improving access to API documentation for developers with docs-as-code-as-a-service. Proc. Assoc. Inf. Sci. Technol. **55**(1), 908–910 (2018)
28. Tsui, R., Davis, D., Sahlin, J.: Digital engineering models of complex systems using model-based systems engineering (MBSE) from enterprise architecture (EA) to systems of systems (SOS) architectures & systems development life cycle (SDLC). In: INCOSE International Symposium, vol. 28, pp. 760–776. Wiley Online Library (2018)
29. Vipavetz, K., Shull, T.A., Infeld, S., Price, J.: Interface management for a NASA flight project using model-based systems engineering (MBSE). INCOSE Int. Symp. **26**(1), 1129–1144 (2016)
30. Wheatcraft, L.S.: 9.2. 2 everything you wanted to know about interfaces, but were afraid to ask. In: INCOSE International Symposium, vol. 20, pp. 1132–1149. Wiley Online Library (2010)
31. Wieringa, Roel J..: Single-case mechanism experiments. In: Design Science Methodology for Information Systems and Software Engineering, pp. 247–267. Springer, Heidelberg (2014). https://doi.org/10.1007/978-3-662-43839-8_18
32. Wieringa, Roel J..: Technical action research. In: Design Science Methodology for Information Systems and Software Engineering, pp. 269–293. Springer, Heidelberg (2014). https://doi.org/10.1007/978-3-662-43839-8_19
33. Yasseri, S.F., Bahai, H.: Interface and integration management for FPSOs. Ocean Eng. **191**, 106441 (2019)
34. Zdravković, M., Panetto, H.: The challenges of model-based systems engineering for the next generation enterprise information systems. Inf. Syst. e-Bus. Manage. **15**, 225–227 (2017)

To Deprecate or to Simply Drop Operations? An Empirical Study on the Evolution of a Large OpenAPI Collection

Fabio Di Lauro$^{(\boxtimes)}$ ⓘ, Souhaila Serbout$^{(\boxtimes)}$ ⓘ, and Cesare Pautasso$^{(\boxtimes)}$ ⓘ

Software Institute, USI, Lugano, Switzerland
{fabio.di.lauro,souhaila.serbout}@usi.ch, c.pautasso@ieee.org

Abstract. OpenAPI is a language-agnostic standard used to describe Web APIs which supports the explicit deprecation of interface features. To assess how APIs evolve over time and observe how their developers handle the introduction of breaking changes, we performed an empirical study on a dataset composed of more than one million API operations described using OpenAPI and Swagger format. Our results focus on detecting breaking changes engendered by operations removal and whether and to which extent deprecation is used to warn clients and developers about dependencies they should no longer rely on. Out of the 41,627 APIs considered, we found only 263 (0.6%) in which some operations are deprecated before being removed, while the developers of 10,242 (24.6%) of them directly remove operations without first informing their clients about the potentially breaking change. Furthermore, we found that only 5.2% of the *explicit-deprecated* operations and 8.0% of the *deprecated-in-description* operations end with a removal, suggesting a tendency to deprecate operations without removing them. Overall, we observed a low negative correlation between the relative amount of deprecated operations and the age of the corresponding APIs.

1 Introduction

Web APIs evolve in different ways (e.g. introduce/alter/refactor/remove endpoints) and for a multitude of reasons [4,5,10]. The extension of an API by adding new features is usually a safe operation, which does not affect existing clients. Conversely, when API maintainers need to remove or alter existing functionalities [2,11], and consequently introduce breaking changes, they should guarantee the stability of their offerings [6] for example announcing those modifications well in advance in order to make clients aware of possible abnormal behaviours of their applications, in case they will not update them [5].

The goal of this study is to determine whether and to which extent Web API maintainers make use of deprecation [7] to announce future potentially breaking changes. One may expect that such practice is well established, given the wide and growing adoption of HTTP-based APIs across the industry.

ⓒ The Author(s), under exclusive license to Springer Nature Switzerland AG 2022
I. Gerostathopoulos et al. (Eds.): ECSA 2022, LNCS 13444, pp. 38–46, 2022.
https://doi.org/10.1007/978-3-031-16697-6_3

To assess whether this is indeed the case, we analyze a large collection of Web APIs [1] described using OpenAPI [8], because of its growing industry adoption [3,9] and its support for explicit deprecation metadata.

In particular, we aim to answer the following research questions:

Q1: How do API operations evolve over time? How stable are they?
Q2: How often an operation is declared deprecated before its removal?
Q3: Does the amount of deprecated operations always increase over the API commit histories?

Overall, we found high stability of API operations over time and that the number of deprecated operations shows a positive correlation with the API age only for a subset of the collected API histories. After mining the operation state model from all observed API changes, we measured that the majority of removed operations had not been deprecated before their removal. This unexpected result requires further study to determine whether it is due to the relative novelty of the deprecation metadata or to a lack of explicit API evolution guidelines and tools to enforce them.

The rest of this paper is structured as follows. Section 2 presents an overview of the dataset used in this study. Section 3 shows our results and we discuss them in Sect. 4. Section 5 summarizes related work. We conclude our study and indicate possible future work in Sect. 6.

2 Dataset Overview

We mined GitHub from December 1st, 2020 to December 31th, 2021 looking for YAML and JSON files, which comply with the OpenAPI [8] standard specification, in order to retrieve API descriptions artifacts. The mining activity produced a total of 271,111 APIs with their histories contained in a total of 780,078 commits. We built a tool, hereinafter called *crawler*, that mines those artifacts and saves associated metadata (commits timestamp, API title, versions, and others), and validates their compliance with Swagger and OpenAPI standards using the *Prance* and *open-api-spec-validator* tools, and finally parse them and extract relevant information for this study. After the validation process, we obtained a dataset of 166,763 valid APIs from which we removed 17,059 APIs with duplicate histories. Subsequently, we removed 12,645 APIs with no operations defined in their histories. This data cleanup resulted in 137,059 APIs with at least one operation and 41,627 unique APIs with valid descriptions, at least one operation, and more than one commit in their history.

3 Results

3.1 Deprecation Detection

In this study we distinguish two types of deprecation: i) *explicit-deprecation* introduced at operations, parameters and schema levels through the dedicated *deprecated* field, defined from OpenAPI 3.0; ii) *deprecation-in-description*,

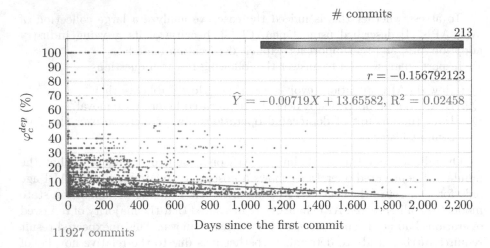

Fig. 1. Deprecated operations ratio φ_c^{dep} vs. API relative age: Does the presence of deprecated operations increase over time?

detected analyzing descriptions fields written in natural language. The latter heuristic is implemented by matching a list of terms, formed by words which start with the prefix *deprecat-*, against the text of description fields. This is similar to the detection heuristic of the earlier study by Yasmin et al. [12].

We detected 5,586 APIs which contain *explicit-deprecated* components and 384 APIs which have *deprecation-in-description* components. Out of these, only 165 APIs make use of both techniques to annotate deprecated components.

3.2 Operation Stability over Time

To assess the relative amount of deprecated operations we define the indicator:

$$\varphi_c^{dep} = \frac{|O_c^{dep}|}{|O_c|} \quad \text{where:} \quad O_c^{dep} \subseteq O_c \tag{1}$$

$$O_c := \{\, op \mid op \text{ is an operation detected in the commit c}\,\}$$
$$O_c^{dep} := \{\, dop \mid dop \text{ is a deprecated operation detected in the commit c}\,\}$$

Figure 1 shows how the indicator φ_c^{dep} changes depending on the commit age (relative to the first commit timestamp of the API history). The dots color shows how many commits we found with the same φ_c^{dep} at the same age. Considering all commits of all APIs together, we can observe a very small negative correlation r^{age} between the two variables. More in detail, we computed the same correlation r_i^{age} separately across each API history i. In Fig. 2 we present the histogram showing the distribution of the $<\varphi_c^{dep}, age>$ correlation over 466 APIs for which

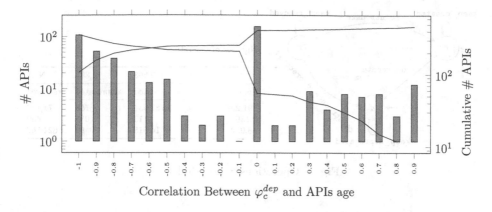

Fig. 2. Distribution of the Correlation r_i^{age} over 453 API histories

it was possible to compute it. We can observe that 157 (33.7%) of the 466 APIs analyzed have $-0.1 \leq r_i^{age} \leq 0.1$ while 251 (53.9%) of the APIs have a negative correlation $-1 \leq r_i^{age} \leq -0.2$.

3.3 Operation State Model

Based on tracking the changes occurring to all API operations for each commit, we inferred the state model shown in Fig. 3. Once created (c), an operation[1] can change its state to deprecated (d) or removed (r). Sometimes the APIs maintainers can choose to reintroduce a removed operation bringing it back to a c (*reintroduce* transition) or d state (*reintroduce_deprecated* transition). We define the **deprecate** transition when a commit introduces an *explicit-deprecation* or a *deprecation-in-description* for an operation. The opposite state change is represented by the **undeprecate** transition which occurs when an operation is not marked anymore as deprecated. Every state has its own self-loop transition which represents operations that remain in the same state between two consecutive commits.

In Fig. 3 we count how many operations were found in each of their initial and final states as well all the transitions between pairs of states. We measured also that 1,188 (2.9%) APIs include *reintroduce* and *reintroduce_deprecated* transitions in their histories and 7,663 (10.9%) of the 70,457 operation removals are later reintroduced.

In Fig. 4 we can observe how widely adopted are different API evolution practices are. For 9,779 APIs, operations are only added, thus ensuring backwards compatibility. In 5,106 APIs, operations are only deprecated, thus avoiding breaking changes. In 603 APIs, operations are only removed, thus potentially breaking clients depending on them. A different set of 9,122 APIs adopts both operation addition and removal, without performing any intermediate deprecation. Overall, deprecated operations are found in 5,805 APIs.

---

[1] To simplify the analysis and reduce its cost, in this section we focus at the operation level neglecting the parameters, responses and schema levels.

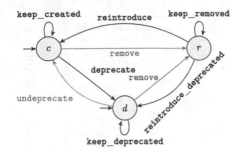

Number of Operations:

	initial	459,593	1,887	N/A
final	→	created	deprecated	removed
391,292	c	3,787,534	758	74,120
2,136	d	113	15,050	490
68,052	r	14,515	80	624,567

Fig. 3. Operations State Model

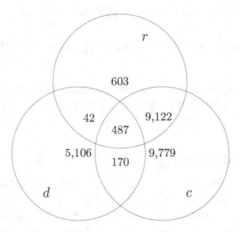

Fig. 4. Number of APIs which present at least one deprecated (d), removed (r), and/or created (c) operation in one commit of their history

We observed that 7,669 (94.8%) of the *explicit-deprecated* operations and 844 (92.0%) of the *deprecated-in-description* operations remain in the deprecated state (d). This means that for most operations, they are not removed after being deprecated and persist in further commits, until the last one. Excluding the transitions which start and terminate in the same state, we counted a total of 559,673 operation state transitions across all commits. Table 1 presents some statistics on their duration. On average, operations get reintroduced much faster than what it takes to remove them. Also, the longest transition from deprecated to removed took 43.2 months. In some cases, few operations did repeatedly get removed but also reintroduced (up to 50 times), as shown with the sub-sequences marked with * in Table 2.

Overall, considering all of the 41,627 APIs analyzed in this study, we detected that only 263 (0.6%) of these APIs include the removal of previously deprecated operations for at least one commit while many more, 10,242 (24.6%) of them directly remove operations (Fig. 5).

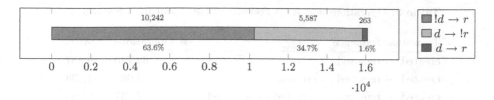

Fig. 5. Number of APIs classified based on the presence in at least one commit of their history, for the same operation undergoing different state transitions: only deprecate ($!d \rightarrow r$), only remove ($d \rightarrow !r$), or deprecated followed by remove ($d \rightarrow r$).

Table 1. Statistics on the Time Between State Transitions

transition	minimum	average	median	maximum
created → removed	0	14.6 wks	9.5 d	67.5 mths
removed → created	0	2 mins	46.4 hrs	37.4 mths
created → deprecated	2 mins	41.9 wks	29.5 wks	50.1 mths
deprecated → created	2 mins	34.1 d	52.5 hrs	13.5 mths
deprecate → removed	0	66 d	9.8 d	43.2 mths
removed → deprecated	64 secs	15.3 d	51.4 hrs	20.6 wks

4   Discussion

Q1: How operations evolve over time? How stable are they? 384,715 (83.4%) of the initial transitions end in a *created* final state passing through only one *create* transition. This result denotes a high stability of the analyzed operations.

We also detect 2,114 (0.2%) operations which remain in a *deprecated* state until the end of their history but only 466 operations follow the *deprecate-remove* path, i.e. they conclude their lifecycle with a *deprecate* transition followed by a *remove*. We also observe that 1,887 (0.4%) of the initial transitions lead directly to the deprecated state, thus indicating that collection includes few artifact histories that lack the initial created state. Furthermore, we can observe from Table 2 that 67,577 (14.7%) operations out of the 459,593 operations that were initially *created* end with a final removal of the involved operations passing through the transitions sequences *create → remove* and *created → removed → (created → removed)**, i.e. with these sequences the developers could potentially introduce breaking changes, due to the absence of the intermediate *deprecate* transition.

Q2: How often an operation is deprecated before its removal? Most operations are removed without being previously deprecated. Out of the 67,577 removed operations, only 466 had been previously deprecated. Furthermore, 419 (5.2%) of the *explicit-deprecated* operations and 73 (8.0%) of the *deprecated-in-description* operations end with a removal.

Table 2. Operations and APIs Following State Transition Sequences

Transition Sequence	# Operations	# APIs
created → removed	64,740	9,837
created → removed → created	4,968	1,234
created → removed → (created → removed)*	2,837	584
created → (removed → created)*	1,555	255
created → deprecated	636	262
created → deprecated → removed	60	25
created → deprecated → created	34	7

Q3: Does the amount of deprecated operations always increase over the API commit histories? According to our measurements the number of deprecated operations, overall, has a small negative correlation with the age of the corresponding API description (Fig. 1). When analyzing individual API histories, we found 59 APIs with a positive correlation between the two variables (Fig. 2).

5   Related Work

Deprecation of Web APIs has been studied by Yasmin et al. in [12]. In this work we are performing a broader-deeper analysis of a recently collected dataset of larger APIs with longer change histories. Yasmin et al. in collected 3,536 OAS belonging to 1,595 unique RESTful APIs and they analyzed RESTful API deprecation on this dataset, proposing a framework called RADA (RESTful API Deprecation Analyzer). The authors filtered the dataset removing duplicate APIs, erroneous OAS and unstable versions, resulting in 2,224 OAS that belongs to histories of 1,368 APIs. In this work, we adopted the same heuristics used by RADA and applied them to a much larger API collection. It consists on determining which OAS components are deprecated by the providers based on the optional boolean `deprecated` field and a list of keywords to be searched in components description fields in order to identify potential components deprecation. Yasmin et al. cluster the considered APIs within three categories: i) *always-follow* for APIs which always deprecate before removing elements. ii) *always-not-follow* for APIs which introduce breaking changes without any deprecation information in previous versions; iii) *mixed* which contains APIs that show an hybrid behavior of i) and ii). While Yasmin et al. consider deprecation at operation, request parameters and responses level, in our study we focus only at operation level. The study performed by Yasmin et al. reveals that the majority of the considered RESTful APIs do not follow the *deprecate-remove* protocol. Our study confirm this conclusion, as stated in Subsect. 3.3.

6   Conclusion

Do developers deprecate or simply remove operations as they evolve their APIs? In this empirical study we found that developers follow backwards compatible practices as they tend to grow their APIs by adding new operations. When removing operations, however, they do not often annotate them as deprecated, thus potentially breaking clients without previously warning them about the operation about to be removed. Another finding is that the operation state model reconstructed from observing API changes is a fully connected graph: there exists at least one operation in some API in which any possible state transition (between the created, deprecated and removed states) occurs. Further work is needed to investigate and gain a better understanding of the reasons for these observations, for example, by further classifying APIs based on whether they are still being developed or they have already been deployed in production.

Acknowledgements. This work is funded by the SNSF, with the API-ACE project nr. 184692.

References

1. Di Lauro, F., Serbout, S., Pautasso, C.: Towards large-scale empirical assessment of web APIs evolution. In: Brambilla, M., Chbeir, R., Frasincar, F., Manolescu, I. (eds.) ICWE 2021. LNCS, vol. 12706, pp. 124–138. Springer, Cham (2021). https://doi.org/10.1007/978-3-030-74296-6_10
2. Hora, A., Etien, A., Anquetil, N., Ducasse, S., Valente, M.T.: APIEvolutionMiner: keeping API evolution under control. In: Proceedings of IEEE Conference on Software Maintenance, Reengineering, and Reverse Engineering (CSMR-WCRE) (2014)
3. Karlsson, S., Čaušević, A., Sundmark, D.: QuickREST: property-based test generation of OpenAPI-described RESTful APIs. In: IEEE 13th International Conference on Software Testing, Validation and Verification (ICST) (2020)
4. Lauret, A.: The Design of Web APIs. Manning (2019)
5. Li, J., Xiong, Y., Liu, X., Zhang, L.: How does web service API evolution affect clients? In: IEEE 20th International Conference on Web Services (2013)
6. Lübke, D., Zimmermann, O., Pautasso, C., Zdun, U., Stocker, M.: Interface evolution patterns—balancing compatibility and flexibility across microservices lifecycles. In: Proceedings of 24th European Conference on Pattern Languages of Programs (EuroPLoP 2019). ACM (2019)
7. Murer, S., Bonati, B., Furrer, F.: Managed Evolution - A Strategy for Very Large Information Systems. Springer, Heidelberg (2010). https://doi.org/10.1007/978-3-642-01633-2
8. OpenAPI Initiative (2022). https://www.openapis.org/. Accessed 11 May 2022
9. Serbout, S., Pautasso, C., Zdun, U.: How composable si the web? an empirical study on openapi data model compatibility. In: Proceedings of IEEE World Congress on Services (ICWS Symposium on Services for Machine Learning), Barcelona, Spain. IEEE, July 2022
10. Sohan, S., Anslow, C., Maurer, F.: A case study of web API evolution. In: IEEE World Congress on Services (2015)

11. Varga, E.: Creating Maintainable APIs. Springer, Heidelberg (2016). https://doi.org/10.1007/978-1-4842-2196-9
12. Yasmin, J., Tian, Y., Yang, J.: A first look at the deprecation of restful APIs: an empirical study. In: IEEE International Conference on Software Maintenance and Evolution (ICSME) (2020)

Architecting for Data-Driven Systems

ProML: A Decentralised Platform for Provenance Management of Machine Learning Software Systems

Nguyen Khoi Tran[1(✉)], Bushra Sabir[1], Muhammad Ali Babar[1], Nini Cui[1], Mehran Abolhasan[2], and Justin Lipman[2]

[1] The University of Adelaide, Adelaide, Australia
nguyen.tran@adelaide.edu.au
[2] University of Technology Sydney, Sydney, Australia

Abstract. Large-scale Machine Learning (ML) based Software Systems are increasingly developed by distributed teams situated in different trust domains. Insider threats can launch attacks from any domain to compromise ML assets (models and datasets). Therefore, practitioners require information about how and by whom ML assets were developed to assess their quality attributes such as security, safety, and fairness. Unfortunately, it is challenging for ML teams to access and reconstruct such historical information of ML assets (ML provenance) because it is generally fragmented across distributed ML teams and threatened by the same adversaries that attack ML assets. This paper proposes ProML, a decentralised platform that leverages blockchain and smart contracts to empower distributed ML teams to jointly manage a single source of truth about circulated ML assets' provenance without relying on a third party, which is vulnerable to insider threats and presents a single point of failure. We propose a novel architectural approach called Artefact-as-a-State-Machine to leverage blockchain transactions and smart contracts for managing ML provenance information and introduce a user-driven provenance capturing mechanism to integrate existing scripts and tools to ProML without compromising participants' control over their assets and toolchains. We evaluate the performance and overheads of ProML by benchmarking a proof-of-concept system on a global blockchain. Furthermore, we assessed ProML's security against a threat model of a distributed ML workflow.

Keywords: SE for AI · Provenance · Machine Learning · Blockchain

1 Introduction

Large-scale Machine Learning (ML) based Software Systems are increasingly developed by distributed interdisciplinary teams [16]. For instance, booking.com, one of the largest online travel agencies, employs *dozens* of multi-functional teams consisting of software developers, user interface designers, ML researchers, and ML engineers to develop and operate ML models [3]. Due to the emerging trend

ⓒ The Author(s), under exclusive license to Springer Nature Switzerland AG 2022
I. Gerostathopoulos et al. (Eds.): ECSA 2022, LNCS 13444, pp. 49–65, 2022.
https://doi.org/10.1007/978-3-031-16697-6_4

of outsourcing and crowdsourcing in ML engineering [3,16], ML teams might not even reside in the same organisation. Let us consider the following running example. A startup A has an ML application idea but lacks the ML skillset and infrastructure to realise it. Therefore, A outsources data collection and model development to companies B and C. The company B acts as a *dataset administrator*, collecting data from relevant sources (social media, open-source intelligence, official statistics) and labelling the data by crowdsourcing via a marketplace such as Amazon Mechanical Turk, a common practice in ML engineering [18]). Model development happens at C, where various *model developers* carry out workflow activities such as preprocessing data, engineering features, training and testing models. The trained models in the form of binaries or neural net architecture and weight values are returned to the *operators* and *auditors* at A for testing in a beta product.

Insider threats can compromise ML assets (models and datasets) at many points in the described ML workflow. For instance, annotators in the crowdsourcing platform can be bribed to mislabel data samples to enable poisoning attacks [9]. Some members of the model development team at C might be bribed to swap the trained model with a poisoned one before delivery. Following problem reports from A, organisation C might detect the model swapping following an internal investigation. However, they might not disclose the issue to protect their reputation, thus harming A. Therefore, all workflow participants, especially the auditors at A, require a complete history of ML assets *(ML provenance)* that show how and by whom workflow activities were performed in order to evaluate various quality attributes of ML assets, such as security, safety, and fairness. Unfortunately, *ML provenance information is generally fragmented* across a distributed ML workflow because participants can only record the provenance related to their activities and store the information in private silos. Moreover, even if the auditors at A can retrieve and reconstruct a complete history of ML assets, *such information might not be trustworthy* as the retrieved provenance records might also have been compromised by the insider threats that attacked ML assets.

This paper proposes **ProML** (**Pro**venance information of **M**achine **L**earning), a *decentralised* platform that leverages blockchain and smart contracts to manage ML provenance in a distributed ML workflow. Unlike the existing centralised provenance management solutions (e.g., [19,20]), ProML does not require workflow participants to appoint a leader or hire a third party to operate it. Instead, the platform distributes the right and responsibility to access and manage ML provenance information across stakeholders of an ML workflow, such as organisations A, B, and C in the running example. Stakeholders join the platform by running identical software clients called *ProML nodes* that maintain a private blockchain and run smart contracts to store and update ML provenance information. On-blockchain records serve as a *single source of truth* about the history of the circulated ML assets, addressing the fragmentation of ML provenance. On-blockchain software programs called smart contracts implement the necessary computation to process provenance updates submitted by workflow participants. Leveraging blockchain and smart contracts brings about various advantages, including data immutability, non-repudiation, integrity, transparency, and fairness [4, 23–25]. It should be noted that ProML directly involves stakeholders in blockchain operations (via ProML nodes) rather than outsourcing the responsibilities to a remote blockchain, an approach taken by many existing blockchain-based provenance systems for ML models [21] and datasets [2, 5, 6, 11, 12, 15, 17, 22, 26]. The direct participation provides stakeholders with complete control and access to the provenance information, reduces costly transaction fees and privacy risks associated with remote blockchains. We propose a novel architectural approach called *Artefact-as-a-State-Machine (ASM)* to utilise blockchain transactions and smart contracts for storing and updating ML provenance information.

Rather than implicitly monitoring and extracting ML provenance from workstations or big data processing clusters, we propose a *user-driven provenance capturing process* to help participants control what and how ML provenance is extracted without exposing them to the underlying complexities. In particular, every ProML node offers services and APIs for submitting provenance updates. Organisation C can embed services offered by ProML into their existing ML training scripts or provenance tools such as MLFlow[1] and Sacred[2] to control the reported information, preventing issues such as Data Use Agreement (DUA) violations. A ProML node belonging to C is considered trusted within C and can only be used by C to access and submit ML provenance.

We evaluate ProML's performance and overheads by deploying and benchmarking a proof-of-concept system on a global test blockchain network called Ropsten[3] to simulate a globally distributed ML workflow. Furthermore, we analysed the security of ProML against a threat model of a distributed ML workflow. On the Ropsten blockchain network, we found that the framework takes around 16 seconds to capture a provenance update and 2.5 minutes to finalise it with high confidence. These figures are negligible to the overall timeframe of a distributed ML workflow, which generally takes at least seven months to bring ML model ideas to production [7] and at least eight days to deploy a trained model [1]. Overhead-wise, according to the conversion rate obtained in April 2022, we found that registering a new asset with ProML costs around USD $160 and submitting a provenance record costs around USD $47. It should be noted that these monetary costs do not apply to private blockchains that ProML targets because participants in a private blockchain can generate an arbitrary amount of cryptocurrency to fund their provenance submission.

The major contributions of this paper include:

– Conceptualisation and architecture of a decentralised platform based on blockchain and smart contracts for secure management of ML provenance in a distributed ML workflow.

---

[1] (mlflow.org).

[2] (Github/IDSIA).

[3] https://ropsten.etherscan.io.

- A novel architectural approach for leveraging blockchain transactions and smart contracts to securely store and update ML provenance information in a distributed ML workflow.
- A user-driven approach to capture ML provenance information that preserves users' control, eases the integration with users' existing scripts and toolchains and abstracts the complexity of blockchain interaction.

2   Preliminary

A *blockchain* is a shared-write database and a secure distributed computer operated by mutually distrusting parties [4]. Formally, it is a transaction-based state machine (Eq. 1) replicated across blockchain participants [23, 24].

$$\sigma_{t+1} \equiv \Upsilon(\sigma_t, T) \tag{1}$$

State transitions are initialised and controlled by *transactions* T, which are instructions coming from *blockchain accounts*. These instructions convey diverse messages, from moving fund between accounts to invoking user-defined software programs, also known as *smart contracts*. Transactions are digitally signed by senders to prevent forgery and tamper as they are distributed amongst blockchain participants. The signatures also prevent senders from falsely denying their transactions.

Blockchain participants calculate the new state σ_{t+1} independently using the deterministic state transition function Υ. Using a fault-tolerant consensus protocol such as Proof-of-Work (PoW), Proof-of-Authority (PoA), Proof-of-Stake (PoS), and Practical Byzantine Fault Tolerance (pBFT), participants reach an agreement on σ_{t+1}. The transaction leading to the accepted σ_{t+1} is added to an ordered transaction list called a *ledger*. All participants hold a copy of the ledger, which represents the canonical history of a blockchain. The ledger is usually stored in a *secure data structure called blockchain*, which uses cryptographic hashes to prevent and detect tampering of content and order of transactions.

Some blockchain protocols such as Ethereum allows users to embed arbitrary software programs called smart contracts to Υ. Smart contracts are generally as stateful objects that has their own blockchain address, internal variables, and functions to act upon those variables.

3   ProML Platform

Every deployment of the ProML platform consists of multiple identical software clients called ProML nodes, deployed and operated independently by workflow participants. The admission, authorisation, and governance of participants are beyond the scope of our paper. We assume that such decisions are in place before ProML is deployed. Figure 1 depicts a ProML deployment for five participants.

Components within a ProML node are structured into three layers. The *client* layer contains software clients implementing blockchain and other distributed protocols used by ProML. This layer also contains a *blockchain wallet*

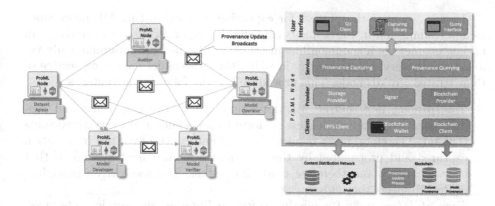

Fig. 1. ProML Platform for a distributed ML workflow with five participants

that holds a participant's private keys to sign blockchain transactions on their behalf. Upon deployment, clients from different ProML nodes connect to form a blockchain and other decentralised infrastructure used by ProML, such as a private content distribution network based on the Interplanetary File System (IPFS[4]). ProML deploys smart contracts on the deployed blockchain to capture and update ML provenance information. Section 3.2 presents our proposed architectural approach called Artefact-as-a-State-Machine (ASM) for engineering these contracts.

The *provider* layer contains service wrappers that abstract the technical complexities and provide a consistent Application Programming Interface (API) to the clients. For instance, the *blockchain provider* can offer a consistent API with high-level services such as "send a transaction" and transform the function calls into proper messages expected by an underlying blockchain client. *Storage provider* and *signer* perform similar tasks for storage clients (e.g., IFPS) and wallets.

The service layer contains high-level services for accessing and updating ML provenance. Participants can invoke these services ad-hoc via the provided software clients or programmatically using a software library. Section 3.1 presents our proposed user-driven approach the leverages these components for capturing ML provenance.

3.1   User-Driven Provenance Capture

The provenance capturing process is a collaboration between participants and their trusted ProML nodes. Participants *initiate the process* and supply the necessary provenance records (pm_i or $Prov_{DS_i}$). ProML nodes *finish the process* by crafting and submitting the corresponding blockchain transactions (tx_{pm_i} or $tx_{Prov_{DS_i}}$) on behalf of the participants with their blockchain credentials.

---

[4] https://ipfs.io.

Figure 2 depicts the process for capturing and submitting ML provenance from a training script. Participants can submit pm_i or $Prov_{DS_i}$ to ProML in an ad-hoc manner via a commandline interface (CLI) client, programmatically via a software library, or directly by invoking the provenance capturing service of their trusted ProML node. This procedure has the following advantages:

– *Transparency and control:* ML development activities can utilise and produce sensitive data, which must conform to predefined Data Use Agreements (DUAs). Therefore, users require visibility and control over the information captured and propagated by the provenance management system so that they can verify and therefore trust the system. The user-driven procedure of ProML meets this ends.
– *Ease of Integration:* By offering software libraries and service interfaces, ProML allows users to integrate the provenance capturing mechanism into their toolchains in a way that is suited to their operating situation and setup.
– *Simplicity:* Having ProML nodes handle the complexities of interacting with blockchain helps to simplify the usage and avoid security mistakes.

The following section presents how different components in a ProML node work to capture some prominent life cycle events of ML assets.

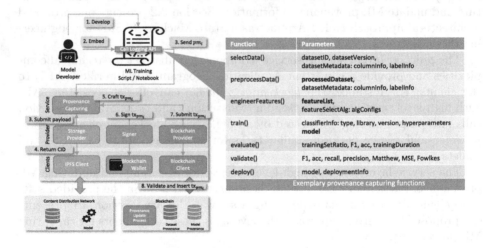

Fig. 2. User-Driven Provenance Capturing Mechanism

Registering a Model or Dataset: Asset registration creates an on-blockchain representative of an ML asset and begins its life cycle with ProML. When registering a dataset, ProML also requires the dataset's metadata, address, and the identifier of its ancestor if available. The *provenance capturing service* uses the provided information (pm_i or $Prov_{DS_i}$) to construct blockchain transactions for deploying smart contracts that represent the given models or datasets. It uses the *signer* service, which holds participants' private keys, to sign the constructed transactions with participants' credentials. Following the signing, the provenance capturing service invokes the *provider* service, which wraps around a blockchain client, to publish the transactions. The registration completes when the transactions have been added to the ledger, making the smart contracts available on the blockchain. ProML returns the addresses of the deployed contracts as asset identifiers. Details of the involved smart contracts would be elaborated in Sect. 3.2.

Recording Model's Life Cycle Events: ProML provides model developers with a software library containing functions that triggers the reporting of different actions performed on a model (selecting and preprocessing data, engineering features, training, evaluating, validating, and deploying model). The parameters passed to these functions are *payload* that describe inputs *in*, outputs *out*, and parameters *param* of actions. The number and types of functions making up the library closely relate to the on-blockchain representatives of ML models and reflect an agreed ML workflow amongst participants. By controlling whether to call these functions and what to provide, participants control the provenance information leaving their trust domain. Figure 2 presents the process and exemplary provenance capturing functions.

When the embedded functions are executed, they submit provenance records pm_i to a trusted ProML node, whose *provenance capturing service* constructs transactions tx_{pm_i} that address the smart contract representing the ML models being recorded, and submits the transactions with the help of the *signer* and *provider* services.

Publishing a Model or Dataset: The provenance records of a model or a dataset publication contain large payloads such as CSV files, databases, executable binaries, or neural network architectures and weight values. Storing such payloads on-chain is discouraged to prevent scalability issues of the distributed ledger. ProML leverages the *off-chain data storage design pattern* [25] to secure the payloads associated with provenance records without keeping those payloads on the blockchain. Specifically, the provenance capturing service can offload the payloads to a distributed content-addressable storage, such as a private IPFS cluster, and keep the pointers to those payloads in the on-chain provenance records. The *storage provider* service is responsible for managing and interacting with off-chain storage such as IPFS.

3.2   Artefact-as-a-State-Machine

Mapping information and processes onto blockchain constructs is a prerequisite for storing and managing them on a blockchain. We propose an architectural approach to guide this mapping based on the following observations:

1. **Every ML asset has a set of states according to its workflow.** For example, an ML model reaches the "trained" state after being fitted to a dataset by a training algorithm.
2. **Actions performed on an ML asset can trigger a state transition.** For instance, the training activity pushes an ML model from a previous stage (engineered features) to the next stage (trained).

3. **ML provenance is the record of a state transition and the responsible party.** In other words, it describes the input, output, parameters of a conducted activity and the identifier of the participant (P_{id}) carrying it out. It should be noted that provenance records are valid and valuable even if the reported activities failed to update the state of an asset. These records show that a participant has conducted a wrong action on it at a certain time.

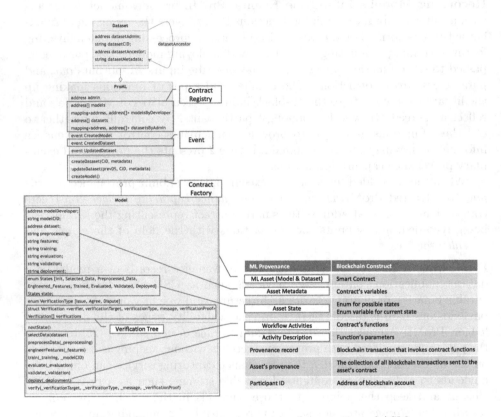

Fig. 3. Exemplary smart contract implementation of ASM

The above observations suggest that ML assets can be modelled as state machines from a provenance perspective. Mapping this state machine representation of ML assets to blockchain constructs is straightforward, as blockchain by design is a replicated state machine (Sect. 2). ML models and datasets map to smart contract instances because they are individually addressable blockchain objects that carry internal variables and functions to act upon those variables. The address of a smart contract becomes an asset's identifier. Internal variables of a smart contract can be used to store an asset's state and metadata. Functions of a smart contract represent workflow activities that update an asset's state. Function parameters can be used to capture the *payload* of a provenance record corresponding to a workflow activity. Participants record a provenance update pm_i by submitting a blockchain transaction to the smart contract to invoke a function corresponding to the reported workflow activity. These transactions serve as provenance records. We call this approach of modelling ML assets as state machines to map them to blockchain constructs for management as *Artefact-as-a-State-Machine, or ASM.* Figure 3 depicts an exemplary implementation of ASM with smart contracts written in Solidity programming language[5].

Implementation Challenges and Solutions: Implementing ASM introduce three challenges listed below. We address these challenges by leveraging the existing design patterns for blockchain-based application [25]. A utility smart contract named ProML was introduced to implement these patterns.

- *Providing a lightweight communication mechanism to notify participants of on-blockchain events such as model publication.* We leverage the embedded event functionality of many blockchain platform to emit events to off-blockchain software via the log portion of a ledger. Events are defined and emitted by the utility contract ProML.
- *Creating and deploying smart contract instances from predefined templates.* We apply the factory contract design pattern by introducing factory functions in the ProML contract, which creates and deploys contract instances based on the templates held by ProML.
- *Maintaining pointers to the registered models and datasets.* We apply the contract registry pattern by adding into ProML arrays of addresses pointing to asset contracts as well as mappings between participants and the registered assets for looking up.

4   Performance and Cost Evaluation

This section presents an evaluation of ProML's performance and operating costs, which impact the platform's feasibility in real-world scenarios. We consider performance as how fast ProML processes and appends provenance updates. The cost aspect indicates the necessary resources for workflow participants to submit ML provenance updates.

4.1   Experimental Design

We evaluated the performance and operating cost of ProML by benchmarking a proof-of-concept (PoC) implementation. The PoC leverages the Solidity programming language (see Footnote 5) to implement smart contracts according to the ASM approach. These smart contracts are compatible with many public and private blockchains that use Ethereum Virtual Machine (EVM) as

---

[5] https://soliditylang.org.

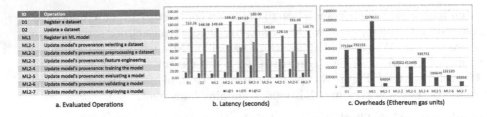

Fig. 4. Latency and overheads of the evaluated operations

the smart contract execution engine. The PoC's smart contracts were deployed on Ropsten, a global Ethereum blockchain network preserved for testing[6]. We chose this blockchain network due to its scale and similarity in configurations and performance characteristics with the Ethereum main network, which operates most high-profile and high-value blockchain-based software applications. We used `Ethers`[7] for implementing the blockchain provider and signer services and `Node` for the provenance capturing and querying services.

Procedure and Data: The experimental workload consisted of ten operations that register and update a dataset and a model (Fig. 4a). We triggered these operations sequentially with ten-second delays and tracked the submitted blockchain transactions to determine their latency and operating cost. This process was replicated ten times. We generated ML provenance for the experiment by training an intrusion detection classifier on the KDD-99 dataset[8] and utilising the provenance capturing procedure described in Sect. 3.1 to capture the data.

Evaluation Metrics: We measured the performance in terms of *latency*, the amount of time between the submission of a provenance update ($tx_{Prov_{DS_i}}$ or tx_{pm_i}) and its inclusion in a blockchain. Every subsequent block represents an additional confirmation of the update, which strengthens its trustworthiness. We formalise a transaction's latency at the confirmation level x as $L@x := t_0 - t_x$, where t_0 is the submission time, and t_x is the time at which a transaction block representing the confirmation x appears in the blockchain.

We measured the operating cost in terms of *gas*, a unit that measures the computational effort required to process and store a transaction on an Ethereum blockchain, on which we deployed the proof-of-concept system. Transactions with higher gas values requires more computation and storage space on a blockchain than transactions with lower gas value. The Ethereum Yellow Paper [24] formally defines gas and a fee schedule.

---

[6] https://ropsten.etherscan.io.
[7] https://docs.ethers.io/v5/.
[8] http://kdd.ics.uci.edu/databases/kddcup99/kddcup99.html.

4.2 Results

Latencies: Figure 4b presents the average latencies of various operations of ProML at one, six, and twelve confirmations. The framework takes around 16 s to record a provenance update to the Ropsten network (L@1). However, achieving confidence that a provenance update has been finalised requires around 2.5 min (L@12).

The existing studies have shown that most companies take at least seven months to bring ML model ideas to production [7] and at least eight days to deploy a trained model [1]. Moreover, ML workflow activities generally do not need to wait for the provenance record of a previous step. Therefore, we argue that the provenance recording latency is negligible and would not impact the overall latency of the workflow.

Operating Cost: Figure 4c compares the operating cost of the evaluation operations. The registration steps (D1, D2, and ML1) are the most costly operations because they involve creating and deploying additional smart contracts on the blockchain. Updating the provenance of an ML model (ML2-1 to ML2-7) incurs a lower cost, averaging at 280000 gas units.

To put these figures in context, we convert them to the dollar value using the conversion rate obtained in April 2022 from the public Ethereum network (USD \$0.000163542 per gas unit[9]). According to the conversion rate, registering a new asset with ProML costs around USD \$160 and submitting a provenance record costs around USD \$47. It should be noted that these monetary costs do not apply to private blockchain networks where ProML aims to operate, because participants in a private blockchain can generate an arbitrary amount of cryptocurrency to fund their provenance submission.

5 Security Evaluation

This section evaluates the security of ProML. First, we define a threat model of a distributed ML workflow where ProML operates. Then, we present the security countermeasures provided by ProML and discuss their effectiveness against the identified threats.

5.1 Threat Model

ProML considers an adversary who aims to corrupt the provenance and verification of ML artefacts to cover up their tampering with a model [10] or a dataset (e.g., poisoning attack [2]). We assume that ML workflow participants are *not anonymous* and possibly bound by legal contracts. We assume that the involved networks and infrastructures are protected by cloud service vendors or enterprise security mechanisms and thus safe from traditional threats, allowing us to focus on insider threats: authorised employees who have gone rogue or compromised by external attackers.

---

[9] https://etherscan.io/gastracker.

Table 1 presents the threat model of ProML. Tampering threats denote unauthorised modification or destruction of artefacts and provenance information. Spoofing threats denote the forgery of provenance updates and verification results. Repudiation denotes that a participant falsely denies their previously provenance records to avoid responsibility. Finally, DoS threats denote attacks that corrupt datasets, models, and provenance information or disrupt the infrastructure necessary to access them.

Table 1. Threat Model of ProML

	Threat	Target
T1	Tampering	At-rest data: Datasets, Models, Provenance Records
T2	Tampering	In-transit data: Datasets, Models, Provenance Records
T3	Spoofing	Provenance records, verification results
T4	Repudiation	Provenance records
T5	DoS	Data stores for datasets, models, provenance records
T6	DoS	Provenance capturing process
T7	DoS	Provenance retrieval process

Secury Countermeasures of ProML. ProML provides the following security countermeasures by leveraging blockchain, smart contracts, and a decentralised architecture.

- **Storing provenance records on a blockchain:** Blockchain data has tamper-resistance and high-availability by design [23,25]. By storing provenance records on a blockchain, we protect them against unauthorised modification and destruction by insider threats. This countermeasure addresses threat T1, T2, and T5.
- **Storing assets on a peer-to-peer content distribution network.** The storage facility of models and datasets presents a single point of failure if it is the only source of those assets. Therefore, ProML nodes form a private, peer-to-peer content network based on the IPFS protocol to offer participants an alternative resilient storage solution. This countermeasure addresses threat T5 and T7.
- **Anchoring off-blockchain artefacts to on-blockchain records using content identifiers.** ProML embeds a cryptographic representation (hash) of the registered models and datasets, allowing users to verify the integrity of any incoming asset. This countermeasure addresses threat T1 and T2.
- **Embedding the provenance recording process in smart contracts.** ProML implements the logic related to the registration and update of assets in smart contracts to prevent an adversary from tampering with or disrupting these processes. This countermeasure addresses threat T6.
- **Embedding provenance updates in blockchain transactions.** This countermeasure leverages digital signatures and the inclusion of transactions

into a transaction block to mitigate the spoofing and repudiation of provenance updates. This countermeasure addresses threat T3 and T4.

6 Discussions

6.1 Usage Scenarios

Auditing ML Assets: The complete and trustworthy provenance information provided by ProML can help auditors detect issues of incoming ML assets more effectively. For instance, auditors at the organisation A in the running example can calculate and compare the cryptographic hash of the received ML model against the one reported by the developers at C to detect the model swapping attack by an insider threat at C. By inspecting the training and testing datasets reported by B and C via ProML, auditors at A can detect fairness risks of the received model early. Even if an organisation omits provenance updates from ProML, the omission itself can serve as an indicator of compromise.

Track and Trace Vulnerabilities and Compromises: Having a complete and trustworthy history helps auditors trace compromised assets to their root causes. For instance, if A determines that the model from C does not match the one reported by the developers at C, then both A and C can trace the compromised model to the employee who carries out the model delivery. After detecting the root cause (i.e., employee-turn-rogue), C can use ProML to track all activities that involve this employee to identify all potential compromises for damage control.

6.2 Where ProML Performs unsatisfactorily

Case 1: Network Fails to Reach a Threshold Size. The security of a decentralised system like ProML depends on the number of participants. Whilst existing surveys have suggested the existence of large-scale ML workflows, some ML workflows might not clear the threshold number of participants. In the future, we plan to explore mechanisms to combine ProML networks to pool their resources for processing blockchain transactions whilst maintaining the confidentiality of the constituting ProML networks.

Case 2: Participants Deliberately Submit Misinformation. Blockchain and smart contracts cannot detect misleading information or omission in the provenance information submitted by participants. However, they maintain trustworthy records of the submitted information that allow other participants to audit and detect misbehaviours. Future research could investigate blockchain-based peer-review protocols to leverage participants' expertise in auditing ML assets and their provenance.

6.3   Threat to Validity

The generalizability of the benchmark results is a validity threat to our evaluation. We mitigated this by choosing Ropsten, the most realistic representation of the Ethereum main net[10] which is one of the most prominent blockchains. Moreover, the performance of ProML would be higher in practice as organisations are likely to adopt consortium blockchains such as Hyperledger Fabric, which exchange openness and anonymity for orders of magnitude performance gain. Therefore, we believe that our benchmark results are helpful because they represent a worst-case scenario.

7   Related Work

This paper aligns with the research on the secure management of the provenance of ML models and datasets. Earlier works on data provenance focused on logging the utilisation of computer files for future privacy compliance audits [17,22] or mitigating poisoning attacks on ML models via datasets [2,21]. Gebru et al. [8] were the first to present a standardized process via question answering to document datasets used in ML projects. Sutton et al. [22] were among the firsts to leverage the Bitcoin blockchain as a security countermeasure to protect the log itself. Since then, blockchain has been and is still commonly used as an alternative secure storage solution for log data (e.g., [12,26]). Recent research has extended blockchain's role by leveraging its programmability via smart contracts to extend its role. For instance, ProVHL [5,6] and [11] employed blockchain as an authoriser and logger for the data stored on an open-source data management system or an IPFS content network. Moller et al. [15] was among the first that captured workflow steps rather than access logs of electronic data on the blockchain as provenance information.

The provenance of ML models has been relatively less explored. Earlier works on model provenance (e.g., [19]) focused on the automated extraction of metadata and provenance of ML experiments, such as details of their training runs, statistics of datasets, evaluation results, and models' metadata. Mitchell et al. [14] proposed a standardized document called model cards to accompanied trained models, presenting their performance characteristics and other metadata. Souza et al. [20] were among the first to advocate for describing the capturing the workflow provenance of ML models to address the increasingly complicated and heterogeneous nature of ML workflows. Recent years have witnessed increased utilisation of blockchain as a security mechanism for the provenance of ML models. For instance, Lo et al. [13] employed smart contracts to store the encrypted hashes of datasets and models appearing in federated learning systems. ProML does more than storing the hashes of models or datasets emerging from an ML workflow. Inspired by [20] and [15], ProML also captures details regarding how workflow activities are performed on ML assets, empowering deeper auditing

---

[10] https://ethereum.org/en/developers/docs/networks/#ropsten.

well as track and trace of compromises. We codified a structured way to capture workflow-centric provenance information on a blockchain with the proposed ASM approach. Moreover, instead of shifting the responsibility for managing provenance from a cloud service to a remote blockchain network, ProML fully embraces decentralisation, allowing relevant participants to secure the provenance information themselves and maintain complete control over how and what information they share.

8 Conclusion

Large-scale Machine Learning based Software Systems are increasingly developed by distributed ML workflows, where provenance information is paramount to secure and verify the circulated models and datasets. This paper proposes a decentralised platform named ProML that leverages blockchain and smart contracts for disseminating, storing, and updating ML provenance securely. ProML proposes a novel architectural approach called Artefact-as-a-State-Machine (ASM) to store and manage ML provenance on a blockchain. Via benchmarks conducted on a global test blockchain network, we showed that ProML's latencies are negligible compared to the average timeframe of ML workflows. Via a security analysis, we also showed that ProML is secure against tampering, spoofing, repudiation, and denial of service threats in a distributed ML workflow environment. Thus, we believe that ProML could be a foundation for developing decentralised software systems that help secure the increasingly remote and distributed engineering process of ML and software systems.

References

1. Algorithmia: 2020 State of Enterprise Machine Learning (2020). https://algorithmia.com/state-of-ml
2. Baracaldo, N., Chen, B., Ludwig, H., Safavi, J.A.: Mitigating poisoning attacks on machine learning models: a data provenance based approach. In: AISec 2017 - Proceedings of the 10th ACM Workshop on Artificial Intelligence and Security, Co-Located with CCS 2017, pp. 103–110 (2017)
3. Bernardi, L., Mavridis, T., Estevez, P.: 150 successful machine learning models: 6 lessons learned at Booking.com. In: Proceedings of the ACM SIGKDD International Conference on Knowledge Discovery and Data Mining, pp. 1743–1751 (2019)
4. Cachin, C., Vukolić, M.: Blockchain consensus protocols in the wild. arXiv preprint arXiv:1707.01873 (2017)
5. Dang, T.K., Anh, T.D.: A pragmatic blockchain based solution for managing provenance and characteristics in the open data context. In: Dang, T.K., Küng, J., Takizawa, M., Chung, T.M. (eds.) FDSE 2020. LNCS, vol. 12466, pp. 221–242. Springer, Cham (2020). https://doi.org/10.1007/978-3-030-63924-2_13
6. Demichev, A., Kryukov, A., Prikhodko, N.: The approach to managing provenance metadata and data access rights in distributed storage using the hyperledger blockchain platform. In: Proceedings - 2018 Ivannikov Isp Ras Open Conference, ISPRAS 2018, pp. 131–136 (2018). https://doi.org/10.1109/ISPRAS.2018.00028

7. Dotscience: The State of Development and Operations of AI Applications. dotscience Survey (2019). https://dotscience.com/assets/downloads/Dotscience_Survey-Report-2019.pdf
8. Gebru, T., et al.: Datasheets for datasets. Commun. ACM **64**(12), 86–92 (2021)
9. He, Y., Meng, G., Chen, K., Hu, X., He, J.: Towards security threats of deep learning systems: a survey. In: IEEE Trans. Softw. Eng. **48**, 1743–1770 (2020)
10. Jentzsch, S.F., Hochgeschwender, N.: Don't forget your roots! using provenance data for transparent and explainable development of machine learning models. In: Proceedings - 2019 34th IEEE/ACM International Conference on Automated Software Engineering Workshops, ASEW 2019, pp. 37–40 (2019)
11. Khatal, S., Rane, J., Patel, D., Patel, P., Busnel, Y.: FileShare: a blockchain and IPFS framework for secure file sharing and data provenance. In: Advances in Machine Learning and Computational Intelligence, pp. 825–833 (2021)
12. Kumar, M., Singh, A.K., Suresh Kumar, T.V.: Secure Log Storage Using Blockchain and Cloud Infrastructure. 2018 9th International Conference on Computing, Communication and Networking Technologies, ICCCNT 2018 pp. 10–13 (2018)
13. Lo, S.K., et al.: Towards trustworthy AI: Blockchain-based architecture design for accountability and fairness of federated learning systems. IEEE Internet of Things J. (2022)
14. Mitchell, M., et al.: Model cards for model reporting. In: Proceedings of the Conference on Fairness, Accountability, and Transparence, pp. 220–229 (2019)
15. Möller, J., Fröschle, S., Hahn, A.: Permissioned blockchain for data provenance in scientific data management. In: Ahlemann, F., Schütte, R., Stieglitz, S. (eds.) WI 2021. LNISO, vol. 48, pp. 22–38. Springer, Cham (2021). https://doi.org/10.1007/978-3-030-86800-0_2
16. Nahar, N., Zhou, S., Lewis, G., Kästner, C.: Collaboration challenges in building ml-enabled systems: communication, documentation, engineering, and process. Organization **1**(2), 3 (2022)
17. Neisse, R., Steri, G., Nai-Fovino, I.: A blockchain-based approach for data accountability & provenance tracking. In: ACM International Conference Proceeding Series (2017)
18. Paolacci, G., Chandler, J., Ipeirotis, P.G.: Running experiments on amazon mechanical turk. Judgm. Decis. Mak. **5**(5), 411–419 (2010)
19. Schelter, S., Böse, J.H., Kirschnick, J., Klein, T., Seufert, S.: Automatically tracking metadata and provenance of machine learning experiments. In: Machine Learning Systems Workshop at NIPS, pp. 1–8 (2017)
20. Souza, R., et al.: Workflow provenance in the lifecycle of scientific machine learning. Concurr. Comput. Pract. Exp. **34**, 1–21 (2020)
21. Stokes, J.W., England, P., Kane, K.: Preventing machine learning poisoning attacks using authentication and provenance. In: MILCOM 2021–2021 IEEE Military Communications Conference (MILCOM) (2021)
22. Sutton, A., Samavi, R.: Blockchain Enabled privacy audit logs. In: d'Amato, C., et al. (eds.) ISWC 2017. LNCS, vol. 10587, pp. 645–660. Springer, Cham (2017). https://doi.org/10.1007/978-3-319-68288-4_38
23. Tran, N.K., Ali Babar, M.: Anatomy, concept, and design space of blockchain networks. In: Proceedings - IEEE 17th International Conference on Software Architecture, ICSA 2020 (2020)
24. Wood, G.: Ethereum: A Secure Decentralized Generalized Transaction Ledger. Ethereum Yellow Paper (2014)

25. Xu, X., Pautasso, C., Zhu, L., Lu, Q., Weber, I.: A pattern collection for blockchain-based applications. In: EuroPLoP 2018: Proceedings of the 23rd European Conference on Pattern Languages of Programs (2018)
26. Zhang, Y., Lin, X., Xu, C.: Blockchain-based secure data provenance for cloud storage. In: Naccache, D., et al. (eds.) ICICS 2018. LNCS, vol. 11149, pp. 3–19. Springer, Cham (2018). https://doi.org/10.1007/978-3-030-01950-1_1

A Systematic Survey of Architectural Approaches and Trade-Offs in Data De-identification

Dimitri Van Landuyt[✉][iD] and Wouter Joosen[iD]

imec-DistriNet, KU Leuven, Leuven, Belgium
{dimitri.vanlanduyt,wouter.joosen}@cs.kuleuven.be

Abstract. Data de-identification refers to the process of removing or hiding the direct and indirect (quasi-)identifiers from data elements through transformation, generalization, or removal. Through active research over twenty years, diverse de-identification approaches, algorithms and tools have emerged. Existing survey studies focus predominantly on the application of de-identification within specific domains and to different data types, with attention to intrinsic characteristics of the algorithms and methods, and the impact on data utility –the extent to which the data can still serve its functional purpose after de-identification.

However, from a software architecture design perspective, de-identification affects a number of additional non-trivial and impactful non-functional attributes, and a comprehensive overview of the involved architectural concerns and trade-offs is currently lacking.

To address this gap, we present the outcome of a systematic literature review (SLR) study that: (1) outlines the current state of the art in an architecture tactic tree which classifies different architectural approaches to de-identification, (2) provides a further exploration of the relevant architectural trade-offs discussed in literature.

Keywords: de-identification · privacy tactics · privacy engineering

1 Introduction

In today's digital society, the automated collection and processing of personal data has become common practice. Activities in which aspects of our personal affairs are systematically recorded by and disclosed to third-parties—service providers, government actors and other individuals—have been normalized and adopted on a scale that generates societal awareness and concern. From a system design perspective, adopting appropriate methods and tools for data protection is essential to avoid harming the fundamental rights to data privacy.

De-identification methods and techniques involve actively reducing or removing the association to a person's identity from data sets or data records. These techniques are used to proactively address risk by reducing the harm to individuals in case of data leaks. A fitting illustration of the relevance of such methods

ⓒ The Author(s), under exclusive license to Springer Nature Switzerland AG 2022
I. Gerostathopoulos et al. (Eds.): ECSA 2022, LNCS 13444, pp. 66–82, 2022.
https://doi.org/10.1007/978-3-031-16697-6_5

comes from studying the diverse contact tracing applications used to identify possible infection paths in the COVID-19 pandemic [3]. In the broader roll-out of these systems, the adoption of suitable de-identification strategies has been a key element in establishing such a system[1] whilst gaining societal acceptance.

Spearheaded mainly in the area of clinical research over twenty years ago, research on data de-identification techniques and algorithms has grown to be diverse and extensive. De-identification is applied to various data types, ranging from unstructured, textual or multimedia formats (video, image, speech), to structured data (key-value, object-oriented, graph, documents, etc.) and at different levels of granularity, ranging from specific attributes of specific records, to entire data records and data sets. De-identification approaches, techniques or algorithms such as data aggregation, encryption, suppression, pseudonymization, rounding, noise addition are *transformative* in nature as they actively modify data elements, some permanently others still reversible. In general, de-identification negatively impacts *data utility*, i.e. the degree to which the transformed data sets can still be used for its intended purposes.

Existing surveys, taxonomies [11,18,31,36] and tools [10,27,34] support practitioners (software architects and developers) in selecting appropriate de-identification techniques. These resources focus predominantly on (i) the implemented approach or algorithm and its intrinsic characteristics, and/or (ii) the interplay between the degree of de-identification (privacy risk reduction) and data utility [7,19,24,30]. However, there is no one-size-fits-all solution, and the establishment of a proper treatment of data depends on a broad set of contextual architectural factors that go beyond the nature of a technique or the utility-privacy trade-off. For example, some de-identification approaches require substantial computational or power resources and are therefore not applicable in resource-constrained environments such as mobile or IoT devices, while others in turn introduce significant architectural complexity, for example as they rely on strict physical separation between pseudonyms and pseudonymous data (and thus impose deployment and data placement constraints).

Limited attention is spent to the broader architectural design implications of de-identification, and an in-depth study of the intrinsic trade-offs is lacking. In this article, we present the results of a systematic literature review (SLR) study [15] involving 163 articles on de-identification of personal data. We (i) identify and summarize recurring architectural approaches for de-identification which we synthesize in tactic trees, and (ii) establish a broader and comprehensive overview of the different trade-offs that come into play in the architectural design of systems that perform de-identification of personal data.

The main contributions of this SLR study are: (i) disambiguation is performed between different methods and algorithms by generalizing them at the basis of the intrinsic approach focusing on the end effects of de-identification (the *architectural tactics*), (ii) we outline the broader architecturally-significant non-functional concerns that come into play when designing a de-identification

---

[1] The adoption of DP3T over the PEPP-PT protocol in some European countries was motivated by privacy concerns [23].

approach, and we highlight the main architectural decision points (sensitivity and trade-off points). Validation is performed in terms of (i) the broad applicability of the tactics to different data types and (ii) the compatibility and coverage when compared to existing catalogs of privacy patterns.

This article is structured as follows: Sect. 2 discussed the background and introduces the overall problem statement. Section 3 presents a reference model for data de-identification, used for disambiguation in the literature study. Section 4 then outlines the design and approach of the SLR study, and Sect. 5 presents the identified architectural tactics. Section 6 then provides an in-depth discussion of the non-functional aspects at play in data de-identification. Section 7 validates our work, and finally Sect. 8 concludes the article.

2   Background and Motivation

Section 2.1 discusses the background on architectural privacy tactics and patterns, after which Sect. 2.2 motivates the work and presents the problem statement.

2.1   Architectural Privacy Tactics and Patterns

An *architectural tactic* is an architectural design decision with a significant impact on the accomplishment of a non-functional property [2]. Alternative tactics for specific quality attributes are typically summarized in taxonomy structures such as tactic trees [2]. Taxonomies of tactics have been established for a wide array of non-functional attributes, including security [8,26], availability [32], performance [2], modifiability [2], safety [38], and for specific technology and application domains [12,21,25,35].

Privacy Design Strategies and Privacy Patterns. Hoepman [13] has established eight distinct privacy design strategies that can be adopted in a *privacy-by-design* approach. These privacy design strategies have been refined by Colesky et al. [5] into tactics. Although these tactics provide a more instructive refinement of the high-level privacy design strategies, the direct applicability to de-identification remains limited.

Privacy patterns [28,29][2] represent common design solutions to common privacy problems. Of the in total 72 privacy patterns in the online resource [29], only 23 involve de-identification, as the remaining privacy patterns focus on other aspects such as legal compliance, user transparency, involvement and awareness, and providing users with explicit controls to enact privacy options. Although the patterns also address de-identification topics, they generally lack a characterization of broader architectural implications.

2.2   Problem Statement and Research Questions

Software systems that have been designed by privacy experts with a strong a-priori emphasis on privacy preservation are shaped by these requirements,

---

[2] It is worth noting that [29] includes most of the patterns of [28].

e.g., contact tracing, online voting, whistleblower submission, online anonymity networks such as Tor, etc. In each such case, the emphasis on privacy has led to non-trivial and highly complex systems that can not easily be mapped to the existing privacy patterns and tactics.

This is indicative of the overall architectural significance of de-identification and shows that adopting a specific approach involves non-trivial architectural trade-offs. In practice, software architects and developers are still required to obtain a substantial degree of expertise to select the most appropriate methods in the context of a concrete system.

To address the above, we target the following two research questions:

RQ1. What are the different design strategies, approaches and architectural tactics used in the state of the art on data de-identification (regardless of data type and application domain)?

RQ2. Which non-functional attributes or requirements (NFRs) are affected by the choice of de-identification tactic and what are the involved trade-offs for each of these methods?

We address these research questions by means of a Systematic Literature Review (SLR) study, which is presented in Sect. 4. To contextualize and harmonize the work, Sect. 3 first presents a reference model for de-identification which delineates three distinct phases.

3   Reference Model for De-identification

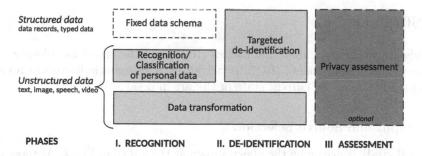

Fig. 1. A high-level reference model for de-identification, distinguishing between three phases involved in the broader context of de-identification.

As a consequence of the diversity in approaches and applications, terminology related 'de-identification' has become ambiguous and overloaded in literature. To increase clarity, Fig. 1 presents a summarizing overview of the different de-identification activities encountered in the current state of the art. De-identification in general is a phased approach, which involves the following three phases (or a subset thereof):

Phase I – the recognition and identification of personal data in unstructured information (e.g. face recognition, or the problem of identifying Named Entities [22] in unstructured text such as clinical notes),

Phase II – the transformation step that involves actively removing from or hiding the identifying information from the data, and/or

Phase III – the privacy assessment of the resulting datasets (e.g. at the basis of privacy models such as those involving differential privacy).

The final two phases can be performed iteratively and/or interchangeably, for example starting with the overall assessment of the privacy risk so that the targeted de-identification can be performed on a more informed basis. Depicted at the bottom of Fig. 1 are holistic transformation-based approaches, i.e. approaches that affect all data elements without making prior distinction between personal data and other data elements.

In some specific research areas (e.g., processing textual clinical notes), Phase I has received so much attention that the term '*de-identification*' has nearly become synonymous with the recognition of identifying information in unstructured data. However, in its strictest interpretation, de-identification refers to the act of fully removing any association to an identity from all data elements in a data set – in this extreme interpretation, de-identification is also called *anonymization*. In practice, however, fully removing any reference to the identity of individuals is often not desirable nor feasible, and the term 'de-identification' also refers to a wide array of approaches to purposely reduce the association between data elements and the identity of an individual in a less binary or destructive fashion.

4   Study Design

The identification of architectural tactics (RQ1) and the broader exploration of non-functional requirements (RQ2) is driven by a systematic literature review (SLR) study [15] of the current state of the art in de-identification.

4.1   Input and Source Selection

The SLR study is driven by the query shown at the left of in Fig. 2. As most de-identification research articles do not focus on the software architecture implications, (the inherent tactics or the involved trade-offs), this search query is intentionally kept broad and inclusive. Including keywords specific to architectural and trade-off decision making would lead to a too restricted data set not representative of the full range of techniques presented in literature.

This query was executed in the following digital libraries: the ACM Digital Library, IEEE Xplore, Springer Link and ScienceDirect. As depicted in Fig. 2, after merging data sets and duplicate removal, we also performed a step to exclude papers (at the basis of article type and scope) to ensure data quality. The resulting literature corpus consists of 163 articles and is accessible [37].

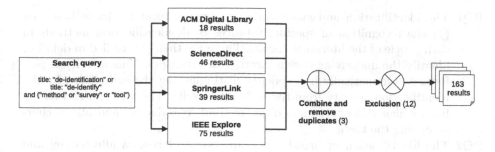

Fig. 2. The applied search strategy in the systematic literature review (SLR).

4.2 SLR Results

Since no further constraints were specified on the query presented above, the final result set of articles is heterogeneous: we identified articles in the domains of medical and health informatics research, legal research, signal processing and telecommunications, big data science, artificial intelligence and machine learning and software engineering and privacy research.

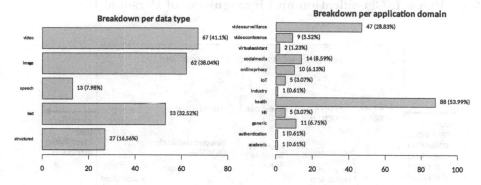

Fig. 3. Descriptive statistics of the obtained article set in terms of (a) the data types to which de-identification is applied and (b) the application domains.

Figure 3 presents a descriptive breakdown of the obtained data set, outlining the different data types and application domains in which de-identification is applied. Not surprisingly, the main application domains and use cases for de-identification are those areas in which privacy and data protection are still considered problematic, and remain high on the societal agenda: health care, (video) surveillance systems, online privacy and social media.

4.3 Research Approach

We adopt the following approach to address the two research questions:

RQ1 The identification and classification of architectural tactics is based on (1) the recognition of specific instances of de-identification methods in each article of the literature corpus. These are then (2) studied in detail to identify the underlying design strategy or strategies. This activity is performed systematically by explicitly distinguishing the end effect of a de-identification activity from the technique itself[3]. The focus on end effects itself makes this effort more objective and reproducible and allows characterizing the tactic.

RQ2 The identification of broader non-functional attributes affected by and involved in de-identification methods is based on a systematic study of the evaluation, validation and discussion sections of each article, and highlighting which aspects, qualities and system properties of architectural relevance have been subject to discussion, validation and/or evaluation.

5   De-identification Tactics

This section summarizes the results of addressing RQ1, more specifically aimed at consolidating and generalizing de-identification tactics.

5.1   Phase I. Classification and Recognition of Personal Data

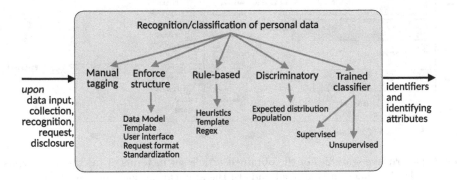

Fig. 4. Tactics for recognition and distinction of personal data, applied before actual de-identification steps.

Many de-identification methods are *targeted*, i.e. they are aimed at specific identifiers or quasi-identifiers under the assumption that identifiers and quasi-identifiers are known beforehand. However, in practice, many re-identification attacks are conducted by adversaries that manage to use data elements not

---

[3] For example, the technique of *recoloring elements of a picture* is considered to be a form of *removal* when it is deliberately used to hide distinguishing characteristics such as tattoos.

considered to be identifiers or quasi-identifiers effectively as identifiers (e.g. the use stylometric features to identify authors [6,14], etc.). Recognizing the direct and quasi-identifying characteristics in data is thus an essential step before performing de-identification. Different approaches have been discussed, explored and implemented in literature, of which a summary tactic tree is presented in Fig. 4[4]. In this tactics tree, five fundamentally different tactic types are defined, each with their own implications in terms of required effort (manual vs. automated), data structure (fixed or flexible), genericity and reusability (rules and heuristics can be domain-specific) and necessity for high-quality data sets in a training phase (classifier-based approaches).

5.2   Phase II. De-identification of Personal Data

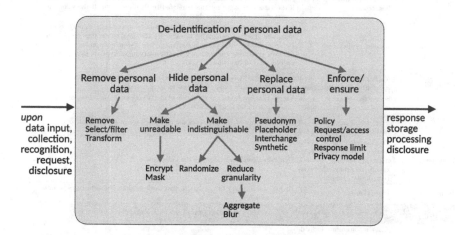

Fig. 5. Tactics tree for de-identification as privacy-preserving activity.

The tactics tree is presented in Fig. 5. A coarse-grained breakdown in four different categories of tactics is proposed, which differ in terms of degree of reversibility (removal of data can not be undone), the visibility of the outcome (replacement with realistic synthetic data can be done in such a way that an adversary would not even be able to see that the data was manipulated), the proactive or reactive nature of de-identification performed (e.g., request or access control). An extensive clarification of the different tactics is provided in Table 1, along with the encountered synonyms for each tactic. Approaches executed in phase III are covered in the Privacy model tactic and are discussed in the final row of Table 1.

---

[4] We have adopted the notation of Bass et al. [2] for creating a comprehensive graphical overview of the different architectural tactics in the form of a *tactics tree*. The left-hand side of the figure presents an overview of the different stimuli and the right-hand side shows the different manifestations in terms of quality attribute response.

Table 1. Glossary description of the different architectural tactics, including synonyms and reversibility consequences.

Tactic name	Synonym/refinement	Description	Reversible
REMOVE PERSONAL DATA	*Tactics in this category involve the removal of personal data (attributes, records, data sets).*		
REMOVE	Scrub, suppress, purge, eliminate, delete, strip, unlinked anonymization	The targeted and deliberate omission of identifying information from the data record or data set.	no
SELECT/FILTER	Sample	Same as REMOVE applied to a copy of the data while keeping the original data.	yes
TRANSFORM	Destructive transformation, permutation	The application of a holistic transformation (not targeted on identifying elements only) on data elements that is destructive in terms of ability to distinguish these data elements.	yes/no
HIDE PERSONAL DATA	*Tactics in this category involve actively hiding identifying information or discriminatory elements (attributes, records, data sets).*		
MAKE UNREADABLE	*Tactics in this category involve the modification of identifying attributes/records so that they have become unreadable or impossible to parse.*		
MASK	Obfuscate, overlay, blackbox, redact.	Overwriting data elements with other values for the purpose of obfuscating the content. If these constant values are randomized, this is related to RANDOMIZE, if the values are constant this is related to PLACEHOLDER. If the values are constant per involved individual, this is a form of PSEUDONYM.	no
ENCRYPT	Encode, cypher, hash	Use cryptographic means to encode the identifying attribute values/records/data sets. Further categories include: (i) Random encryption (probabilistic encryption), (ii) Deterministic encryption (searchable encryption such as Order-preserving encryption, Format-preserving encryption, Homomorphic encryption, Convergent encryption, . . .).	yes
MAKE INDISTINGUISHIBLE	*Tactics that involve the modification of identifying attribute values/records so that they have become more difficult to distinguish from other attribute values or records in the data set.*		
RANDOMIZE	Scramble, degrade, noise introduction, perturbation	Tactics that involve the modification of identifying attribute values/records by injecting artificial random elements.	no
REDUCE GRANULARITY	*Tactics that involve the systematic reduction of granularity of the data enclosed in the data set so that identifying becomes indiscernible.*		
AGGREGATE	Top/bottom coding, summarize, generalization, combination, binning, bucketization, rounding, abbreviation, outlier removal	Generalize, combine and group data elements.	no
BLUR	Pixelation	Reduce the accuracy of the data so that distinguishing characteristics become indiscernible	no
REPLACE PERSONAL DATA	*Tactics in this category involve the targeted replacement of personal data with different values.*		
PSEUDONYM	Alias replacement, individual surrogate, deterministic hash, individual replacement	The systematic replacement of direct identifiers with surrogates, whereby the mapping between surrogate and identity is kept separately	yes
PLACEHOLDER	Tagging, annotating, constant or fixed surrogate, role indication, text redacting, mask	The systematic replacement of direct identifiers with a surrogate that is the same for all member of the population	no
INTERCHANGE	Swapping, replacement, shuffling	The targeted mingling of data elements across members of the population	no
SYNTHETIC	Artificial surrogate, constructed replacement	The replacement of with a synthetic placeholder which is a constructed representation specifically aimed at conveying discriminatory features.	no
ENFORCE/ENSURE	*Tactics in this category involve the enforcement of de-identification (a priori through control mechanisms and a posterio through filtering and measurement).*		
DE-IDENTIFICATION POLICY	Sticky policy, data management policy	The operationalization of de-identification in separate policy and the enactment thereof	n/a
REQUEST/ACCESS CONTROL	Query rewriting, fine-grained access control (e.g., role-based, attribute-based, purpose-based)	Request manipulation or control (e.g. query transformation as to not to involve disclosure of PII), denying unpermitted requests based on the request content and request context (request purpose, credentials and permissions)	n/a
RESPONSE LIMITING	Query result filtering, query response limiting, sampling, selective disclosure	Enforcing constraints on the data disclosed (volume of the response, number of records, filtering out specific records/attributes)	n/a
PRIVACY MODEL	k-anonymity, t-closeness, l-diversity, ϵ-differential privacy	The utilization of statistical privacy models to assess the risk of re-identification (based on statistical variance), or (dis)similarity metrics	n/a

6 Non-functional Attributes and Trade-Offs Involved in De-identification

As discussed in Sect. 4, we address RQ2 by systematically studying the evaluation, validation and discussion sections of each article included in the literature corpus and highlighting which non-functional attributes (NFRs) have been discussed in the context of de-identification.

A detailed clarification of the different NFRs identified in this manner is presented in Table 2, distinguishing between (i) qualities of the recognition system used for identifying personal data (phase I), (ii) qualities and assessment criteria used to discuss and evaluate the outcome of de-identification itself (phases II and III), (iii) system properties, and (iv) development-centric concerns, related to the practical adoption of a technique. The final column of Table 2 shows the frequency of occurence of the different NFRs. These quantitative results confirm that de-identification literature is predominantly focused on the trade-off between privacy (performance) and utility, and on the performance in the recognition phase (precision and recall). Other system aspects of architectural relevance when adopting de-identification technologies are much less frequently discussed, and especially system aspects such as system performance (scalability) and memory consumption, and development-centric aspects such as the ability to customize de-identification approaches and policies, the testability (to continuously measure performance, or to assess the performance beforehand), are given much less consideration, yet are relevant in this broader scope.

We shortly discuss the main architectural considerations that will influence the selection of a suitable de-identification approach below. This discussion is structured along a number of recurring themes and is exploratory in nature.

Deployment Context for De-identification. If performed in a device controlled by the user (e.g., smartphone apps that perform de-identification), or very near the information source (e.g., on IoT gateways), discriminatory approaches such as differential privacy that act upon comparison of data records within a broader context (representative of a population) can not be adopted. In addition, concerns of resource utilization come into play when adopting costly classifier-based recognition systems. In such cases, tactics to hide (e.g., aggregation or encryption) or holistic transformation become most relevant [1,16].

Trust Models and Involved Parties. Complementary to the above, the organizations and parties involved in the data processing and the trust bestowed upon these will affect the de-identification choices made. De-identification commonly occurs when data is passed over organizational boundaries (e.g., sharing medical information among hospitals for the purpose of clinical research, sharing video information to a third party conferencing service, who in turn shares the video data to other participants). In privacy-preserving federated or decentralized learning and analytics approaches [4,17], different organizations that mutually mistrust each other set up collaborations, typically relying on the tactic of aggregation, i.e. by sharing intermediate or generalized outcomes, without having to share the source data.

Table 2. Overview of the different non-functional aspects discussed in literature.

NFR	Description	Frequency
Classifier properties (phase I)		
Classifier performance	The degree to which the trained classifier or recognition system can correctly recognize personal data (precision, recall, F-measure, false positives and true negative rates)	87 (53.37%)
Robustness	The degree to which the trained classifier or recognition system can withstand evolution or adversarial perturbations	3 (1.84%)
Postconditions after de-identification (phase II)		
Utility	The degree to which the data set can still serve its purpose after de-identification; this evidently depends highly on the intended purpose.	69 (42.33%)
Dissimilarity	The degree to which the result after de-identification differs from the original data set	9 (5.52%)
Risk (reduction)	An assessment of the residual risk of identification or the ability to re-identify individuals from the de-identified data.	9 (5.52%)
Irreversibility	The degree to which the de-identification step can be reversed (e.g. through inverse transformation steps, such as decryption)	2 (1.23%)
System impact (Phase I and II)		
System performance (incl. scalability)	The required time to de-identify, for example to indicate necessity to prepare classifers or perform de-identification in real-time	19 (11.66%)
Memory consumption	Determination whether the de-identification method can be used in a memory-constrained context.	2 (1.23%)
Energy consumption	Determination whether the de-identification method can be used in battery-powered devices.	1 (0.61%)
Security	Security impact of the de-identification approach (beyond the risk to re-identification highlighted above)	4 (2.45%)
Design properties (Phases I, II and III)		
Customizability	The degree to which automated steps (phase I and phase II) can be customized by the application developer.	6 (3.68%)
Testability	The ability to test the de-identification method and assess its performance during development.	1 (0.61%)
Human effort	The degree of human effort required (e.g. to verify the outputs, or provide training data).	11 (6.75%)

Threat Models and Adversaries. An untrusted and interested involved party is but one source of re-identification risk and different de-identification solutions will be required to guard against possible re-identification attacks from for example insiders (e.g., a database administrator), an external 'script kiddie' that has gained access to the network, a developer or technology provider that inserts backdoors, a nation state with virtually unlimited computational resources. A proper characterization of the adversaries against whom to protect will be essential. In this analysis, the nature and capabilities of adversaries or attackers against which the de-identification solution must act will heavily determine the selection of appropriate de-identification techniques, their strength and many other factors such as deployment, taking into account who has access to devices, data sources, etc. To accomplish this, we advocate in favor of adopting threat modeling and risk analysis approaches which allow identifying the most pertinent risks to re-identification, further characterizing its sources and provide a baseline to assess the overall effectiveness of the adopted de-identification approaches.

Proactive Versus On-demand De-identification. The decision between de-identifying entire data sets upon acquisition or initial storage and having to de-identify on demand (e.g., upon request and perhaps even in real-time processing) will heavily determine the de-identification approach.

For example, in [20] a dedicated classifier is pre-trained to allow for run-time transformation of speech in the context of speaker de-identification. Similarly, [33] presents a system in which image data is pro-actively de-identified and run-time access control mechanisms (including query manipulation mechanisms) are used to further reduce to risk to re-identification in the context of health research. Gafni et al. [9] have presented a dedicated transformation approach tailored to live (real-time) de-identification of human faces in video data. This approach as such does not include an explicit recognition activity (nor a targeted de-identification step) to allow meeting real-time processing constraints.

7   Validation

We first discuss the threats to validity. Then, we validate the tactic trees, first in terms of the applicability of tactics to different data types, then in terms of coverage in the existing privacy patterns.

7.1   Threats to Validity

Coverage. The architectural tactics presented in this paper are a synthesis of the studied (in total 163) articles. De-identification as a broader topic area is rife with ambiguity in terminology, which leads us to consider the risk that the adopted search query may not capture the most relevant work on de-identification. For example, we did not explore the literature at the basis of broadened formulations such as *"privacy-preserving data sharing"* which may lead to relevant articles currently not included. Regardless, as clearly illustrated in the descriptive statistics of Sect. 4, our search query did yield a data set that includes diverse approaches applied to different data types and application areas (cf. Fig. 3), and the diversity of the approaches is clearly illustrated in the presented tactic trees.

Researcher Bias. As discussed in Sect. 4.3, the construction of the tactics trees is based on a generalization and classification activity that was mainly driven by focusing on the objective end effects or outcomes of a de-identification approach. The survey was conducted by the same researchers at the basis of a shared understanding of the SLR goals. However, as no consensus mechanism was used, there is a potential risk of researcher bias which may impact overall reproducibility. The study does not draw statistical conclusions, but mainly focuses on synthesis of the de-identification approaches and algorithms, as established through the means of a systematic literature review (SLR) study.

7.2 Applicability of the De-identification Tactics to Data Types

We confirm the genericity of the established architectural tactics by considering the applicability of the tactics to different data types at different levels of granularity (data set, data record, data attribute). Table 3 provides the main outcome. In this table, we explicitly annotate which tactics have effectively been encountered in our SLR in their specific application to data types, and complement that with our assessment of theoretical applicability of specific tactics.

Table 3. Applicability of de-identification tactics to data types.

Tactic / Data type	* Entire data set	Structured — Entire record	Structured — Identifying attribute	Text — Entire (stream)	Text — Annotated text	Text — Stylometric features	Image/video — Entire (stream)	Image/video — Feature (face...)	Speech — Entire (stream)	Speech — Feature (intonation...)
REMOVE	×	⊗	⊗	×	⊗		×	⊗	×	×
SELECT/FILTER	×	⊗	⊗	⊗	⊗		×	⊗		
TRANSFORM	×	×	⊗	⊗	⊗	×	⊗	⊗	⊗	×
MASK			⊗		⊗			⊗		
ENCRYPT	⊗	⊗	⊗	⊗	⊗		⊗	⊗		
RANDOMIZE			⊗		⊗		⊗	⊗	×	×
AGGREGATE			⊗		⊗			⊗	×	×
BLUR			⊗		⊗		⊗	⊗	⊗	×
PSEUDONYM			⊗		⊗			⊗		
PLACEHOLDER			⊗		⊗			⊗		
INTERCHANGE			⊗		⊗			⊗		
SYNTHETIC			×		⊗			⊗	⊗	
POLICY	⊗	×	⊗	×	⊗		×	×	×	×
REQUEST/ACCESS CONTROL	×	×	⊗	×	×		×	×	×	×
RESPONSE LIMITING	×	×	⊗	×	×		×	⊗	×	×
PRIVACY MODEL	⊗		⊗		×	×		×		×

×: theoretically possible but not encountered in the SLR,
⊗: theoretically possible and encountered in literature.

Literature predominantly focuses on methods and their characteristics, and less on the architectural mechanisms in which de-identification is enforced, such as policy systems, control layers and retroactive manipulation of responses. This is reflected in the lower direct coverage at the bottom part of the table.

7.3 Coverage of the Privacy Strategies and Privacy Patterns

In this part of the validation, we assess the extent to which these existing catalogs of privacy patterns [28,29] actually involve the tactics discussed in this article. As discussed above, of the 72 patterns provided in [29], only 23 involve a form of de-identification. As a result of our mapping effort, we found that all of these 23 privacy patterns could be further concretized in terms of the proposed architectural tactics. Table 4 lists the tactics used within these patterns and shows that the four different types of strategies are generally addressed in these privacy patterns.

This analysis also shows that any privacy patterns and best practices related to the recognition phase (Phase I) itself are largely lacking, despite the significant architectural impact.

Table 4. Mapping between the privacy patterns of [29] and the tactics.

Privacy patterns (from [29])	Architectural Tactics
Anonymity Set, Location Granularity, Trustworthy Privacy Plug-in	AGGREGATE
Encryption with user-managed keys, Onion Routing	ENCRYPT
Added-noise measurement obfuscation	RANDOMIZE
Active broadcast of presence	REQUEST/ACCESS CONTROL
Masquerade, Preventing mistakes/reducing impact, Protection Against Tracking, Strip Invisible Metadata	SELECT/FILTER
Federated Privacy Impact Assessment, Pseudonymous Messaging, Pseudonymous Identity, Use of dummies	PSEUDONYM
Support Selective Disclosure	SELECT/FILTER, RESPONSE LIMITING
Aggregation Gateway	ENCRYPT, AGGREGATE
Attribute Based Credentials	AGGREGATE, SELECT/FILTER
Decoupling content and location information visibility	SELECT/FILTER, DE-IDENTIFICATION POLICY
Identity Federation Do Not Track, Selective access control, Single Point of Contact, Sticky Policies, Reasonable Level of Control	REQUEST/ACCESS CONTROL, RESPONSE FILTERING, SELECT/FILTER
Obligation Management	DE-IDENTIFICATION POLICY, REQUEST/ACCESS CONTROL

8 Conclusion

This article addresses a gap in the consolidation of common architectural tactics for de-identification of personal data: where existing privacy strategies and patterns are either high-level or incomplete in capturing the diversity of the approaches used in practice, existing de-identification surveys fail at generalizing beyond specific application domains or data types.

As contemporary systems increasingly involve multi-model data sets—heterogeneous in both origin and form—, maintaining a holistic architecture-centric perspective is becoming increasingly difficult yet simultaneously gains in importance. The establishment of a de-identification approach in a system involves the decision when in the data life-cycle to apply which technique (upon data collection, persistence, processing, data sharing), taking into account the consequential privacy and security risks (and the further mitigation thereof), and the distribution of these data sets across distributed storage architectures, and these are all aspects of relevance in a software architecture. The establishment of a reference model of architectural tactics presented in this article is a stepping stone towards a more grounded characterization of the complex privacy architectures that emerge from practice.

Acknowledgements. This research is partially funded by the Research Fund KU Leuven, and by the Flemish Research Programme Cybersecurity.

References

1. Banerjee, S., Ross, A.: Smartphone camera de-identification while preserving biometric utility. In: 2019 IEEE 10th International Conference on Biometrics Theory, Applications and Systems (BTAS), pp. 1–10 (2019). https://doi.org/10.1109/BTAS46853.2019.9185996
2. Bass, L., Clements, P., Kazman, R.: Software Architecture in Practice. Addison-Wesley Professional, Boston (2003)
3. Bradford, L.R., Aboy, M., Liddell, K.: COVID-19 contact tracing apps: a stress test for privacy, the GDPR and data protection regimes. J. Law Biosci. **7**(1), lsaa034 (2020)
4. Briggs, C., Fan, Z., Andras, P., et al.: A review of privacy-preserving federated learning for the internet-of-things (2020)
5. Colesky, M., Hoepman, J.H., Hillen, C.: A critical analysis of privacy design strategies. In: IEEE Security and Privacy Workshops (SPW), pp. 33–40. IEEE (2016)
6. El Emam, K., Jonker, E., Arbuckle, L., Malin, B.: A systematic review of re-identification attacks on health data. PLoS ONE **6**(12), e28071 (2011)
7. Fefferman, N.H., O'Neil, E.A., Naumova, E.N.: Confidentiality and confidence: is data aggregation a means to achieve both? J. Public Health Policy **26**(4), 430–449 (2005)
8. Fernandez, E.B., Astudillo, H., Pedraza-García, G.: Revisiting architectural tactics for security. In: Weyns, D., Mirandola, R., Crnkovic, I. (eds.) ECSA 2015. LNCS, vol. 9278, pp. 55–69. Springer, Cham (2015). https://doi.org/10.1007/978-3-319-23727-5_5
9. Gafni, O., Wolf, L., Taigman, Y.: Live face de-identification in video. In: Proceedings of the IEEE International Conference on Computer Vision, pp. 9378–9387 (2019)
10. Gardner, J., Xiong, L.: HIDE: an integrated system for health information de-identification. In: 21st IEEE International Symposium on Computer-Based Medical Systems, pp. 254–259. IEEE (2008)
11. Garfinkel, S.L.: De-identification of personal information. National institute of standards and technology (2015)
12. Gesvindr, D., Buhnova, B.: Architectural tactics for the design of efficient PaaS cloud applications. In: 2016 13th Working IEEE/IFIP Conference on Software Architecture (WICSA), pp. 158–167. IEEE (2016)

13. Hoepman, J.-H.: Privacy design strategies. In: Cuppens-Boulahia, N., Cuppens, F., Jajodia, S., Abou El Kalam, A., Sans, T. (eds.) SEC 2014. IAICT, vol. 428, pp. 446–459. Springer, Heidelberg (2014). https://doi.org/10.1007/978-3-642-55415-5_38

14. Hurtado, J., Taweewitchakreeya, N., Zhu, X.: Who wrote this paper? Learning for authorship de-identification using stylometric featuress. In: Proceedings of the 15th International Conference on Information Reuse and Integration (IEEE IRI), pp. 859–862. IEEE (2014)

15. Kitchenham, B., Brereton, O.P., Budgen, D., Turner, M., Bailey, J., Linkman, S.: Systematic literature reviews in software engineering-a systematic literature review. Inf. Softw. Technol. **51**(1), 7–15 (2009)

16. Lee, D., Park, N., Kim, G., Jin, S.: De-identification of metering data for smart grid personal security in intelligent CCTV-based P2P cloud computing environment. Peer Peer Netw. Appl. **11**(6), 1299–1308 (2018)

17. Lee, G.H., Shin, S.Y.: Federated learning on clinical benchmark data: performance assessment. J. Med. Internet Res. **22**(10), e20891 (2020)

18. Leevy, J.L., Khoshgoftaar, T.M., Villanustre, F.: Survey on RNN and CRF models for de-identification of medical free text. J. Big Data **7**(1), 1–22 (2020)

19. Li, T., Li, N.: On the tradeoff between privacy and utility in data publishing. In: Proceedings of the 15th ACM SIGKDD International Conference on Knowledge Discovery and Data Mining, pp. 517–526 (2009)

20. Magariños, C., Lopez-Otero, P., Docio-Fernandez, L., Rodriguez-Banga, E., Erro, D., Garcia-Mateo, C.: Reversible speaker de-identification using pre-trained transformation functions. Comput. Speech Lang. **46**, 36–52 (2017)

21. Márquez, G., Astudillo, H.: Identifying availability tactics to support security architectural design of microservice-based systems. In: Proceedings of the 13th European Conference on Software Architecture, vol. 2, pp. 123–129 (2019)

22. Nadeau, D., Sekine, S.: A survey of named entity recognition and classification. Lingvisticae Investigationes **30**(1), 3–26 (2007)

23. Nanni, M., et al.: Give more data, awareness and control to individual citizens, and they will help COVID-19 containment. Ethics Inf. Technol. **23**, 1–6 (2021). https://doi.org/10.1007/s10676-020-09572-w

24. Narayanan, A., Felten, E.W.: No silver bullet: de-identification still doesn't work. White Paper, pp. 1–8 (2014)

25. Osses, F., Márquez, G., Astudillo, H.: Exploration of academic and industrial evidence about architectural tactics and patterns in microservices. In: Proceedings of the 40th International Conference on Software Engineering: Companion Proceedings, pp. 256–257 (2018)

26. Pedraza-Garcia, G., Astudillo, H., Correal, D.: A methodological approach to apply security tactics in software architecture design. In: IEEE Colombian Conference on Communications and Computing (COLCOM), pp. 1–8. IEEE (2014)

27. Prasser, F., Kohlmayer, F.: Putting statistical disclosure control into practice: the ARX data anonymization tool. In: Gkoulalas-Divanis, A., Loukides, G. (eds.) Medical Data Privacy Handbook, pp. 111–148. Springer, Cham (2015). https://doi.org/10.1007/978-3-319-23633-9_6

28. privacypatterns.eu: Collecting patterns for better privacy. http://privacypatterns.eu/

29. privacypatterns.org: Privacy pattern catalog. https://privacypatterns.org/

30. Rastogi, V., Suciu, D., Hong, S.: The boundary between privacy and utility in data publishing. In: Proceedings of the 33rd International Conference on Very Large Data Bases, pp. 531–542 (2007)

31. Ribaric, S., Ariyaeeinia, A., Pavesic, N.: De-identification for privacy protection in multimedia content: a survey. Signal Process. Image Commun. **47**, 131–151 (2016)
32. Scott, J., Kazman, R.: Realizing and refining architectural tactics: availability. Technical report, Carnegie-Mellon University SEI (2009)
33. Silva, J.M., Pinho, E., Monteiro, E., Silva, J.F., Costa, C.: Controlled searching in reversibly de-identified medical imaging archives. J. Biomed. Inform. **77**, 81–90 (2018)
34. Steinkamp, J.M., Pomeranz, T., Adleberg, J., Kahn, C.E., Jr., Cook, T.S.: Evaluation of automated public de-identification tools on a corpus of radiology reports. Radiol. Artif. Intell. **2**(6), e190137 (2020)
35. Ullah, F., Ali Babar, M.: Architectural tactics for big data cybersecurity analytics systems: a review. J. Syst. Softw. **151**, 81–118 (2019). https://doi.org/10.1016/j.jss.2019.01.051
36. Uzuner, Ö., Luo, Y., Szolovits, P.: Evaluating the state-of-the-art in automatic de-identification. J. Am. Med. Inform. Assoc. **14**(5), 550–563 (2007)
37. Van Landuyt, D., Joosen, W.: A systematic survey of architectural approaches and trade-offs in data de-identification: data sets and auxiliary materials, June 2022. /home/dimitri/Documents/papers/dvl/de-identification/ecsa2022/dvanlanduyt_ecsa2022_datasets.zip
38. Wu, W., Kelly, T.: Safety tactics for software architecture design. In: Proceedings of the 28th Annual International Computer Software and Applications Conference, COMPSAC 2004, pp. 368–375. IEEE (2004)

Accurate Performance Predictions with Component-Based Models of Data Streaming Applications

Dominik Werle[✉][iD], Stephan Seifermann[iD], and Anne Koziolek[iD]

Karlsruhe Institute of Technology (KIT), Karlsruhe, Germany
{dominik.werle,stephan.seifermann,koziolek}@kit.edu

Abstract. Data streaming applications are an important class of data-intensive systems and performance is an essential quality of such systems. Current component-based performance prediction approaches are not sufficient for modeling and predicting the performance of those systems, because the models require elaborate manual engineering to approximate the behavior of data streaming applications that include stateful asynchronous operations, such as windowing operations, and because the simulations for these models do not support the metrics that are specific to data streaming applications. In this paper, we present a modeling language, a simulation and a case-study-based evaluation of the prediction accuracy of an approach for modeling systems that contain stateful asynchronous operations. Our approach directly represents these operations and simulates their behavior. We compare measurements of relevant performance metrics to performance simulation results for a system that processes smart meter readings. To assess the prediction accuracy of our model, we vary both the configuration of the streaming application, such as window sizes, as well as the characteristics of the input data, i.e., the number of smart meters. Our evaluation shows that our model yields prediction results that are competitive with a state-of-the-art baseline model without incurring the additional manual engineering overhead.

Keywords: software performance · model-driven software engineering · computer aided software engineering · software architecture · data streaming · big data applications

1 Introduction

Systems that process large amounts of data from varied sources are becoming a more and more important class of software systems in recent years, for which numerous frameworks, middlewares and overall implementation techniques exist. Reasons for the increased demand for this type of systems are the increasing amount of data sources from which data is collected and a steady increase in the number of models and methods for data analysis. One manifestation of this is the ongoing growth in popularity for machine learning models.

© The Author(s), under exclusive license to Springer Nature Switzerland AG 2022
I. Gerostathopoulos et al. (Eds.): ECSA 2022, LNCS 13444, pp. 83–98, 2022.
https://doi.org/10.1007/978-3-031-16697-6_6

However, it is challenging for software engineers to build systems that process large amounts of data [8]. Part of the challenge is planning how the system will perform for future workloads that are either larger in scale or that have different characteristics that influence how data is grouped and processed. One approach to systematically analyze the quality of a software system are models, which allow exploring different implementation alternatives without fully implementing and running them. They allow analyzing the performance of the system under changing workloads without investing the resources needed for extensive load tests. Recent research to reduce the cost of automatically building and maintaining models of software systems for which asynchronous communication is a major performance influence factor [17] has made the use of models for these software systems a relevant alternative in comparison to building and load-testing implementations.

In this paper, we examine whether component-based performance models that include stateful operations can be used to predict the performance of data-intensive software systems as accurately as the state of the art while using models that are better aligned with the systems. We call these operations *stateful asynchronous operations (SAOs)*. This question is relevant because our previous research [19] indicates that some of the timing effects present in this type of system cannot be suitably predicted with stateless models and require approximations and workarounds. An example of a stateful operation is when data is collected and emitted as a group after a specified duration has passed or after a specified number of elements has arrived. Such stateful operations are common in data stream processing applications, for example as sliding windows that are created on data streams [1]. We use a case study to evaluate the benefit of models extended with SAOs. We extend our previous research in performance modeling for data-streaming applications [19] with a generalization of the model and simulation and with an evaluation of the resulting approach.

Derived from the presented problem, we address the following research question: RQ_1: Does explicitly modeling stateful asynchronous operations allow modelers to create architecture-level performance models that are better aligned with the system architecture without reducing the prediction accuracy of the models?

To answer RQ_1, we model different configurations of a case study system both with our approach (*model with stateful asynchronous operations (MSAO)* hereafter), which includes SAOs, and with systematically created baseline models using a state-of-the-art modeling approach (*baseline (BL)* hereafter), which does not include SAOs. We discuss the process that these models are derived by and how the models align with changes in configuration and workload. We furthermore evaluate the accuracy of these models in comparison with measurements on an implementation of the case study system. The metric that we consider in this evaluation is the data age after analysis, which is the time from the creation of a data item to the point of time it is included in an analysis result. We focus on the metric data age because a) it is suited better for asynchronous processing than the more commonly supported metric *user response time* because one call to the system interface providing one data element can imply multiple, delayed

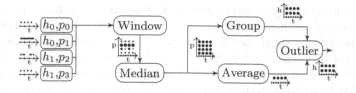

Fig. 1. Illustration of the case study system (Source: [18])

calls within the system, and b) it is not as well supported with current modeling approaches. Our evaluation shows that MSAO yields prediction results that are competitive with BL without incurring the additional manual engineering overhead. Our evaluation investigates the usefulness of MSAO in comparison with the state of the art and we do not intend to formally prove that current approaches theoretically are not able to represent streaming behavior. Thus, we create a baseline model that is as accurate as possible and explain the behavior that the analyst has to manually represent in the baseline by calculating stochastic descriptions of the behavior by hand. In contrast, our approach provides explicit modeling constructs for the behavior. Measuring the modeling effort in a statistically sound way requires a controlled experiment, which is out of scope for this article. Thus, we use a discussion for presenting the reduced manual overhead as clearly as possible. We plan to evaluate increases in the accuracy of the prediction in future work for scenarios where the performance of the system heavily depends on the underlying technical realization of the middleware in cases where delays caused by scheduling on active resources dominate the performance.

We present the following contributions: C_1: A simulation approach for system models that incorporate stateful asynchronous operations. C_2: A case-study based evaluation of our modeling and simulation approach. The data and models used in the experiment are available in the companion data set [20].

2 Running Example

For our case study, we implemented and instrumented a case study system that we described and published in previous work [18,19]. It is based on the grand challenge of the DEBS Conference on Distributed and Event-based Systems 2014 [9,10]. The system creates sliding windows of smart meter readings to calculate outlier values for each house and time window. The outlier value of a house for a window is the percentage of smart plugs in the house that have a median reading value for the window that is above the overall average median reading value of all plugs for this window. We chose this system since its complexity is manageable for implementation and measuring with different system setups. The case study system is illustrated in Fig. 1. It is structured in five components: *Window* creates groups of data elements via sliding windows. The groups are partitioned according to plugs. The component emits one collection of readings for each smart plug p and time window. *Median* takes readings, calculates a median of the values and emits this median value. Therefore, the component emits one median per plug for each time window. *Group* collects the medians and groups them by the house h the plugs belong to. Thus, it emits one collection of medians for each house and window. *Average* calculates one overall average of all medians for each window and emits it. *Outlier* joins the medians that have been grouped per house together with the overall average of all medians. It operates once per house and time window to calculate one outlier per house per time window.

For our running example, the question that a software designer wants to answer during the design of the systems are about the configuration of the operations and for the behavior in different load scenarios. For example, they want to know how a change in the windowing operator, e.g., by increasing the spacing between windows, impacts the performance of the system, or how the system will perform when the amount of smart meters is doubled.

3   Related Work

We see two groups of works related to the approach presented in this paper: The first group provides modeling approaches for data-intensive applications (DIAs) in the architectural design phase. The second group supports the implementation of DIAs without a particular focus on the architectural design phase.

In the first group focusing on the architectural design phase, the approaches can be divided into approaches for streaming and approaches for batch processing. The work of Kroß et al. [11,12] targets stream processing. They extract Palladio performance models [14] for the Big Data frameworks Apache Spark and Hadoop, which they use for predicting the performance of DIAs. In contrast to our approach, Kroß et al. do not model stateful operations but derive their effect based on impact factors, such as the number of partitions in data streams, which architects have to identify first. The DICE project [5] provides methods for modeling and simulating [7] Big Data systems. The models distinguish the platform, technology and deployment and various combinations of these. For instance, the model supports Apache Storm topologies using different types of bolts. The simulation of the systems is based on Petri nets. However, the models do not consider stateful operations, to the best of our knowledge. Maddodi et al. [13] analyze the performance of event-sourcing applications by Layered Queuing Networks (LQNs). In contrast to our approach, they only support aggregating multiple calls but do not support other interactions of calls including windowing or joining data. There are various other approach for batch processing, which focus on different aspects of the analysed systems. Castiglione et al. [6] focus on predicting metrics relevant for operating highly concurrent applications in cloud infrastructure such as performance, number of virtual machines or energy efficiency. Aliabadi et al. [2] focus on predicting the performance of batch applications in different Big Data analysis frameworks using Stochastic Activity Networks. These approaches for batch processing do not support the metrics required for stream processing, which we focus on.

The second group of approaches does not focus on the architectural design phase, resulting in models with inappropriate abstractions for this phase. Sachs [16] suggests a model-based approach for predicting the performance of event-based systems based on Queueing Petri Nets. The presented Petri Net patterns support state-based behavior, such as time windows. In contrast to our approach, Sachs does not consider the decomposition of systems, which is essential for describing software architectures. The approach furthermore does not derive characteristics of resulting data elements and groups of elements after processing which can be measured or used as input for subsequent behavior. Wu et al. [21] provide an approach to formulate information needs in form of queries on event streams and provide instructions on implementing the queries with good performance, however not providing means of abstracting from the actual query plan, e.g., via stochastical descriptions of the used data or the load on the system.

4 Problem Analysis

In this section, we structure the influence factors for the performance of data-streaming applications in more detail. The benefit of this structuring is that we can align our modeling concepts (Sect. 5) and our evaluation (Sect. 7) with the identified factors. We then introduce required capabilities of the modeling language and simulation to represent stateful asynchronous operations in an architecture-level performance model. The collected factors are derived from current state-of-the-art in component-oriented performance modeling [14] and from work in defining operations that are used in data streaming applications (Apache Beam, Apache Flink, Dataflow Model [1]). Overall, our analysis is aligned with our previous work in component-oriented modeling of the performance of data streaming applications [19]. However, we generalize the state-of-the-art to allow a model that is as flexible as possible regarding the type of operations that can be represented. This is achieved by allowing the person that creates stateful asynchronous operations to implement the behavior of an operation as code that is included in the simulation.

4.1 Types of Delays

First, we identify different factors that influence the time it takes for a data item from its creation to its inclusion in an analysis result.

Active Resource Delays are introduced because scheduled resources such as CPUs are contested by different processes. Requests are scheduled and processing time depends on the ressource's characteristics.

Lock Delays occur when parts of the system can only be entered by one process concurrently, resulting in wait times for other processes.

Collective Operation Delays occur when the application waits for some time or event to further process a data. This is for example the case, when sliding windows of incoming data are created and emitted periodically.

4.2   Required Capabilities of the Modeling Language and Simulation

We identify the following required capabilities of the modeling language and simulation to represent stateful asynchronous operations and motivate each of the capabilities with a type of system behavior or with a requirement that comes from the way systems are modeled.

Asynchronous forks and joins of calls. The modeling language has to be able to express calls that result in multiple, parallel calls and a join of multiple, parallel calls. Forked calls do not have to be joined but can result in different computations in the system and can be included in different types of calculations and results.

Metrics for collective operations need to allow tracing a data item across different calls, e.g., a relevant metric can be the age of a data item since it has entered the system. If data is passed between asynchronous calls, this implies that the age has to be traced back to the entry point of the system. A data item does not necessarily have a single origin or a single time of processing, e.g., when a group of elements is calculated and further processed.

Characteristics of data must be representable by the modeler of the system, if they are performance-relevant. Characteristics means that a value is associated with the data. The value is not necessarily the payload of the data itself, but an abstract representation of the information that performance-relevant, i.e., it influences the observable timing of the system in some way. For example, the number of elements that have to be processed in a group of data elements or the characterization of the data that is used for filtering has an observable effect on the timing. This is in line with the way current component-oriented performance models represent characteristics [14].

References to characteristics of data must be possible in the model, i.e., the system can be expressed in a way that depends on characteristics of data. An example is filtering data elements by a characteristic, e.g., discarding elements that are larger that some threshold.

Reference to internal component state. Components need to be able to have state *during execution* which can influence the observable behavior for incoming calls. An example for why internal component state is required is implementing a maximum capacity of a queuing component that may block processes with new data, when the capacity is surpassed. This is only possible, if the component actively manages a queue of data elements.

Collective operations that derive characteristics. If the behavior can depend on the characteristics of data, we need to accurately compute the characteristics of data derived in the system. An example is when a stateful asynchronous operation partitions data based on its characteristics. Subsequently, the number of elements in each partition can be relevant for timing of further processing.

Stochastical behavior description is needed to define how operators and components behave based on stochastic distributions, for example taken from measurements. Stochastics are beneficial when we do not want invest the resources to model in detail the characteristics of data that is relevant for the behavior of the system. An example is a filtering component for which we provide a probability for a data item to be filtered instead of modeling the data characteristic that leads to filtering.

5   Modeling Concepts

In this section, we present and discuss the different modeling concepts for stateful asynchronous operations, which our approach introduces. While our approach addresses a similar problem as our previous work [19], we provide a more general and more flexible modeling and simulation approach. We structure the required concepts in three groups: a) stateful operations, b) (asynchronous) data-oriented call flow, c) metrics.

Stateful operations. In principle, a stateful operation can implement any type of behavior. Note that if the expressiveness is not constrained, we do not claim static analysability of the models. This means that we trade unrestricted expressiveness of the state and analysis by simulation for a reduction in the static analysability. To reduce the overall complexity, we can introduce some reusability for parts of the specification of stateful asynchronous operations. One possibility is to do this as a reduced modeling language for operators as introduced in our previous work [19]. While the previously described language introduces a predefined structure for queues and operations between them, we rely on blackbox operations that can be implemented as Java code as part of the simulation. However, we allow similar composability by code reuse, e.g., by inheritance or composition of classes. To reduce the complexity of implementing the used SAOs in the simulation, we provide some common patterns.

Each stateful asynchronous operation has an internal time which it is certain has already passed. This concept is called watermarks or event time/processing time in literature [1] and in state-of-practice implementations (Apache Beam[1], Apache Flink[2]). Depending on the configuration, this time can be advanced either a) periodically to a reference clock, or b) when a new data item with a timestamp arrives. When the clock is advanced, the stateful asynchronous operation can decide whether it should process the current data. This is for example the case, when the new advanced time surpasses the end of a window that can in turn be created and emitted.

(Asynchronous) Data-oriented Call Flow. Calls through the system can be triggered in different ways. Periodic calls that are triggered according to operator properties, e.g., because windows are emitted periodically. Calls that are triggered because some predicate over previous calls is true, e.g., because the maximum distance to a previous call is surpassed. Furthermore, we can differentiate active data retrieval operations, where a call retrieves data from a data source and might block if no data is available, and pushing calls that are triggered as new processes in the system because data becomes available at a data source. Apart from the initial spawning of a process, calls may need to access

---

[1] https://beam.apache.org/documentation/basics/#watermarks.
[2] https://nightlies.apache.org/flink/flink-docs-stable/.

shared resources that represent a data structure, e.g., for retrieving or storing the actual data, e.g., in some type of shared concurrent data structure.

Metrics. When we focus on data that flows through the system, the simulation and model have to provide metrics that are data-oriented. Instead of investigating users that get a response from a business system, resulting in a response time metric, the model has to provide metrics that represent the timeliness of data elements at different points in the system. Particularly, for asynchronous operations (data elements can be forked and joined or otherwise replicated), we need a way to measure the time from the inception of the data (i.e., when it is created, e.g., in a sensor or in a clickstream) to points in the execution, for example the point of time when a data element is incorporated in an analysis (i.e., a specific computation), or when it becomes part of the active behavior of a stateful asynchronous operation (for example because it is discarded). Utilizing these metrics, the system designer can evaluate whether timeliness and quality requirements at different points in the system are met by different system designs and the configuration of the processing system while also considering the tradeoff with the characteristics of the processed data. For example, lowering the number of elements that are waited for, grouped, and processed can reduce the data age at the point of analysis. However, including less elements in the processing might provide less stable results, e.g., for a smoothed average.

6   Implementation

Our approach is an extension to an existing architecture description language designed for software quality predictions, the Palladio Component Model (PCM) [14], and an extension to a discrete event simulation for this modeling language, the SimuLizar [4] simulator. The components that are used in PCM to describe entities that provide or consume services and are deployed as a unit are called *basic components*. In contrast, we will call our components *data channels*. Basic components provide and require services and have a service effect description (SEFF) for each provided service. The SEFF describes the behavior of a call of a provided service in terms of resource demands and calls to other services. The behavior described in a SEFF (and thus a basic component) can only be triggered by an incoming call, either by a user or another component. In contrast, our approach includes two new types of role that a stateful asynchronous operations can play: data source role and data sink role. A data source role means that a component can act as a data source for a specific type of data item, i.e., it can emit this type of data. A data sink role means that a component can accept this type of data. In contrast to SEFFs, the behavior description for a stateful asynchronous operations has access to the aforementioned types of state (see Subsect. 4.2) and can actively emit data that can result in additional processing threads in the system. Our approach does not restrict the passing of data to push behavior (actively triggering processing in another part of the system) or pull behavior (consumers decide when they consume data from a data source) but allows to model both. To support simulating asynchronously processed data and grouping of different data in the system, we also make the chain of calls that a data item has passed through available in the simulation.

7 Evaluation

The aim of our evaluation is to show that our approach (MSAO) performs as well as a baseline state-of-the-art modeling approach that does not incorporate stateful asynchronous operations (BL). In this section, we will first define our evaluation goal and derive evaluation questions and metrics from it. We then describe the state-of-the-art baseline model without stateful asynchronous operations, and the model in our approach with stateful asynchronous operations. We then discuss how both models are calibrated. Last, we describe the space of scenarios that the models are not calibrated for and for which we predict the performance of the system.

7.1 Goals, Questions, Metrics

Our evaluation is structured along the Goal-Question-Metric (GQM) approach [3]. The evaluation goals are: G_1: Evaluate the accuracy of MSAO in comparison to BL for data streaming applications. G_2: Evaluate the modeling overhead for MSAO in comparison to BL for data streaming applications.

Therefore, the evaluation concerns systems using our modeling approach (contribution C_1). We derive the following evaluation questions from G_1: $EQ_{1.1}$: How accurate is the prediction of the distribution of data age at the time it is processed using BL? $EQ_{1.2}$: How accurate is the prediction of the distribution of data age at the time it is processed using MSAO?

We address these questions with the following metrics: M_1: Relative error of predicted average data age. M_2: Wasserstein metric between measured and predicted distribution of data age. We evaluate metrics M_1 and M_2 for all scenarios in our test set and also provide statistical data about the metrics (mean and maximum). Thus, $EQ_{1.1}$ and $EQ_{1.2}$ are evaluated quantitatively.

We derive the following evaluation question from G_2: $EQ_{2.1}$: What is the increase in complexity of modeling the system from BL to MSAO? We address this question by elaborating on the overhead of creating BL in Subsect. 7.4. Thus, $EQ_{2.1}$ is evaluated qualitatively via discussion.

7.2 Evaluation Design

To evaluate G_1 and G_2, we create both BL and MSAO for a case-study system. We calibrate both models using the same calibration measurements from our real implementation (training set). However, the active resource delays are negligible in comparison with the collective operation delays in the scenarios that we observed. For our test set, we choose different scenarios that change aspects of the input data or configuration of the system. For each of the scenarios, we again measure the behavior of the real implementation. We then compare the results of each of the models with the real measurements using M_1 and M_2 for the measured data age.

7.3   Experiment Setup

We have measured all combinations of the following configuration dimensions and values, leading to a total of $3 \cdot 10 = 30$ scenarios: i) window size/shift: 5/5, 10/10, 20/20, ii) workload: 1s1p1h, 1s2p2h, 1s4p4h, 1s8p8h, 1s10p10h, debs-2, debs-4, debs-all-2, debs-all-4, debs-all-6 The 5 workloads with identifiers of the form *1s2p2h* describe artificial workloads that have a fixed amount of houses and plugs. Each plug sends a power consumption measurement with a fixed frequency. In this case, the identifier 1s2p2h means that the frequency is 1 s, there are 2 plugs per house and 2 houses, leading to a total of 4 messages per second. We use these as training for our calibration. For our test set, we use 5 reduced excerpts of the original DEBS data set which are filtered variants of the first five minutes. Here, *debs-n* is a subset which only includes the first n houses. *debs-all-n* is a subset that only includes the first n plugs of the first n households of the first n houses. All of our measurements result in a steady state, i.e., they do not lead to a congestion behavior that overloads the system indefinitely.

The measurements are done on a machine with an AMD Ryzen 9 3900X 12-Core Processor running Windows 10, Version 21H1. All of the measurements are executed in the Windows Subsystem for Linux (WSL) running Ubuntu 20.04.3 LTS. The application is executed as a Java program that runs inside one instance of the Java Virtual Machine (JVM). The Java version we use is OpenJDK 11.0.11. Each component is run as one thread inside the JVM. We pin the `java` executable to the first processor core using `taskset -pc 0`. We further allow limiting the CPU usage of the process using `cpulimit -b -m -l <percentage>`. For our experiments, we use a limit of 100%, i.e., to a maximum of one CPU.

7.4   Models

In this section, we describe how both BL as well as MSAO are created and how the models are derived for the different modeling scenarios. The goal of this section is to answer $EQ_{2.1}$. The proposed benefit of creating models with first-class entities for SAOs is twofold: i) architects do not need to create workarounds with current techniques that only capture a specific configuration of the system, ii) they can directly measure the metrics of interest instead of relying on proxy metrics. In the following, we will illustrate these workarounds for BL.

We implemented an automated tool that uses measurements from the training set for calibrating the resource demands that occur in the system. Our tool creates models for both BL and MSAO for each scenario from the test set, automatically executes the simulation and stores the simulation results. We define which of the measurements belong to the test set and which belong to the training set and automatically derive M_1 and M_2.

Baseline Model. Figure 2 illustrates our generated baseline model. The model consists of four components that represent the different parts of the system that incur active resource delays. The usage model of the baseline model reproduces

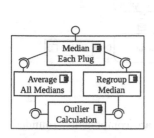

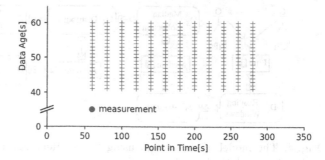

Fig. 2. Baseline Model

Fig. 3. Measurement for artificial scenario 1s4p4h, window size/shift 20/20.

the windowing behavior of the first part of the processing. It contains one periodically arriving user per house that calls the system for each window, thus arriving every *window shift* time units. The call to the system is parameterized with a distribution of the number of elements contained in the window. The different usage scenarios for the system are generated from the workload. For this purpose, our model generator implements the operation that is first evaluated in the system (windowing the incoming data) and derives the characteristics from the resulting data. The result is a distribution of the number of elements per window for each house. The components additionally contain delays that model the behavior of the system when waiting for new data that advances its timer. For example, Fig. 3 shows the measurements and predictions of BL and MSAO for an artificial scenario with 4 houses with 4 plugs. In this case, the earliest time for the first window, spanning elements from 0 to 20 time units, can be processed at 60 time units. This is because the window is created after the first element after the window has been received by the *Median* component, resulting in a delay of $T_1 \geq$ *window size*. The component for creating medians can immediately process the window. The components that group the medians again for the time window have to wait for the first group of the next window to arrive, resulting in an additional delay of $T_2 =$ *window shift*. Additionally, the join has to wait for both sides of the processing to finish and for the next group of elements to arrive, resulting in additional delay of $T_3 =$ *window shift*. The overall collective operation delay is thus at least $T_1 + T_2 + T_3 =$ *window size* $+ 2 \cdot$ *window shift* time units. The result that we get from the simulation of the model is a response time for each of the users providing windows, which is equivalent to the point in time T_W that the whole window has been processed. To calculate the ages of single data elemente, we apply a distribution that we have measured in the data: we generate $[T_W -$ *window size*$, T_W]$ measurements that are spaced by the average interarrival time for the house this process represents. For example, for a house for which plugs send data with an average interarrival time of 2 s and a window size of 20 s, a window that has finished processing at 60 s results in the data age metric $[40, 42, 44, \ldots, 60]$.

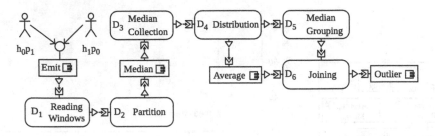

Fig. 4. The model of the system using SAOs. Rectangles are components, rounded rectangles are data channels.

Model with Stateful Asynchronous Operations. Figure 4 illustrates the model of the system using our approach. The model separates the operations for collecting and regrouping the arriving data. In summary, the components have the following functions: − *Emit*: emits a sensor reading when called, − D_1: emits group of all plug readings in sliding window, − D_2: partitions readings by plug identifier and emits a collection per plug and sliding window − *Median*: calculates median for each plug − D_3: collects all medians for a time window − D_4: duplicates data item and distributes it to both *Average* and D_5 − D_5: groups the medians per house − *Average*: calculates an overall average across all medians − D_6: joins the overall average and house median groups − *Outlier*: calculates one outlier per average and house median group Each of the parts of the case study system (see Fig. 1) is realized by one or more of components in MSAO: system ingress is realized by *Emit*, windowing is realized by D_1 and D_2, *Median* is realized by component Median, *Average* is realized by D_3 and component Average, *Outlier* is realized by D_6 and Outlier.

Comparison of BL and MSAO. Altogether, the BL requires the performance engineer to understand the timing behavior of the system in much detail and to adapt the model in case of changes to the underlying system. If a wall clock with discarding was used, the baseline would have to be modeled differently: we would have to first create a model for the percentage that are discarded by measuring the delay of elements before the windowing step. This percentage would then have to be included in a second model that includes the next components to accurately represent the discarding and the resulting characterization of the windowed group. In case of the MSAO, the mode the component operates in is directly associated with the data channel and can be changed as a model parameter for the element. BL also requires the performance analyst to take the metrics provided by the constructed model, i.e., the processing time of *windows* and derive the actual metric of interest from this metric via an additional step, which further increases the overhead of using BL in comparison with MSAO.

7.5   Calibration

We use the measurements in the training set for the calibration of resource demands. While there are different methods for deriving resource demands for a performance model, we use isolated measurements of the different components in our case study system. We measure both the time and the number of elements for i) calculating the median value per plug, ii) calculating the overall plug median average, iii) calculating the outlier value. We then use linear regression to derive a parameterized resource demand value assuming an empty queue and a processing rate of 1 per time unit. The same calibrated and parametrized resource demands are used for both BL as well as MSAO. This means that the resulting time behavior depends on the data characteristics that arrive at the components, e.g., the correct characterization of the number of smart meter readings in a sliding window, and would be the same for BL and MSAO if both provide the same characterization.

7.6 Results

Example results of the model and MSAO and BL can be seen in Fig. 5. In our evaluation, we can see that the models can successfully approximate the measurements of the case study system. The overall accuracy of the models is high due to two factors: i) the active resource delays in the case study system are small to emphasize the collective operation delays, ii) the collective operation delay can replicate the behavior of the system.

We expect both the accuracy of MSAO as well as the accuracy of BL to reduce with more complicated operation pipelines and with a more complex interplay between active resource delays and collective operation delays. However, the evaluation supports our thesis that MSAO can model the collective operation delays that occur in our case study system at the same level as BL. Table 1 and Fig. 6 show the results of our evaluation across all 30 scenarios, including the 15 test scenarios. The difference between MSAO and BL is negligible in both M_1 (mean: 0.17 percentage points (pp), median: 0.01 pp) and M_2 (mean: 0.046, median: 0.023). As a result, we see an improvement in the capabilities of the performance modeling approach we presented while retaining the prediction quality.

Table 1. Aggregated metrics M_1 and M_2 for BL and MSAO for all 30 scenarios.

		Relative Error (M_1)			Wasserstein (M_2)		
		Mean	Median	Max	Mean	Median	Max
Training	BL	0.05%	0.04%	0.12%	0.013	0.009	0.037
	MSAO	0.02%	0.03%	0.05%	0.008	0.005	0.029
Test	BL	0.32%	0.17%	1.66%	0.101	0.064	0.311
	MSAO	0.15%	0.16%	0.35%	0.055	0.041	0.142
All	BL	0.19%	0.07%	1.66%	0.057	0.024	0.311
	MSAO	0.09%	0.04%	0.35%	0.031	0.021	0.142

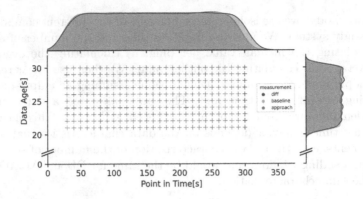

Fig. 5. Exemplary result for DEBS scenario debs-full-4 with window size/shift 10/10.

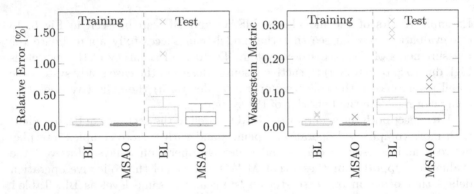

Fig. 6. Aggregated metrics M_1 and M_2 for BL and MSAO for all 30 scenarios.

8   Threats to Validity

In this section, we address threats to validity as proposed by Runeson and Höst [15, sec. 5.2.3] for case-study-based research in software engineering.

Internal Validity. Addresses whether all influence factors on the investigated causal relations have been considered. In our case study, we analyzed whether including SAOs in a modeling language allows models that are better aligned with the system architecture without reducing the prediction accuracy (RQ_1). Our focus on collective operation delays helps to minimize other influence factors such as interaction between collective operation delays and active resource delays. Furthermore, we also evaluate and present the behavior for artificial simple scenarios in the training set to show that simple behavior is accurately predicted without unknown influence factors. We also present the factors that influence the alignment of our approach with the system and the baseline with the system in a structured argumentation. One factor that is hard to eliminate is the expertise of the architect modeling the system. We mitigate this factor by creating a baseline that is as sophisticated and accurate as possible to avoid that our approach has an unfair and hidden advantage in the comparison.

External Validity. Addresses whether the findings of the case study can be generalized to other cases of interest. According to Runeson and Höst [15, sec. 6.1], case studies does not need to be representative of a population. We aim to increase the external validity by focusing on a case description that comes from the research community. Furthermore, we derive our model elements of interest from operations that are discussed both in the seminal work in the research area [1] and are also used in popular frameworks (Apache Beam, Apache Flink).

Construct Validity. Addresses whether the metrics that are studied answer the research question. We derive the evaluation goals, questions and metrics according to the established Goal-Question-Metric (GQM) approach [3]. This helps to make the connection between the evaluation and the presented goal transparent. We also use metrics that are established to evaluate performance prediction approaches.

Reliability. Addresses whether the findings depend on the specific researcher that conducted the research. We address this threat by automating the experiment pipeline, from execution and measurement of the case study system to the analysis and derivation of our target metrics and by publishing the whole experiment pipeline. Thus, it is available to other researches who can freely study the experiment setup and also replicate or change the experiments.

9   Conclusion and Future Work

In this paper we have introduced an approach for modeling and simulating stateful asynchronous operations (SAOs) and have demonstrated that we can build performance models that more explicitly represent the behavior of software systems that include SAOs while retaining the accuracy of a state-of-the-art baseline model crafted by an expert performance engineer. The expected benefit of this approach is that software architects are supported in making design decisions for systems that include stateful operations, such as data-streaming systems. One direction in need of further investigation are scenarios where a system becomes overloaded recovers from the load in a phase with reduced load to assess whether models can reproduce the transient behavior of the system. A second direction of research is regarding the modeling language for SAOs. We currently do not restrict their functionality, but there might be cases where it is beneficial to do so to ensure that the simulation results are accurate, for example, if the effects that are modeled rely on events that are very rare and thus are not sufficiently captured by a simulation that only runs for a limited time frame.

Acknowledgements. This work was supported by KASTEL Security Research Labs and by the German Research Foundation (DFG) under project number 432576552, HE8596/1-1 (FluidTrust).

References

1. Akidau, T., et al.: The dataflow model: a practical approach to balancing correctness, latency, and cost in massive-scale, unbounded, out-of-order data processing. Proc. VLDB Endow. 8(12) (2015). https://doi.org/10.14778/2824032.2824076

2. Aliabadi, S.K., et al.: Analytical composite performance models for big data applications. J. Netw. Comput. Appl. **142**, 63–75 (2019)
3. Basili, V.R., Caldiera, G., Rombach, H.D.: The goal question metric approach. In: Encyclopedia of Software Engineering - 2 Volume Set. Wiley (1994)
4. Becker, M., et al.: Performance analysis of self-adaptive systems for requirements validation at design-time. In: ACM SIGSOFT QoSA 2013. ACM (2013). https://doi.org/10.1145/2465478.2465489
5. Casale, G., Li, C.: Enhancing big data application design with the DICE framework. In: Advances in Service-Oriented and Cloud Computing - Workshops of ESOCC (2017)
6. Castiglione, A., et al.: Modeling performances of concurrent big data applications. Softw. Pract. Exper. **45**(8), 1127–1144 (2015)
7. DICE consortium: Deliverable 3.4 DICE simulation tools (2017). http://www.dice-h2020.eu/deliverables/. European Union's Horizon 2020 Programme
8. Hummel, O., et al.: A collection of software engineering challenges for big data system development. In: Euromicro SEAA. IEEE (2018)
9. Jerzak, Z., Ziekow, H.: DEBS 2014 Grand Challenge: Smart homes - DEBS.org. https://debs.org/grand-challenges/2014/
10. Jerzak, Z., Ziekow, H.: The DEBS 2014 grand challenge. In: DEBS 2014. ACM, New York (2014). https://doi.org/10.1145/2611286.2611333
11. Kroß, J., Krcmar, H.: Model-based performance evaluation of batch and stream applications for big data. In: MASCOTS. IEEE (2017)
12. Kroß, J., Krcmar, H.: Pertract: model extraction and specification of big data systems for performance prediction by the example of apache spark and hadoop. Big Data Cogn. Comput. **3**(3), 47 (2019)
13. Maddodi, G., Jansen, S., Overeem, M.: Aggregate architecture simulation in event-sourcing applications using layered queuing networks. In: ICPE 2020. ACM (2020)
14. Reussner, R.H., et al.: Modeling and Simulating Software Architectures - The Palladio Approach. MIT Press, Cambridge (2016)
15. Runeson, P., Höst, M.: Guidelines for conducting and reporting case study research in software engineering. Empir. Softw. Eng. **14**(2), 131–164 (2009)
16. Sachs, K.: Performance modeling and benchmarking of event-based systems. Ph.D. thesis, Darmstadt University of Technology (2011)
17. Singh, S., et al.: Towards extraction of message-based communication in mixed-technology architectures for performance model. In: ICPE 2021. ACM (2021). https://doi.org/10.1145/3447545.3451201
18. Werle, D., Seifermann, S., Koziolek, A.: Data stream operations as first-class entities in palladio. In: SSP 2019. Softwaretechnik Trends (2019)
19. Werle, D., Seifermann, S., Koziolek, A.: Data stream operations as first-class entities in component-based performance models. In: Jansen, A., Malavolta, I., Muccini, H., Ozkaya, I., Zimmermann, O. (eds.) ECSA 2020. LNCS, vol. 12292, pp. 148–164. Springer, Cham (2020). https://doi.org/10.1007/978-3-030-58923-3_10
20. Werle, D., Seifermann, S., Koziolek, A.: Data Set of Publication on Accurate Performance Predictions with Component-based Models of Data Streaming Applications (2022). https://doi.org/10.5281/zenodo.6762128
21. Wu, E., Diao, Y., Rizvi, S.: High-performance complex event processing over streams. In: SIGMOD. ACM (2006)

Microservices and Middleware

Assessing Architecture Conformance to Coupling-Related Infrastructure-as-Code Best Practices: Metrics and Case Studies

Evangelos Ntentos[1]([envelope]), Uwe Zdun[1], Jacopo Soldani[2], and Antonio Brogi[2]

[1] Faculty of Computer Science, Research Group Software Architecture,
University of Vienna, Vienna, Austria
{evangelos.ntentos,uwe.zdun}@univie.ac.at
[2] Faculty of Computer Science, University of Pisa, Pisa, Italy
{jacopo.soldani,antonio.brogi}@unipi.it

Abstract. Infrastructure as Code (IaC) is an IT practice that facilitates the management of the underlying infrastructure as software. It enables developers or operations teams to automatically manage, monitor, and provision resources rather than organize them manually. In many industries, this practice is widespread and has already been fully adopted. However, few studies provide techniques for evaluating architectural conformance in IaC deployments and, in particular, aspects such as loose coupling. This paper focuses on coupling-related patterns and practices such as deployment strategies and the structuring of IaC elements. Many best practices are documented in gray literature sources, such as practitioner books, blogs, and public repositories. Still, there are no approaches yet to automatically check conformance with such best practices. We propose an approach based on generic, technology-independent metrics tied to typical architectural design decisions for IaC-based practices in microservice deployments to support architecting in the context of continuous delivery practices. We present three case studies based on open-source microservice architectures to validate our approach.

Keywords: Infrastructure as Code · metrics · software architecture · architecture conformance · IaC best practices

1 Introduction

Today, many microservice-based systems are being rapidly released, resulting in frequent changes not only in the system implementation but also in its infrastructure and deployment [7,13]. Furthermore, the number of infrastructure nodes that a system requires is increasing significantly [13] and the managing and structuring of these elements can have a significant impact on the development and deployment processes. *Infrastructure as Code* enables automating the provisioning and management of the infrastructure nodes through reusable scripts, rather than through manual processes [11]. IaC can ensure that a provisioned environment remains the same every time it is deployed in the same configuration, and configuration files contain infrastructure specifications making the process of editing and distributing configurations easier [1,11].

© The Author(s), under exclusive license to Springer Nature Switzerland AG 2022
I. Gerostathopoulos et al. (Eds.): ECSA 2022, LNCS 13444, pp. 101–116, 2022.
https://doi.org/10.1007/978-3-031-16697-6_7

IaC can also contribute to improving consistency and ensuring loose coupling by separating the deployment artifacts according to the services' and teams' responsibilities. The deployment infrastructure can be structured using infrastructure stacks. An infrastructure stack is a collection of infrastructure elements/resources that are defined, provisioned, and updated as a unit [11]. A wrong structure can result in severe issues if coupling-related aspects are not considered. For instance, defining all the system deployment artifacts as only one unit in one infrastructure stack can significantly impact the dependencies of system parts and teams as well as the independent deployability of system services. Most of the established practices in the industry are mainly reported in the so-called "grey literature," consisting of practitioner blogs, system documentation, etc. The architectural knowledge is scattered across many knowledge sources that are usually based on personal experiences, inconsistent, and incomplete. This creates considerable uncertainty and risk in architecting microservice deployments.

In this work, we investigate such IaC-based best practices in microservice deployments. In this context, we formulate a number of coupling-related *Architectural Design Decisions (ADDs)* with corresponding decision options. In particular, the ADDs focus on *System Coupling through Deployment Strategy* and *System Coupling through Infrastructure Stack Grouping*. For each of these, we define a number of generic, technology-independent metrics to measure the conformance of a given deployment model to the (chosen) ADD options. Based on this architectural knowledge, our goal is to provide an automatic assessment of architecture conformance to these practices in IaC deployment models. We also aim for a continuous assessment, i.e., we envision an impact on continuous delivery practices, in which the metrics are assessed with each delivery pipeline run, indicating improvement, stability, or deterioration in microservice deployments. In order to validate the applicability of our approach and the performance of the metrics, we conducted three case studies on open source microservice-based systems that also include the IaC-related scripts. The results show that our set of metrics is able to measure the support of patterns and practices.

This paper aims to answer the following research questions:

- **RQ1.** How can we measure conformance to coupling-related IaC best practices in the context of IaC architecture decision options?
- **RQ2.** What is a set of minimal elements needed in an IaC-based deployment and microservice architecture model to compute such measures?

This paper is structured as follows: Sect. 2 discusses related work. Next, we describe the research methods and the tools we have applied in our study in Sect. 3. In Sect. 4 we explain the ADDs considered in this paper and the related patterns and practices. Section 5 introduces our metrics in a formal model. Then, three case studies are explained in Sect. 6. Section 7 discusses the RQs regarding the evaluation results and analyses the threats to validity of our study. Finally, in Sect. 8 we draw conclusions and discuss future work.

2   Related Work

Several existing works target collecting IaC bad and best practices. For instance, Sharma et al. [17] present a catalog of design and implementation language-specific smells for Puppet. A broad catalog of language-agnostic and language-specific best and bad practices related to implementation issues, design issues, and violations of essential IaC principles is presented by Kumara et al. [9]. Schwarz et al. [16] offer a catalog of smells for Chef. Morris [11] presents a collection of guidance on managing IaC. In his book, there is a detailed description of technologies related to IaC-based practices and a broad catalog of patterns and practices. Our work also follows IaC-specific recommendations given by Morris [11], as well as those more microservice-oriented given by Richardson [15]. We indeed build on their guidelines and catalogs of bad/best practices to support architecting the deployment of microservices, while also enabling us to assess and improve the quality of obtained IaC deployment models.

In this perspective, it is worth relating our proposal with existing tools and metrics for assessing and improving the quality of IaC deployment models. Dalla Palma et al. [4,5] suggest a catalog of 46 quality metrics focusing on Ansible scripts to identify IaC-related properties and show how to use them in analyzing IaC scripts. A tool-based approach for detecting smells in TOSCA models is proposed by Kumara et al. [10]. Sotiropoulos et al. [18] provide a tool to identify dependency-related issues by analyzing Puppet manifests and their system call trace. Van der Bent et al. [2] define metrics reflecting IaC best practices to assess Puppet code quality. All such approaches focus on the use of different metrics to assess and improve the quality of IaC deployment models, showing the potential and effectiveness of metrics in doing so. We hence follow a similar, metrics-based approach but targeting a different aspect than those of the above mentioned approaches, namely *system coupling*. To the best of our knowledge, ours is the first solution considering and tackling such aspects.

Other approaches worth mentioning are those by Fischer et al. [6] and Krieger et al. [8], who both allow automatically checking the conformance of declarative deployment models during design time. They both model conformance rules in the form of a pair of deployment model fragments. One of the fragments represents a detector subgraph that determines whether the rule applies to a particular deployment model or not. The comparison of the model fragments with a given deployment model is done by subgraph isomorphism. Unlike our study, this approach is generic and does not introduce specific conformance rules, such as checking coupling-related ADDs in IaC models.

Finally, it is worth mentioning that architecture conformance can also be checked with other techniques such as dependency-structure matrices, source code query languages, and reflexion models as shown by Passos et al. [14]. So far, methods based on various interrelated IaC-based metrics to check pattern/best practice conformance like ours do not yet exist. Also, none are able to produce assessments that combine different assessment parameters (i.e., metrics). Such metrics, if automatically computed, can be used as a part of larger assessment models during development and deployment time.

3   Research and Modeling Methods

Figure 1 shows the research steps followed in this study. We first studied knowledge sources related to IaC-specific best practices from practitioner books and blogs, and the scientific literature (such as [9,11,15–17]) as well as open-source repositories (such as the case studies discussed in Sect. 6). We then analyzed the data collected using qualitative methods based on Grounded Theory [3] coding methods, such as open and axial coding, and extracted the two core IaC decisions described in Sect. 4 along with their corresponding decision drivers and impacts. We followed the widely used pattern catalogs by Morris [11] and Richardson [15] closely to obtain the necessary information since both are well documented, detailed, and address many relevant concerns in the IaC domain. Among the many design decisions, covered in these catalogs, we selected those that are directly connected to IaC practices, operate at a high abstraction level (i.e., they are "architectural" design decisions), and are related to architectural coupling issues. We then defined a set of metrics for automatically computing conformance to each coupling-related pattern or practice per decision described in Sect. 4. We studied and modeled three case studies following the *Model Generation* process. Finally, we evaluated our set of metrics using the case studies. Furthermore, in our work [12], we have introduced a set of detectors to automatically reconstruct an architecture component model from the source code. Combining the automatic reconstruction with the automatic computation of metrics, the evaluation process can be fully automated.

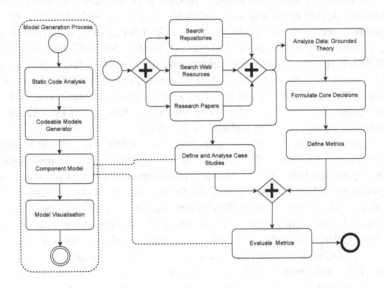

Fig. 1. Overview of the research method followed in this study

The systems we use as case studies were developed by practitioners with relevant experience and are supported by the companies Microsoft, Instana, and Weaveworks as microservice reference applications, which justifies the assumption that they provide a good representation of recent microservice and IaC practices. We performed a fully manual static code analysis for the IaC models that are in the repositories together with the application source code. To create the models, we used our existing modeling tool Codeable Models. The result is a set of decomposition models of the software systems along with their deployments (see Sect. 5.1). The code and models used in and produced as part of this study have been made available online for reproducibility[1].

---

[1] https://doi.org/10.5281/zenodo.6696130.

Figure 2 shows an excerpt of the resulting model of *Case Study 1* in Sect. 6. The model contains elements from both application (e.g., *Service, Database*) and infrastructure (e.g., *Container, Infrastructure Stack, Storage Resources*). Furthermore, we have specified all the deployment-related relationships between these elements. In particular, a *Service* and a *Web Server* are *deployed on* a *Container*. A *Database* is *deployed on Storage Resources* and also on a separate *Container*. An *Infrastructure Stack defines deployment of* a *Container* as well as a *Web Server*. All the containers *run on* a *Cloud Server* (e.g., ELK, AWS, etc.).

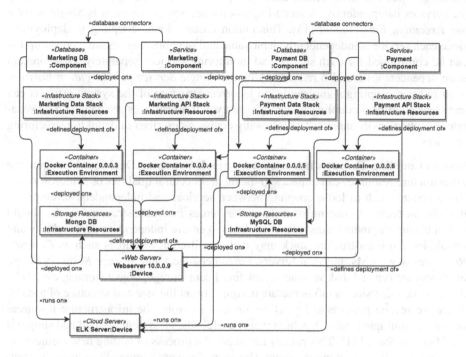

Fig. 2. Excerpt of the reconstructed model CS1 from Table 1

4 Decisions on Coupling-Related, IaC-Specific Practices

In this section, we briefly introduce the two coupling-related ADDs along with their decision options which we study in this paper. In one decision, we investigate the deployment strategy between services and execution environments, and in the second, we focus on the structure of all deployment artifacts.

System Coupling Through Deployment Strategy Decision. An essential aspect of deploying a microservice-based system is to keep the services independently deployable and scalable and ensure loose coupling in the deployment strategy. Services should be isolated from one another, and the corresponding development teams should be able to build and deploy a service as quickly as possible. Furthermore, resource consumption per service is another factor that should be considered, since some services might have constraints on CPU or memory consumption [15]. Availability and behavior monitoring are additional factors for each independent service that should be ensured in a deployment. One option, which hurts the *loose coupling* of the deployment, is *Multiple Services per Execution Environment*[2] In this pattern, services are all deployed in the same execution environment making it problematic to change, build, and deploy the services independently. A second option for service deployment is *Single Service per Execution Environment* [15]. This option ensures loose coupling in deployment since each service is independently deployable and scalable, and resource consumption can be constrained for each service and monitoring services separately. Development team dependencies are also reduced. Although *Single Service per Execution Environment* reduces coupling significantly, an incorrect structure of the system artifacts can introduce additional coupling in deployment even if all services are deployed on separate execution environments. The following decision describes in detail the structuring practices.

System Coupling Through Infrastructure Stack Grouping Decision. Managing the infrastructure resources can impact significant architectural qualities of a microservice-based system, such as loose coupling between services and independent development in different teams. Grouping of different resources into infrastructure stacks should reflect the development teams' responsibilities to ensure independent deployability and scalability. An infrastructure stack may include different resources such as *Compute Resources* (e.g., VMs, physical servers, containers, etc.) and *Storage Resources* (e.g., block storage (virtual disk volumes), structured data storage, object storage, etc.) [11]. An important decision in infrastructure design is to set the size and structure of a stack. There are several patterns and practices on how to group the infrastructure resources into one or multiple stacks. A pattern that is useful when a system is small and simple is the *Monolith Stack* [11]. This pattern facilitates the process of adding new elements to a system as well as stack management. However, there are some risks to using this pattern. The process of changing a larger monolith stack is riskier than changing a smaller one, resulting in more frequent changes. Also, services cannot be deployed and changed independently and different development teams may be dependent on each other [11]. A similar pattern is the *Application Group Stack* [11]. This kind of stack includes all the services of multiple related applications. This pattern is appropriate when there is a single development team for the infrastructure and deployment of these services and has similar consequences as the *Monolith Stack* pattern.

A structuring that can work better with microservice-based systems is the *Service Stack* [11]. In this pattern, each service has its own stack which makes it easier to

---

[2] The term *Execution Environment* is used here to denote the environment in which a service runs such as a VM, a Container, or a Host. Please note that execution environments can be nested. For instance, a VM can be part of a Production Environment which in turn runs on a Public Cloud Environment. Execution environments run on Devices (e.g., Cloud Server).

manage. Stacks boundaries are aligned to the system and team boundaries. Thus, teams and services are more autonomous and can work independently. Furthermore, services and their infrastructure are loosely coupled since independent deployability and scalability for each service are supported. The pattern *Micro Stack* [11] goes one step further by breaking the *Service Stack* into even smaller pieces and creates stacks for each infrastructure element in a service (e.g., router, server, database, etc.). This is beneficial when different parts of a service's infrastructure need to change at different rates. For instance, servers have different life cycles than data and it might work better to have them in separate stacks. However, having many small stacks to manage can add complexity and make it difficult to handle the integration between multiple stacks [11].

5 Metrics Definition

In this section, we describe metrics for checking conformance to each of the decision options described in Sect. 4.

5.1 Model Elements Definition

In this paper, we use and extend a formal model for metrics definition based on our prior work [19]. We extend it here to model the integration of component and deployment nodes. A microservice decomposition and deployment architecture model M is a tuple $(N_M, C_M, NT_M, CT_M, c\_source, c\_target, nm\_connectors, n\_type, c\_type)$ where:

- N_M is a finite set of component and infrastructure **nodes** in Model M.
- $C_M \subseteq N_M \times N_M$ is an ordered finite set of **connector edges**.
- NT_M is a set of **component types**.
- CT_M is a set of **connector types**.
- $c\_source : C_M \rightarrow N_M$ is a function returning the component that is the **source** of a link between two nodes.
- $c\_target : C_M \rightarrow N_M$ is a function returning the component that is the **target** of a link between two nodes.
- $nm\_connectors : \mathbb{P}(N_M) \rightarrow \mathbb{P}(C_M)$ is a function returning the set of connectors for a set of nodes: $nm\_connectors(nm) = \{c \in C_M : (\exists n \in nm : (c\_source(c) = n \land c\_target(c) \in C_M) \lor (c\_target(c) = n \land c\_source(c) \in C_M))\}$.
- $n\_type : N_M \rightarrow \mathbb{P}(NT_M)$ is a function that maps each node to its set of **direct and transitive node types**. (for a formal definition of node types see [19]).
- $c\_type : C_M \rightarrow \mathbb{P}(CT_M)$ is a function that maps each connector to its set of **direct and transitive connector types**. (for a formal definition of connector types see [19]).

All deployment nodes are of type *Deployment_Node*, which has the subtypes *Execution_Environment* and *Device*. These have further subtypes, such as *VM* and *Container* for *Execution_Environment*, and *Server*, *IoT Device*, *Cloud*, etc. for *Device*. Environments can also be used to distinguish logical environments on the same kind of infrastructure, such as a *Test_Environment* and a *Production_Environment*. All types can be combined, e.g. a combination of *Production_Environment* and *VM* is possible.

The microservice decomposition is modeled as nodes of type *Component* with component types such as *Service* and connector types such as *RESTful HTTP*.

The connector type *deployed_on* is used to denote a deployment relation of a *Component* (as a connector source) on an *Execution_Environment* (as a connector target). It is also used to denote the transitive deployment relation of *Execution_Environments* on other ones, such as a *Container* is deployed on a *VM* or a *Test_Environment*. The connector type *runs_on* is used to model the relations between execution environments and the devices they run on.

The type *Stack* is used to define deployments of *Devices* using the *defines_deployment_of* relation. Stacks include environments with their deployed components using the *includes_deployment_node* relation.

5.2   Metrics for System Coupling Through Deployment Strategy Decision

The *System Coupling through Deployment Strategy* related metrics, introduced here, each have a continuous value with range from 0 to 1, with 0 representing the optimal case where the coupling is minimized by applying the recommended IaC best practices.

Shared Execution Environment Connectors Metric (SEEC). This metric $SEEC$: $\mathbb{P}(C_M) \to [0,1]$ returns the number of the *shared* direct connectors from deployed service components to execution environments (e.g., containers or VMs) in relation to the total number of such service to environment connectors. For instance, the connectors of two services that are deployed on the same container are considered as shared. This gives us the proportion of the shared execution environment connectors in the system. In this context, let the function $service\_env\_connectors : \mathbb{P}(C_M) \to \mathbb{P}(C_M)$ return the set of all connectors between deployed services and their execution environments: $service\_env\_connectors(cm) = \{c \in cm : Service \in n\_type(c\_source(c)) \land Execution\_Environment \in n\_type(c\_target(c)) \land deployed\_on \in c\_type(c)\}$. Further, let the function $shared\_service\_env\_connectors : \mathbb{P}(C_M) \to \mathbb{P}(C_M)$ return the set of connectors from multiple components to the same execution environment: $shared\_service\_env\_connectors(cm) = \{c1 \in service\_env\_connectors(cm) : \exists c2 \in C_{EE} : c\_source(c1) \neq c\_source(c2) \land c\_target(c1) = c\_target(c2)\}$. Then SEEC can be defined as:

$$SEEC(cm) = \frac{|shared\_service\_env\_connectors(cm)|}{|service\_env\_connectors(cm)|}$$

Shared Execution Environment Metric (SEE). The metric $SEE : \mathbb{P}(N_M) \to [0,1]$ measures the shared execution environments that have service components deployed on them (e.g., a container/VM that two or more services are deployed on) in relation to all executions environments with deployed services:

$$SEE(nm) = \frac{|\{n \in nm : (\exists c \in nm\_connectors(nm) : c \in shared\_service\_env\_connectors(cm) \land c\_target(c) = n)\}|}{|\{n \in nm : (\exists c \in nm\_connectors(nm) : c \in service\_env\_connectors(cm) \land c\_target(c) = n)\}|}$$

5.3 Metrics for System Coupling Through Infrastructure Stack Grouping Decision

The metrics for *System Coupling through Infrastructure Stack Grouping* decision are return boolean values as they detect the presence of a decision option. Please note that the boolean metrics are defined for arbitrary node sets, i.e. they can be applied to any subset of a model to determine sub-models in which a particular practice is applied.

For the metrics below, let the function $services : \mathbb{P}(N_M) \rightarrow \mathbb{P}(N_M)$ return the set of services in a node set: $services(nm) = \{n \in nm : Service \in n\_type(n)\}$. Further, let the function $stack\_deployed\_envs : N_M \times \mathbb{P}(N_M) \rightarrow \mathbb{P}(N_M)$ return environments included in a Stack s with $stack\_included\_envs(s, nm) = \{e \in nm : (\exists c \in nm\_connectors(cm) : Stack \in n\_type(s) \land c\_source(c) = s \land c\_target(c) = e \land includes\_deployment\_node \in c\_type(c))\}$. Let the function $stack\_deployed\_components : N_M \times \mathbb{P}(N_M) \rightarrow \mathbb{P}(N_M)$ return the components deployed via an environment by a Stack s with $stack\_deployed\_components(s, nm) = \{n \in nm : (\exists c \in nm\_connectors(cm) : Component \in n\_type(c\_source(c)) \land c\_target(c) \in stack\_included\_envs(s) \land deployed\_on \in c\_type(c))\}$. With this, $stacks\_deploying\_services : \mathbb{P}(N_M) \rightarrow \mathbb{P}(N_M)$ can be defined, which returns all stacks that deploy at least one service: $stacks\_deploying\_services(nm) = \{s \in nm : Stack \in n\_type(s) \land (n \in services(nm) : n \in stack\_deployed\_components(s))\}$ Finally, we can define $stacks\_deploying\_non\_service\_components(nm) : \mathbb{P}(N_M) \rightarrow \mathbb{P}(N_M)$ as $stacks\_deploying\_non\_service\_components(nm) = \{s \in nm : Stack \in n\_type(s) \land (n \in nm : n \in stack\_deployed\_components(s) \land n \notin services(nm))\}$.

Monolithic Stack Detection Metric (MSD). The metric $MSD : \mathbb{P}(N_M) \rightarrow Boolean$ returns $True$ if only one stack is used in a node set that deploys more than one service via stacks (e.g., a number of/all system services are deployed by the only defined stack in the infrastructure) and $False$ otherwise.

$$MSD(nm) = \begin{cases} True : & if \ |stacks\_deploying\_services(nm)| = 1 \\ False : & otherwise \end{cases}$$

Application Group Stack Detection Metric (AGSD). The metric $AGSD : \mathbb{P}(C_M) \rightarrow Boolean$ returns $True$ if multiple stacks are used in a node set to deploy services and more services are deployed via stacks than there are stacks (e.g., system services are deployed by one stack and other elements such as routes are deployed by different stack(s)). That is, multiple services are clustered in groups on at least one of the stacks.

$$AGSD(nm) = \begin{cases} True : & \text{if } |stacks\_deploying\_services(nm)| > 1 \land \\ & |stacks\_deploying\_services(nm)| < |services(nm)| \\ False : & otherwise \end{cases}$$

Service-Stack Detection Metric (SES). The metric $SES : \mathbb{P}(N_M) \rightarrow Boolean$ returns $True$ is the number of services deployed by stacks equals the number of stacks (e.g., each system service is deployed by its own stack).

$$SES(nm) = \begin{cases} True : & \text{if } |stacks\_deploying\_services(nm)| = |services(nm)| \\ False : & otherwise \end{cases}$$

Micro-stack Detection Metric (MST). The metric $MST : \mathbb{P}(C_M) \rightarrow Boolean$ returns $True$ if SES is $True$ and also there is one or more stacks that deploy non-service components (e.g., databases, monitoring components, etc.). For instance, a service is deployed by one stack and its database is deployed by another stack as well as a router is deployed by its own stack, etc.:

$$MST(nm) = \begin{cases} True : & \text{if } SES(nm) = True \land \\ & |stacks\_deploying\_non\_service\_components(nm)| > 0 \\ False : & otherwise \end{cases}$$

Services per Stack Metric (SPS). To measure how many services on average are deployed by a service-deploying stack, we define the metrics $SPS : \mathbb{P}(C_M) \rightarrow \mathbb{R}$ as:

$$SPS(nm) = \frac{|\{n \in services(nm) : (\exists s \in nm : Stack \in n\_type(s) \land\ n \in stack\_deployed\_components(s))\}|}{|stacks\_deploying\_services(nm)|}$$

Components per Stack Metric (CPS). To measure how many components on average are deployed by a component-deploying stack, we define the metrics $CPS : \mathbb{P}(C_M) \rightarrow \mathbb{R}$ as:

$$CPS(nm) = \frac{|\{n \in nm : (\exists s \in nm : Stack \in n\_type(s) \land\ n \in stack\_deployed\_components(s))\}|}{|stacks\_deploying\_services(nm) \cup\ stacks\_deploying\_non\_service\_components(nm)|}$$

6   Case Studies

In this section, we describe the case studies used to evaluate our approach and test the performance of the metrics. We studied three open-source microservice-based systems. We also created variants that introduce typical violations of the ADDs described in the literature or refactorings to improve ADD realization to test how well our metrics help to spot these issues and improvements. The cases are summarized in Table 1 and metrics results are presented in Table 2.

Table 1. Overview of modeled case studies and the variants (size, details, and sources)

Case Study ID	Model Size	Description / Source
CS1	68 components 167 connectors	E-shop application using pub/sub communication for event-based interaction as well as files for deployment on a Kubernetes cluster. All services are deployed in their own infrastructure stack (from https://github.com/dotnet-architecture/eShopOnContainers).
CS1.V1	67 components 163 connectors	Variant of Case Study 1 in which half of the services are deployed on the same execution environment and some infrastructure stacks deploy more than one service.
CS1.V2	60 components 150 connectors	Variant of Case Study 1 in which some services are deployed on the same execution environment and half of the non-services components are deployed by a component-deploying stack.
CS2	38 components 95 connectors	An online shop that demonstrate and test microservice and cloud-native technologies and uses a single infrastructure stack to deploy all the elements (from https://github.com/microservices-demo/microservices-demo).
CS2.V1	40 components 101 connectors	Variant of Case Study 2 where multiple infrastructure stacks are used to deploy the system elements as well as some services are deployed on the same execution environment.
CS2.V2	36 components 88 connectors	Variant of Case Study 2 where two infrastructure stacks are used to deploy the system elements (one for the services and one for the rest elements) as well as some services are deployed on the same execution environment.
CS3	32 components 118 connectors	Robot shop application with various kinds of service interconnections, data stores, and Instana tracing on most services as well as an infrastructure stack that deploys the services and their related elements (from https://github.com/instana/robot-shop).
CS3.V1	56 components 147 connectors	Variant of Case Study 3 where some services are deployed in their own infrastructure stack as well as some services are deployed on the same execution environment.
CS3.V2	56 components 147 connectors	Variant of Case Study 3 where all services are deployed in their own infrastructure stack as well as all services are deployed on their own execution environment.

Case Study 1: eShopOnContainers Application. The *eShopOnContainers* case study is a sample reference application realized by Microsoft, based on a microservices architecture and Docker containers, to be run on Azure and Azure cloud services. It contains multiple autonomous microservices, supports different communication styles (e.g., synchronous, asynchronous via a message broker). Furthermore, the application contains the files required for deployment on a Kubernetes cluster and provides the necessary IaC scripts to work with ELK for logging (Elasticsearch, Logstash, Kibana).

To investigate further, we performed a full manual reconstruction of an architecture component model and an IaC-based deployment model of the application as ground truth for the case study. Figure 2 shows the excerpt component model specifying the component types (e.g., *Services, Facades, and Databases*), and connector types (e.g., *database connectors*, etc.) as well as all the IaC-based deployment component types (e.g., *Web Server, Cloud Server, Container, Infrastructure Stack, Storage Resources*, etc.) and IaC-based deployment connector types (e.g., *defines deployment of, deployed on*, etc.) using types as introduced in Sect. 5 shown here as stereotypes.

The component model, consists of in total 235 elements such as component types, connector types, IaC-based deployment component types and IaC-based deployment connector types. More specifically, *19 Infrastructure Stacks, 19 Execution Environments, 6 Storage Resources, 7 Services, 6 Databases, 19 Stack-to-Execution Environment connectors, 7 Stack-to-Service connectors* and *6 Storage Resources-to-Database connectors*. There are also other 146 elements in the application (e.g., *Web Server, Cloud Server, Stack-to-Web Server connectors*, etc.).

The values of metrics *SEEC* and *SEE* show that *Single Service per Execution Environment* pattern is fully supported. We treat both components and connectors as equally essential elements; thus, we use two metrics to assess coupling in our models. Given that *SEE* returns the shared execution environments, it is crucial to measure how strongly these environments are shared. The *SEEC* value indicates this specific aspect by returning the proportion of the shared connectors that these environments have.

The application uses multiple stacks to deploy the services and the other elements, and this is shown by the outcomes of the metrics for the *System Coupling through Infrastructure Stack Grouping* decision. Since multiple stacks have been detected the metrics *MSD* and *AGSD* return *False*. The *SES* metric returns *True* meaning that the *Service Stack* pattern is used. The *MST* returns *True* which means the *Micro-Stack* pattern for the node sub-set *Storage Resources* is also used. The *SPS* value shows that every service is deployed by a service-deploying stack. Furthermore, *CPS* also shows that components that belong to node sub-set *Storage Resources* are deployed by a component-deploying stack. Overall the metrics results in this case study show no coupling issue in deployment, and all best practices in our ADDs have been followed.

For further evaluation, we created two variants to test our metrics' performance in more problematic cases. Our analysis in *CS1.V1* shows that half of the execution environments are shared, and around two-thirds of the connectors between services and execution environments are also considered as shared, meaning these execution environments are strongly coupled with the system services. Using both values, we have a more complete picture of the coupling for all essential elements in this model. Furthermore, the *SPS* value indicates that the *Service Stack* pattern is partially supported, meaning some services are grouped in the same stacks. The analysis in *CS1.V2* shows that our metrics can measure all the additional violations that have been introduced.

Case Study 2: Sock Shop Application. The *Sock Shop* is a reference application for microservices by the company Weaveworks to illustrate microservices architectures and the company's technologies. The application demonstrates microservice and cloud-native technologies. The system uses *Kubernetes* for container-orchestration and services are deployed on *Docker* containers. *Terraform* infrastructure scripts are provided to deploy the system on *Amazon Web Services (AWS)*. We believe it to be a good representative example of the current industry practices in microservice-based architectures and IaC-based deployments.

The reconstructed model of this application contains in total 133 elements. In particular, *1 Infrastructure Stack, 13 Execution Environments, 3 Storage Resources, 7 Services, 4 Databases, 13 Stack-to-Execution Environment connectors, 7 Stack-to-Service connectors* and *4 Storage Resources-to-Database connectors*. There are also another 74 elements in the application such as *Web Server, Cloud Server, Stack-to-Web Server connectors* and *Execution Environment-to-Cloud Server connectors*.

We have tested our metrics to assess the conformance to best patterns and practices in IaC-based deployment. The outcome of the metrics related to *System Coupling through Deployment Strategy* decision shows that also this application fully supports the *Single Service per Execution Environment* pattern. That is, all services are deployed in separate execution environments. Regarding the *System Coupling through Infrastructure Stack Grouping* decision, we detected the *Monolith Stack* pattern, which means one stack defines the deployment of all system elements, resulting in a highly coupled deployment. The metrics *AGSD*, *SES*, and *MST* are all *False*, and *SPS* and *CPS* return 0, since a monolith stack has been detected. These values can guide architects to improve the application by restructuring the infrastructure to achieve the desired design.

In our variants, we introduced gradual but not perfect improvements. The metrics results for *CS2.V1* show an improvement compared to the initial version. That is, *Monolith Stack* pattern is not used since three infrastructure stacks have been detected, and some services are deployed by service-deploying stacks. In *CS2.V2* there is a slight improvement since *Application Group Stacks* has been detected. However, *SEEC* and *SEE* metrics indicate that there is a strong coupling between services and execution environments. In both variants, the metrics have well detected the improvements made.

Case Study 3: Robot-Shop Application. *Robot-Shop* is a reference application by the company Instana provides to demonstrate polyglot microservice architectures and Instana monitoring. It includes the necessary IaC scripts for deployment. All system services are deployed on *Docker* containers and use *Kubernetes* for container-orchestration. Moreover, *Helm* is also supported for automating the creation, packaging, configuration, and deployment to *Kubernetes* clusters. End-to-end monitoring is provided, and some services support *Prometheus* metrics.

The reconstructed model of this application contains in total 150 elements. In particular, *2 Infrastructure Stacks, 18 Execution Environments, 2 Storage Resources, 10 Services, 3 Databases, 13 Stack-to-Execution Environment connectors, 10 Stack-to-Service connectors* and *3 Storage Resources-to-Database connectors*. There are also 89 additional elements in the application.

The metrics results for the *System Coupling through Deployment Strategy* decision are both optimal, showing that in this application all services are deployed in separate execution environments. For the *System Coupling through Infrastructure Stack Structuring* decision, the *AGSD* metric return *True* which means that the *Application Group Stack* pattern is used, resulting in highly coupled services' deployment. Thus, the metrics *SES* and *MST* are *False* and *SPS* and *CPS* return 0. According to these values, architects can be supported to address the detected violations (e.g., as done in *CS3.V2*).

In the variants, we introduced one gradual improvement first and then a variant that addresses all issues. Our analysis in *CS3.V1* shows significant improvement in infrastructure stack grouping. Most of the services are deployed on their own stack, and components that belong to node sub-set *Storage Resources* are completely deployed by a separate stack. However, coupling between services and execution environments has also been detected. Variant *CS3.V2* is even more improved since, in this case, all services are deployed by service-deploying stacks, and no coupling has been detected. In both variants, the metrics have faithfully identified the changes made.

7 Discussion

Discussion of Research Questions. To answer **RQ1**, we proposed a set of generic, technology-independent metrics for each IaC decision, and each decision option corresponds to at least one metric. We defined a set of generic, technology-independent

Table 2. Metrics Calculation Results

Metrics	CS1	CS1.V1	CS1.V2	CS2	CS2.V1	CS2.V2	CS3	CS3.V1	CS3.V2
System Coupling through Deployment Strategy									
SEEC	0.00	0.71	0.42	0.00	0.25	0.62	0.00	0.37	0.00
SEE	0.00	0.50	0.20	0.00	0.14	0.40	0.00	0.16	0.00
System Coupling through Infrastructure Stack Grouping									
MSD	False	False	False	True	False	False	False	False	False
AGSD	False	False	False	False	False	True	True	False	False
SES	True	False	False	False	False	False	False	False	True
MST	True	True	False	False	False	False	False	False	True
SPS	1.00	0.20	0.57	0.00	0.12	0.00	0.00	0.62	1.00
CPS	1.00	1.00	0.50	0.00	0.00	0.00	0.00	1.00	1.00

metrics to assess each pattern's implementation in each model automatically and conducted three case studies to test the performance of these metrics. For assessing pattern conformance, we use both numerical and boolean values. In particular, *SEEC* and *SEE* measures return a range from 0 to 1, with 0 representing the optimal case where a set of patterns is fully supported. Having this proportion, we can assess not only the existence of coupling but also how severe the problem is. However, this is not the case for the *MSD*, *AGSD*, *SES*, and *MST* metrics that return *True* or *False*. Using these metrics, we intend to detect the presence of the corresponding patterns. For *Service Stack* and *Micro Stack* decision options, we introduce two additional metrics with numerical values that can be applied on node subsets to assess the level of the pattern support when patterns are not fully supported. However, applying them on node subsets has the limitation that many runs need to be made, leading to ambiguous results. Our case studies' analysis shows that every set of decision-related metrics can detect and assess the presence and the proportion of pattern utilization.

Regarding **RQ2**, we can assess that our deployment meta-model has no need for significant extensions and is easy to map to existing modeling practices. More specifically, to fully model the case studies and the additional variants, we needed to introduce 13 device type nodes and 11 execution environment nodes types such as *Cloud Server* and *Virtual Machine* respectively, and 9 deployment relation types and 7 deployment node relations. Furthermore, we also introduced a deployment node meta-model to cover all the additional nodes of our decisions, such as *Storage Resources*. The decisions in *System Coupling through Deployment Strategy* require modeling several elements such as the *Web Server*, *Container*, and *Cloud Server* nodes types and technology-related connector types (e.g. *deployed on*) as well as deployment-related connector types (e.g. *Runs on, Deployed in Container*). For the *Coupling through Infrastructure Stack Grouping* decision, we have introduced attributes in the system nodes (e.g., in *Infrastructure Stack, Storage Resources*) and connector types (e.g., *defines deployment of, includes*).

Threats to Validity. We mainly relied on third-party systems as the basis for our study to increase internal validity and thus avoid bias in system composition and structure. It is possible that our search procedures resulted in some unconscious exclusion of specific sources; we mitigated this by assembling a team of authors with many years of experience in the field and conducting a very general and broad search. Because our search was not exhaustive and the systems we found were created for demonstration purposes, i.e., were relatively modest in size, some potential architectural elements were not included in our metamodel. Furthermore, this poses a potential threat to the external validity of generalization to other, more complex systems. However, we considered widely accepted benchmarks of microservice-based application as reference applications, in a way to reduce this possibility. Another potential risk is that the system variants were developed by the author team itself. However, this was done following best practices documented in the literature. We were careful to change only certain aspects in a variant and keep all other aspects stable. Another possible source of internal validity impairment is the modeling process. The author team has considerable experience with similar methods, and the systems' models have been repeatedly and independently cross-checked, but the possibility of some interpretive bias remains. Other researchers may have coded or modeled differently, resulting in different models. Because our goal was only to find a model that could describe all observed phenomena, and this was achieved, we do not consider this risk to be particularly problematic for our study. The metrics used to assess the presence of each pattern were deliberately kept as simple as possible to avoid false positives and allow for a technology-independent assessment.

8 Conclusions and Future Work

We have investigated the extent to which it is possible to develop a method to automatically evaluate coupling-related practices of ADDs in an IaC deployment model. Our approach models the critical aspects of the decision options with a minimal set of model elements, which means it is possible to extract them automatically from the IaC scripts. We then defined a set of metrics to cover all decision options described in Sect. 4 and used the case studies to test the performance of the generated metrics. Before, for the coupling aspects of IaC deployment models, no general, technology-independent metrics have been studied in depth. Our approach treats deployment architectures as a set of nodes and links, considering the technologies used, which were not supported in prior studies. The goal of our approach is a continuous evaluation, taking into account the impact of continuous delivery practices, in which metrics are evaluated continuously, indicating improvements and loose coupling of deployment architecture compliance.

In future work, we plan to study more decisions and related metrics, test further in larger systems, and integrate our approach in a systematic guidance tool.

Acknowledgments. This work was supported by: FWF (Austrian Science Fund) project IAC^2: I 4731-N.

References

1. Artac, M., Borovssak, T., Di Nitto, E., Guerriero, M., Tamburri, D.A.: DevOps: introducing infrastructure-as-code. In: 2017 IEEE/ACM 39th International Conference on Software Engineering Companion (ICSE-C), pp. 497–498 (2017)

2. van der Bent, E., Hage, J., Visser, J., Gousios, G.: How good is your puppet? An empirically defined and validated quality model for puppet. In: 2018 IEEE 25th International Conference on Software Analysis, Evolution and Reengineering (SANER), pp. 164–174 (2018). https://doi.org/10.1109/SANER.2018.8330206

3. Corbin, J., Strauss, A.L.: Grounded theory research: procedures, canons, and evaluative criteria. Qual. Sociol. **13**, 3–21 (1990). https://doi.org/10.1007/BF00988593

4. Dalla Palma, S., Di Nucci, D., Palomba, F., Tamburri, D.A.: Toward a catalog of software quality metrics for infrastructure code. J. Syst. Softw. **170**, 110726 (2020)

5. Dalla Palma, S., Di Nucci, D., Tamburri, D.A.: AnsibleMetrics: a Python library for measuring infrastructure-as-code blueprints in ansible. SoftwareX **12**, 100633 (2020)

6. Fischer, M.P., Breitenbücher, U., Képes, K., Leymann, F.: Towards an approach for automatically checking compliance rules in deployment models. In: Proceedings of The Eleventh International Conference on Emerging Security Information, Systems and Technologies (SECURWARE), pp. 150–153. Xpert Publishing Services (XPS) (2017)

7. Humble, J., Farley, D.: Continuous Delivery: Reliable Software Releases Through Build, Test, and Deployment Automation. Addison-Wesley Professional (2010)

8. Krieger, C., Breitenbücher, U., Képes, K., Leymann, F.: An approach to automatically check the compliance of declarative deployment models. In: Papers from the 12th Advanced Summer School on Service-Oriented Computing (SummerSoC 2018), pp. 76–89. IBM Research Division, October 2018

9. Kumara, I., Garriga, M., Romeu, A.U., Di Nucci, D., Palomba, F., Tamburri, D.A., van den Heuvel, W.J.: The do's and don'ts of infrastructure code: a systematic gray literature review. Inf. Softw. Technol. **137**, 106593 (2021)

10. Kumara, I., et al.: Towards semantic detection of smells in cloud infrastructure code. In: Proceedings of the 10th International Conference on Web Intelligence, Mining and Semantics, WIMS 2020, pp. 63–67. Association for Computing Machinery, New York (2020)

11. Morris, K.: Infrastructure as Code: Dynamic Systems for the Cloud, vol. 2. O'Reilly (2020)

12. Ntentos, E., et al.: Detector-based component model abstraction for microservice-based systems. Computing **103**(11), 2521–2551 (2021). https://doi.org/10.1007/s00607-021-01002-z

13. Nygard, M.: Release It! Design and Deploy Production-Ready Software. Pragmatic Bookshelf (2007)

14. Passos, L., Terra, R., Valente, M.T., Diniz, R., das Chagas Mendonca, N.: Static architecture-conformance checking: an illustrative overview. IEEE Softw. **27**(5), 82–89 (2010)

15. Richardson, C.: A pattern language for microservices (2017). http://microservices.io/patterns/index.html

16. Schwarz, J., Steffens, A., Lichter, H.: Code smells in infrastructure as code. In: 2018 11th International Conference on the Quality of Information and Communications Technology (QUATIC), pp. 220–228 (2018). https://doi.org/10.1109/QUATIC.2018.00040

17. Sharma, T., Fragkoulis, M., Spinellis, D.: Does your configuration code smell? In: Proceedings of the 13th International Conference on Mining Software Repositories, MSR 2016, pp. 189–200. Association for Computing Machinery, New York (2016)

18. Sotiropoulos, T., Mitropoulos, D., Spinellis, D.: Practical fault detection in puppet programs. In: Proceedings of the ACM/IEEE 42nd International Conference on Software Engineering, ICSE 2020, pp. 26–37. Association for Computing Machinery, New York (2020)

19. Zdun, U., Navarro, E., Leymann, F.: Ensuring and assessing architecture conformance to microservice decomposition patterns. In: Maximilien, M., Vallecillo, A., Wang, J., Oriol, M. (eds.) ICSOC 2017. LNCS, vol. 10601, pp. 411–429. Springer, Cham (2017). https://doi.org/10.1007/978-3-319-69035-3_29

Teaching Microservice Architecture Using DevOps—An Experience Report

Henrik Bærbak Christensen[✉]

Computer Science, Aarhus University, 8200 Aarhus, Denmark
hbc@cs.au.dk

Abstract. In this education paper we outline a course and exercise design aimed at teaching students knowledge and skills in refactoring ("strangling") a monolith architecture into a microservice equivalent using a cross team DevOps process. The core aim of our proposed exercise design is that students are engaged in a realistic DevOps process by working in teams on team specific microservices, negotiating interfaces with other teams while ensuring all microservices will interact seamlessly to provide correct system behavior. Our main contribution is to outline the challenges faced when designing such an exercise, our proposals for solving them, the exercise design itself, guidelines for exercise design, as well as present experiences from two courses using this approach.

1 Introduction

Novel software development practices and architectural styles have over the last decade revolutionized how companies develop, deploy, and maintain software. A key driver has been the agile manifesto's first principle *provide value to customers*: from having a time scale of month or even years between a new feature is envisioned until it is bringing value to the customer, these practices allow new features to be designed, tested, and deployed within hours.

The development process, "DevOps"—short for "Development and Operation", and the architectural style, "Microservices" are key techniques to make this agile and responsive development paradigm work, and in a number of ways breaks fundamentally with more classic development paradigms. It is thus not surprising that teaching these techniques poses new challenges for how to design, structure, and execute our teaching, which has spurred research interest over the last years [1,2,4,7,12–15,17,20,26].

In this education and teaching paper, we will outline a course curriculum in general and an exercise design in particular that successfully addresses some of the challenges facing a DevOps/Microservice teacher.

Our main contributions are outlining a concrete exercise design requiring students to work in DevOps teams on disjoint microservices, negotiating interfaces, and ensuring correct integration over three different microservices, and outlining some general guidelines for exercise design based upon instructor's and students' experience. We report our general curriculum design along with experiences from the courses and the exercise design in particular.

© The Author(s), under exclusive license to Springer Nature Switzerland AG 2022
I. Gerostathopoulos et al. (Eds.): ECSA 2022, LNCS 13444, pp. 117–130, 2022.
https://doi.org/10.1007/978-3-031-16697-6_8

The paper describes the challenges in teaching DevOps and microservices in Sect. 2 followed by our particular course context in Sect. 3. The microservice and DevOps exercise design is detailed in Sect. 4, and followed by results (Sect. 5), discussion (Sect. 6), and finally conclusion (Sect. 7).

2   Challenges in Teaching

While the concepts and techniques of DevOps and microservice architectures have matured over the last decade, the challenges in teaching the topics have received attention only recently. DevOps has received the most attention and some of the earliest work is that of Pengxiang [27] and Christensen [7]. Pengxiang identified a central challenge, namely that DevOps requires *hybrid skills*, i.e. skills in combining techniques and elements from a large set of classic topics in computer science. It is not just "databases" or "software architecture" or "security" etc.; it is picking elements from all of them, which is challenging for both students and teachers. Christensen outlines further challenges, notably the challenge of offering a realistic environments of many servers, the challenge of marking student's solutions as these complex environments have to be reproduced to do the evaluation, and that most academic teachers lack operational experiences, a point also noted later by Jones et al. [17].

Case studies of DevOps courses have been reported [4,12,14,15,17,20] that provide ideas for course design, technologies, and teaching techniques. However, a recent study by Fernandes et al. [13] uses a more systematic approach, and identifies central challenges in teaching DevOps by conducting a systematic literature review combined with structured interviews with teachers coming from an industrial background. They list 83 challenges and identify the eight most mentioned challenges. Our work addresses five of these identified challenges, namely:

- Insufficient Time to Teach DevOps (8 occurrences)
- Large number of DevOps tools (7 occurrences)
- Challenging to balance theory and practice (6 occurrences)
- DevOps culture hard to teach (4 occurrences)
- Challenge to find right sized examples (4 occurrences)

One may argue that the commonality of all these issues is that DevOps is a large subject which spans a lot of disciplines: To do successful DevOps you need to master and combine software architecture, databases, requirements engineering, testing, tooling, processes, communication, etc. On top of that, a lot of essential tools are required to fulfill the automation aspect, each with their own learning curve.

Research on teaching the microservice architectural style seems more scarce. Lange et al. [18] presents a bachelor practical project, in which teams of students migrated a legacy insurance system to a microservice architecture with four microservices representing bounded contexts in the domain. A similar project is reported by Cordeiro et al. [11]. Both report student learning outcomes and evaluations to be good, but provides little detail concerning the actual structure of exercises and exercise guidelines, which is a central contribution of this paper.

A recent European effort, the Microservice Education Group [22], brought teachers and researchers together to present and discuss teaching formats, and interestingly two different approached emerged: one approach was project oriented/problem based as students engaged in a collaboration with an industrial partner and working with processes and tools dictated by the partner; the other approach was topic based as the teacher decided on tooling, exercises, and progression. While the former may be more realistic, the latter offers more control over the set of methods, theory, and practices covered. Our course falls in the latter category.

3   Course Description

The course context is a 15 European Credit Transfer System (ECTS)[1] module, divided in three courses of 5 ECTS each, that is taught at Computer Science, Aarhus University, as part of Danish lifelong education effort. Each of the three courses are quarter length, with 7 weeks each. The course is at Master's level, and students are part-time students, typically between 25–60 years old, and employed as programmers and software architects in the software and electronic industry.

The three courses are a progression, building upon the previous course, and forms a whole. The two first courses, "DevOps and Container Technology" and "Scalable Microservices", are topic based while the third course is a project course in which students define their own subject area to study under supervision. The module has been taught twice, in 2020 and 2021.

3.1   Pedagogical Considerations

Our teaching is grounded in the *constructivist paradigm* using elements from constructive alignment [3], cognitive apprenticeship [5] and using a story-telling approach [6]. In short, we emphasize and value that learners must use their *own activity* to construct knowledge and skills, that teachers must state the intended learning outcomes clearly, and that the activities students engage in must be aligned so they directly aim at the learning outcome.

These requirements pose a major challenge when trying to design a course on the topics of MS and DevOps: these techniques are specifically designed for big company large scale development which does not align well with our much more limited teaching context.

Our approach generally follows recommendations in [13] and in particular emphasizes two of these: *Teaching method based on practical activities* and *Use relevant industrial tools*.

Regarding the *teaching method based on practical activities*, we argue that a *story-telling approach* [6] serves well—defining a scaled-down but realistic context/project in which learning topics are introduced as a response to realistic

---

[1] ECTS is a workload measure, 15 ECTS is around 400 h.

requirements in a number of iterations of increasing complexity. We have defined a concrete system, SkyCave, detailed in Sect. 3.3, which serves as grounding case for all exercises and all learning topics in the courses.

Regarding the *use relevant industrial tools*, the selection is daunting, but from a theory and teaching point of view, many solve the same underlying problem, so the theory can be taught in general, and a suitable tool selected to support practical work on exercises.

In this selection process, it is important to select tools that strike a balance between industrial relevance and shallow learning curve. As a concrete example, we have chosen Docker Swarm as orchestration tool rather than Kubernetes. While the latter is more adopted in industry, the learning curve of Swarm is lower especially as Docker Engine was selected as the container technology— and Swarm is already part of that tool and well integrated.

3.2 Learning Goals and Week Plan

Our teaching plan encompassed the following learning goals, and associated tools/techniques.

Course 1: DevOps & Container Technology		Course 2: Scalable Microservices	
Week	Theme	Week	Theme
1	Broker Pattern, SkyCave intro	8	Microservice Design
2	Cloud, Virtualization, Docker	9	Architectural Modernization
3	REST, OAuth 2.0	10	Stability Antipatterns
4	Testing, NoSQL Databases	11	Stability Patterns
5	DevOps, Orchestration, Swarm	12	Logging, Monitoring
6	Scaling, Continuous Integration	13	Versioning, Messaging
7	Continuous Deployment, TLS	14	Security, Event Sourcing

The first course, *"DevOps and Container Technology"*, is heavily biased towards establishing a strong theoretical framework and practical experience with the tool chains, as evident from the learning goals outlined above. Central learning goals are mastering containerization (Docker Engine) and orchestration (Docker Swarm), communication patterns (Broker and REST), and continuous integration (CI) and deployment (CD) (Bitbucket pipelines). Throughout a strong focus is kept on all aspects of testing: unit testing (JUnit 5), service and contract testing, as well as end-to-end testing (TestContainers). Security (TSL, OAuth) as well as NoSQL databases (MongoDB, Redis) are also covered.

All exercises in the first course revolve around enhancing and refactoring the SkyCave system from a Java project into a containerized system, with a Redis backend, well-tested and deployed through a CI/CD pipeline. This happens through six iterations of exercises [7] of which only some are mandatory, allowing for some adjustment of workload and ambition. Most exercises are marked by the instructor, however, some are marked by an automated system, Crunch [8]. Each exercise grants a number of points for solving, which are accumulated and converted to a final exam grade for the course.

The second course, *"Scalable Microservices"*, is biased towards the architectural aspects of microservices. Central learning goals is architectural modernization (aka. "strangling the monolith"), patterns for stability [25]/high availability, redundancy, monitoring, versioning, messaging and security.

Exercises for the second course are fewer but larger, with a strong emphasis on the modernization exercise, which is the main focus of this paper, and treated in detail below in Sect. 4. The following two exercises are focussing upon *design for failure* using Nygard stability patterns, and a "free" exercise in which students pick some topic from the course to try out in context of the SkyCave project. Concretely, groups explored various topics, like logging tools, secure containers, correlation IDs, chaos engineering, a.o. The exercises are documented in reports which are defended orally at the final exam. For full details, please consult [9].

3.3   SkyCave

Our goal is to support student's constructive learning activities through a realistic case striking an appropriate balance between complexity and challenges on one hand, and avoiding accidental complexity which takes time but does not support learning on the other.

Our proposal is "SkyCave": a massive, multi-user, online (MMO) exploration experience with elements of social networking. SkyCave is inspired by the first adventure game, Colossal Cave Adventure [16]; however, game elements have been removed and replaced by social networking and massive multi-user aspects: Friends can log into the SkyCave, meet in specific rooms, post and read messages on that room's notice board ("wall"), and extend the cave by creating new rooms. One student called it a "a text based MineCraft".

As the core topics of the courses are *architectural* and not *functional* the students are provided with high quality source code of a fully operational Sky-Cave system at the onset of the course [10]; however, central aspects (notably authentication and persistence) are provided by stub (or more correctly test double [21]) implementations. Throughout the course, students work on improving architectural aspects of the code base more than developing new functionality.

The handed-out SkyCave code base is a classic three-tier architecture: A client application, *cmd*, provides a text-based user interface similar to the original Colossal Cave's read-eval-print-loop. Every command is sent to a server application, *daemon*, which updates the cave's state by querying and updating a persistence layer, *CaveStorage*.

A client interaction that demonstrate "look" in current room, posting and reading messages in the room, navigation to a new room, and finally creating ("dig") a new room (user commands after the > prompt) may look like this:

```
== Welcome to SkyCave, player Mikkel ==
Entering command loop, type "q" to quit, "h" for help.
```

```
> look
You are standing at the end of a road before a small brick building.
  Creator: Will Crowther, in 1972.
There are exits in directions:
  NORTH  EAST  WEST  UP
You see other players in this room:
  [0] Joe [1] Carla [2] Mikkel
> post Let us solve some exercises.
You posted a message.
> read
  0: [Mikkel, just now] Let us solve some exercises.
  1: [Magnus, 2 minutes ago] Looking forward to dig my own rooms...
  2: [Mathilde, 3 minutes ago] I have just started exploring SkyCave!
> north
You moved NORTH
You are in open forest, with a deep valley to one side.
> dig east This is a newly dug room in SkyCave.
You dug a new room in direction EAST
> east
You moved EAST
> look
This is a newly dug room in SkyCave.
  Creator: Mikkel, just now.
There are exits in directions:
  SOUTH  WEST
You see other players:
  [0] Mikkel
```

3.4 Technical Environment

The provided SkyCave code base is Java 8 and Gradle 6 based, so students initially start the server *daemon* in one shell and the client *cmd* in another.

The set of exercises given to the students during the first course migrate the provided code base towards a full three-tier architecture in which *daemon* and its associated persistence layer (Redis or MongoDB) is containerized as Docker containers and orchestrated by Docker Swarm, horizontally scaled over multiple *daemon* instances, and deployed in the cloud (DigitalOcean) through CI/CD via bitbucket pipelines.

4 Modernization: From Monolith to Microservices

The first large exercise in the second course has DevOps and Microservices as the central learning goal.

The exercise requires the students, working in groups ranging from 1–3 students in size, to do a number of tasks:

– Develop a microservice REST API. Each group is assigned a specific microservice to develop.

- Negotiate this REST API with other groups that depend on ("consume") their API using peer review.
- Develop Contract Tests [19]/Consumer Driven Tests (CDTs) [23] for the group's microservice. These CDTs were provided to consuming groups. Alongside this work, of course, the microservice itself must be developed. Groups were free to choose any technology stack they wished.
- Refactor the *daemon* from its current business logic + database architecture into using the group's own microservice as well as the microservices developed by two other groups.
- Deploy the full MS architecture in production using Docker Swarm.

We initially considered making a collaborative exercise with the aim at identifying the bounded contexts, but decided against it to lower the workload. Therefore the "seams"/bounded contexts were given a priori. The SkyCave *daemon* essentially covers three bounded context:

- **PlayerService.** Responsibilities: Manage the cave's players: knows names and attributes of players, update player's position in the cave, compute list of players in given room, etc. The "north" and "east" commands in the example in Sect. 3.3 are examples of client commands that interact with the PlayerService.
- **CaveService.** Responsibilities: Manage the cave's 3D matrix of rooms: digging new rooms, retrieval of existing rooms, computing exits from a room, etc. The "dig" and "look" commands interact with the CaveService.
- **MessageService.** Responsibilities: Manage the notice board messages in rooms: adding a message, retrieve a subset of the messages from a room, etc. The "post" and "read" commands interact with the MessageService.

Thus, the core challenge of this exercise is to refactor ("modernize" [28] or "strangle" [24]) the existing *daemon* code base so it becomes an *API Gateway* between the *cmd* and the three developed microservices.

As a concrete example, the Java code to create/"dig" a new room in the Redis database in the monolith version:

```
public UpdateResult digRoom(Position position, Room room) {
    result = redisDatabase.addRoom(position, room);
    return result;
}
```

may be refactored in the microservice version so something like:

```
public UpdateResult digRoom(Position position, Room room) {
    String asJson = gson.toJson(room);
    String pos = translateToString(position);
    int statusCode =
        caveService.doPOSTonPath("room/" + pos, asJson);
    result = translateStatusCode(statusCode);
    return result;
}
```

Each bounded context/microservice is assigned to one group, and three groups are paired to form a "migration team", as this example from the course illustrate:

```
Group          | Produce         | Consumes from groups
-----------------------------------------------------------

Migration Team One

Alfa           | CaveService     | Bravo, Charlie
Bravo          | MessageService  | Alfa, Charlie
Charlie        | PlayerService   | Alfa, Bravo
```

That is, group Alfa will design and implement a containerized microservice for CaveService, but have to review and integrate the two services provided by groups Bravo and Charlie to deploy a fully functional *daemon*, essentially doing DevOps with these two groups[2].

To ensure progress and avoid groups waiting unnecessarily for each other, the exercise was organized with five intermediate deadlines before the final hand-in of the exercise report, containers (for daemon and for assigned service), and code base:

- Deadline 1: Version 1 REST API proposal. Output: API specification.
- Deadline 2: REST API review. Output: Review comments.
- Deadline 3: Version 2 REST API proposal. Output: API specification.
- Deadline 4: Release 1 of service + CDT (only in-memory storage). Output: Docker container for service + code base of CDT (Java 8 based).
- Deadline 5: Release 2 of service + CDT (Redis/MongoDB persistence). Output: Container + CDT.
- Deadline 6: Modernization complete with *daemon* refactored to use the three microservices, deployed in cloud, and report hand-in. Output: Report, containers (daemon + service), running system in cloud.

Thus, the first deadlines require quite a lot of communication between groups. In the 2020 instance of the course, this was done exchanging e-mails. However, as reported below, quite a few groups reported it to be a poor medium, so in the 2021 instance, we created three discussion forums, one for each migration team, on our e-learning platform.

The timespan covered for the six deliveries were about three weeks. Remember that it is part-time students, doing their studies in their spare time besides a full time job.

---

[2] In the second instance of the course, the number of groups was not divisible by three, and we as instructors acted as the third group.

5   Results

Data for the process was collected primarily by each group being required to write a section entitled "Reflections on DevOps" in their final report. The 2020 instance had nine groups (three migration teams) while the 2021 instance had seven groups (three migration teams, two of which collaborated with the instructor as the third team). The summary and quotes below are from these sections.

A second source is from the 2021 course, in which the full exchange of all messages regarding API proposals and review comments could be extracted from the e-learning discussion forum module.

The final source is university course evaluations, asking questions on learning outcomes and relevance.

The overall impression about the DevOps process and the exercise is positive. Most groups report that the exchange of information went smoothly and that groups responded timely in order to update APIs or fix breaking bugs in the service implementations or container configurations: "People were open minded about the direct feedback they received which was nice" (Whisky team, 2020), "The teams were all open to feedback, and quickly made new versions of their API specifications" (Bravo team, 2021).

The communication format is important. The 2020 instance was e-mail based, leading to quite some frustration: "As soon as we have more than version (of the API), mail is a bad format" (Romeo, 2020). Even more grave was exchanging CDTs (Java and gradle code) by e-mail: "CDT exchange via e-mail is inefficient, a repository would have been better" (Uniform, 2020). This of course lead us to use discussion forums in the next course instance.

The discussion forum for the 2021 course was divided into three, one for each migration team, which were again divided into three threads, one for each service API (proposals, reviews, discussions, clarification). There were between 4–17 postings in each thread, and 8.78 on average. No bad experiences were reported in the 2021 instance regarding the communication format.

Somewhat to our surprise, no group chose to pick a totally different technology stack (such as Python, Go, or C#) even though most students used other languages (notably C#) in their normal industrial worklife. However, there were quite a diversity in picking Java technologies and libraries, some used Spring Boot, Java 11's HTTP library, UniRest, and others. This diversity lead to some frustration for consuming groups, as groups also exchanged their developed CDT's (required to be in Java 8), and these then had their own requirements in terms of libraries to include in the Gradle build file. Thus, groups faced the issue of either including received CDT's verbatim which bloats the tests with numerous libraries only used by one service and not the others; or refactoring the received CDTs to use the groups own choice of libraries; or even rewriting the CDT's from scratch. Comments like "We never saw much use for the other groups's CDTs on our end." (Whisky, 2020), "There can be some difficulty adding these CDTs from other groups, when they use other libraries than we do." (Xray 2020), "The CDT should be delivered by all teams. But it is possible to write the CDT yourself" (Alfa, 2021).

The diversity in ambition level and working habits of the groups also influenced the experience. "Groups does not work at the same pace or direction. Some groups prefer to make everything the day before delivery, I myself prefer to work in advance, so I can realize my errors and fix them before it is too late" (Papa, 2020) (author's translation).

Our approach to counter this issue was organizing the deadline as a sequence of partial deliveries with deadlines as reported in the previous section. However, it had the consequence of making the DevOps process feel a bit "waterfall" like. "(The strict deadlines) means that the room for experimenting with different types of API's and responsibility of the services is very limited. The agreements on the boundaries between the services need to be finalized early in the process, to allow each team to start working. But because it may take some iterations before you 'get it right', then you may end up having defined and published an API, that you later want to change" (Romeo, 2020). A reflection and an experience that often also occur in industrial practice.

While the first course did require groups to organize *daemon* deployment as a bitbucket pipeline for both CI and CD, no such requirement was made for their own assigned microservice. Some groups though they could handle release and deployment easier by a manual process, but concluded that "As part of the collaboration experience we learned that we had some inconveniences/issues in our implementation, which meant that we had to rebuild and republish our server and thereby its docker image. Seeing how much valuable development time this manual republish consumed, we noted that it would have been worth the effort to set up a CI pipeline to automate the process, even though the service is relatively small" (Quebec, 2020).

A central learning point of DevOps is of course that the boundary between services are more than just agreeing on interfaces. Once integration starts, bugs pop up: "Thus introducing a worse bug than the one we had asked them to fix. While this is a classic and relatable situation among developers, that does not change the fact that our pipeline is still broken" (Whisky, 2020).

The aspect of deployment was open in the exercise—it did not dictate whether group A's service X (and associated database) was deployed on group A's cloud infrastructure; or if the consuming group just started the service and associated database as part of their own Docker Swarm stack. All groups adopted the latter approach, as it was considered easier. However, it lessens the ability of group A to ensure consuming groups migrate to an updated/bug fixed version of the service: "Another detail is that 'my' service is running in my 'clients' stack. Thus nothing forces them to update, when I make breaking changes. In essence, the service ought to run on my stack, and to be reached by an endpoint that I expose" (Papa, 2020) (author's translation).

Both courses were evaluated through the university's course evaluation system and achieved good scores. The evaluation was based upon statements that students had to evaluate on a Lickert scale. 92% (2020)/100% (2021) rated course outcome as "very great" or "great" with the last 8% (2020) rated it as "some". 100% (both courses) rated the relevance for professional development as either to a "high extent" or "great extent". A similar 100% rated that the knowledge and skills could be used in present or future practice as "high extent" or "great extent".

6 Discussion

From a teaching point of view, we find the above reflections by the groups align with our learning goal in particular, and in the aspects of DevOps in general. Benefits and liabilities of the DevOps approach are felt first-hand and reflected upon by the students as is also evident from the many subtle issues in DevOps and microservice architectures that emerge naturally during the student's process of solving the exercise. Furthermore, the evaluation comments reflect that students find the process and learning outcomes valuable and relevant for their industrial practice.

While our SkyCave project and our execution is of course highly specific, we do find some guidelines can be extracted as inspiration for teachers wanting to define other projects. A summary of design considerations are:

- Learning a DevOps process and splitting a monolith are major tasks by themselves, so avoid requiring additional/new functionality to be implemented. Instead, provide a functionally correct, well tested, and well designed system at the onset that is architecturally inadequate in terms of availability, scalability, and deployability.
- Ensure the technology stack/tooling proficiency is established before hand, again to avoid overwhelming the students with tasks. In our context, the first course covered Docker, orchestration, continuous integration and deployment, and that was well known *before* the DevOps and microservice assignment[3].
- Ensure that the initial monolithic system contains well defined bounded contexts of about equal size, and that these boundaries already are rather well encapsulated via interfaces or similar in the provided code base.
- The microservices themselves should not add new features nor complexity, the complexity will arise in the DevOps process itself. Realistically the implementation effort code wise should be small for each group, in that most code can be "copied/moved" from the existing code base to the microservice. No group reported that our exercise was small, on the contrary.
- Organize the communication between groups using the right medium, such as discussion forums. In particular, e-mail is not the right medium.
- Organize the process via partial deliveries with deadlines. Avoid big bang processes where some groups wait endlessly on unresponsive producing groups.

It is of course difficult to get bounded contexts of equal size, so it is a balancing task of assigning microservices to groups. While in our case, that were about

---

[3] One participant actually quit the first course as "there are so many tools to learn". This is the back-side of the automation medal.

equal size in terms of endpoints (PlayerService: 3 REST endpoints; CaveService: 4 endpoints; MessageService: 4 endpoints), the message service was the more complex as it deals with lists of data and pagination. We balanced this by assigning the more complex services to those groups that showed the most proficiency during the course.

Finally, a source of uncertainty should be noted, as our students are all industrial developers or architects, most of which are seasoned developers, typically with 5–25 years of development experience. However, some reported that they had not coded anything for the last 20 years, and felt going back to programming was a tough challenge.

7   Conclusion

We have reported our experiences on an exercise design aimed at teaching students the process of DevOps on refactoring a system with a monolith architecture into a microservice equivalent. The aim has been to mimic properties of an industrial process, and in particular the issue of each team developing a specific microservice that must interact and integrate with other team's microservices.

Data from student's reflections and evaluation generally support the exercise design as the reflections align with properties of real industrial DevOps challenges.

While our exercise design of course is rooted in a specific course setting, we argue that some general guidelines can be formulated, that can be used by teachers as inspiration for their own course and exercise design. A central guideline is to avoid requesting students to develop new functionality as part of the exercise—instead provide mostly functionally complete systems (or build upon systems already completed by the students) that must be refactored along well defined bounded contexts. Then the challenge facing students align with the central learning goal: the DevOps process and the inter-team communication and API negotiation process in particular, as well as the integration of services; rather than overwhelming the students with non-essential work. Another important guideline is to have a communication form that supports a DevOps process. A final guideline is to support the progression with partial deadlines, to avoid groups waiting for each other.

References

1. Alves, I., Rocha, C.: Qualifying software engineers undergraduates in DevOps-challenges of introducing technical and non-technical concepts in a project-oriented course. In: IEEE/ACM 43rd International Conference on Software Engineering and Training (ICSE-SEET) (2021)
2. Benni, B., Collet, P., Molines, G., Mosser, S., Pinna-Déry, A.-M.: Teaching DevOps at the graduate level. In: Bruel, J.-M., Mazzara, M., Meyer, B. (eds.) DEVOPS 2018. LNCS, vol. 11350, pp. 60–72. Springer, Cham (2019). https://doi.org/10.1007/978-3-030-06019-0_5

3. Biggs, J., Tang, C.: Teaching for Quality Learning at University. Open University Press, McGraw-Hill (2007)
4. Bobrov, E., Bucchiarone, A., Capozucca, A., Guelfi, N., Mazzara, M., Masyagin, S.: Teaching DevOps in academia and industry: reflections and vision. In: Bruel, J.-M., Mazzara, M., Meyer, B. (eds.) DEVOPS 2019. LNCS, vol. 12055, pp. 1–14. Springer, Cham (2020). https://doi.org/10.1007/978-3-030-39306-9_1
5. Caspersen, M.E., Bennedsen, J.: Instructional design of a programming course: a learning theoretic approach. In: Proceedings of the Third International Workshop on Computing Education Research, ICER 2007, pp. 111–122. ACM, New York (2007). https://doi.org/10.1145/1288580.1288595
6. Christensen, H.B.: A story-telling approach for a software engineering course design. In: Proceedings of the 14th Annual ACM SIGCSE Conference on Innovation and Technology in Computer Science Education, ITiCSE 2009, pp. 60–64. ACM, New York (2009). https://doi.org/10.1145/1562877.1562901
7. Christensen, H.B.: Teaching DevOps and cloud computing using a cognitive apprenticeship and story-telling approach. In: Proceedings of the 2016 ACM Conference on Innovation and Technology in Computer Science Education, pp. 174–179 (2016)
8. Christensen, H.B.: Crunch: automated assessment of microservice architecture assignments with formative feedback. In: Cuesta, C.E., Garlan, D., Pérez, J. (eds.) ECSA 2018. LNCS, vol. 11048, pp. 175–190. Springer, Cham (2018). https://doi.org/10.1007/978-3-030-00761-4_12
9. Christensen, H.B.: Microservices and DevOps Website, March 2022. https://baerbak.cs.au.dk/c/msdo-ecsa/
10. Christensen, H.B.: SkyCave Bitbucket Repository, March 2022. https://bitbucket.org/henrikbaerbak/skycaveopen/src/master/
11. Cordeiro, R., Rosa, T., Goldman, A., Guerra, E.: Teaching complex systems based on microservices. GROUP 1, 1 (2019)
12. Demchenko, Y., et al.: Teaching DevOps and cloud based software engineering in university curricula. In: 2019 15th International Conference on eScience (eScience), pp. 548–552. IEEE (2019)
13. Fernandes, M., Ferino, S., Fernandes, A., Kulesza, U., Aranha, E., Treude, C.: DevOps education: an interview study of challenges and recommendations. In: 44nd International Conference on Software Engineering: Software Engineering Education and Training (ICSE-SEET 2022), Pittsburgh, PA, USA, May 2022
14. Hobeck, R., Weber, I., Bass, L., Yasar, H.: Teaching DevOps: a tale of two universities. In: Proceedings of the 2021 ACM SIGPLAN International Symposium on SPLASH-E, pp. 26–31 (2021)
15. Jennings, R.A.K., Gannod, G.: DevOps-preparing students for professional practice. In: 2019 IEEE Frontiers in Education Conference (FIE), pp. 1–5. IEEE (2019)
16. Jerz, D.G.: Somewhere nearby is colossal cave: examining will Crowther's original "adventure" in code and in Kentucky. Digit. Humanit. Q. 1(2) (2007)
17. Jones, C.: A proposal for integrating DevOps into software engineering curricula. In: Bruel, J.-M., Mazzara, M., Meyer, B. (eds.) DEVOPS 2018. LNCS, vol. 11350, pp. 33–47. Springer, Cham (2019). https://doi.org/10.1007/978-3-030-06019-0_3
18. Lange, M., Koschel, A., Hausotter, A.: Microservices in higher education. In: International Conference on Microservices (2019)
19. Lewis, J.: Microservices, March 2014. https://martinfowler.com/articles/microservices.html

20. Mazzara, M., Naumchev, A., Safina, L., Sillitti, A., Urysov, K.: Teaching DevOps in corporate environments. In: Bruel, J.-M., Mazzara, M., Meyer, B. (eds.) DEVOPS 2018. LNCS, vol. 11350, pp. 100–111. Springer, Cham (2019). https://doi.org/10. 1007/978-3-030-06019-0_8
21. Meszaros, G.: xUnit Test Patterns: Refactoring Test Code. Addison-Wesley (2007)
22. Microservices Community-Education Group (2022). https://microservices.sdu.dk/ community-groups/education.html
23. Newman, S.: Building Microservices-Designing Fine-Grained Systems. O'Reilly (2015)
24. Newman, S.: Monolith to Microservices: Evolutionary Patterns to Transform Your Monolith. O'Reilly (2015)
25. Nygard, M.T.: Release It! Design and Deploy Production-Ready Software, 2nd edn. Pragmatic Bookshelf (2018)
26. Pang, C., Hindle, A., Barbosa, D.: Understanding DevOps education with grounded theory. In: Proceedings of the ACM/IEEE 42nd International Conference on Software Engineering: Software Engineering Education and Training, pp. 107–118 (2020)
27. Pengxiang, J., Leong, P.: Teaching work-ready cloud computing using the DevOps approach. In: Proceedings of International Symposium on Advances in Technology Education (ISATE), September 2014
28. Richardson, C.: Microservice Patterns. Manning Publications (2019)

Should Microservice Security Smells Stay or be Refactored? Towards a Trade-off Analysis

Francisco Ponce[1](✉) [iD], Jacopo Soldani[2] [iD], Hernán Astudillo[1] [iD],
and Antonio Brogi[2] [iD]

[1] Universidad Técnica Federico Santa María, Valparaìso, Chile
francisco.ponceme@usm.cl, hernan@inf.utfsm.cl
[2] University of Pisa, Pisa, Italy
{jacopo.soldani,antonio.brogi}@unipi.it

Abstract. Securing microservice-based applications is crucial, as many
IT companies are delivering their businesses through microservices. Security smells, i.e. possible symptoms of (often unintentional) bad design
decisions, can occur in microservice-based applications, resulting in violations of key security properties as well as design soundness (i.e. adherence
to microservice design principles). However, it is non-trivial to decide in
each case whether to apply a refactoring to mitigate the effects of a smell,
or whether it is more convenient to keep the smell in the application (at
least at that specific time), since its refactoring may impact both the
application quality and design soundness. This paper argues for trade-off
analysis to help determining whether to keep a security smell or to apply
a refactoring, based on their positive/negative impacts on specific quality attributes and design soundness. The method enacts and supports
this trade-off analysis using *Softgoal Interdependency Graphs* (SIGs), a
visual formalism that provides a holistic view of the positive/negative
impacts of, in our case, security smells and refactorings on software quality attributes and design soundness. We also illustrate our method with
a detailed analysis of a well-known security smell and its possible refactoring. Further development and empirical validation of this method will
allow to deploy automatic recommendations on trade-offs and appropriateness of possible refactorings of microservice applications.

Keywords: Security smells · Security refactoring · Trade-off analysis ·
Soft-goal Interdependency Graphs

1 Introduction

Microservices are on the rise for architecting enterprise applications nowadays,
with big players in IT (e.g., Amazon, Netflix, Spotify, and Twitter) already
delivering their core businesses through microservices [13]. Microservice-based
applications are essentially service-oriented applications adhering to an extended

© The Author(s), under exclusive license to Springer Nature Switzerland AG 2022
I. Gerostathopoulos et al. (Eds.): ECSA 2022, LNCS 13444, pp. 131–139, 2022.
https://doi.org/10.1007/978-3-031-16697-6_9

set of design principles [14], which include the independent deployability and horizontal scalability of microservices, failure isolation, and decentralization.

Microservices also pose new security challenges, including so-called *security smells* [12]. These are possible symptoms of a bad decisions (though often unintentional) while designing or developing an application, which may impact the overall application's security. The effects of security smells can be mitigated by refactoring the application or the services therein while not changing the functionalities offered to clients. Even if applying refactorings requires effort from development teams, they can help improving the overall application quality [1].

Consider, for instance, the *centralized authorization* security smell, which occurs when a single component centrally authorizes all external requests sent to a microservice-based application [12]. When this occurs, the requests exchanged among an application's microservices are trusted without further authorization controls, making them prone to, e.g., confused-deputy attacks, which may compromise the application's authenticity [4]. To mitigate the effects of *centralized authorization*, application architects may *use decentralized authorization*, which consists of refactoring applications to enforce fine-grained authorization controls at microservices-level [12]. This would improve the application's authenticity, while also impacting on other quality attributes and on the adherence of the application to microservices' key design principles.

Whether to keep a security smell, or to apply a refactoring to mitigate its effects, is a design decision that deserves careful analysis. This can indeed impact on several aspects of an application, including other quality attributes besides security, like performances and maintainability [9], and on its adherence to microservices' key design principles [8]. Architects must therefore analyze the possible different trade-offs among such aspects, to balance them and take informed decisions [5]. This is inherently complex, as it requires to holistically consider the impact of keeping a smell/applying a refactoring on security and other quality attributes, and on the adherence to microservices' key design principles.

In this work-in-progress paper, we introduce a first support for analyzing the possible trade-offs related to keeping a security smell in a microservice-based application or applying some refactoring. More precisely, we introduce a method to enact such trade-off analysis using *Softgoal Interdependency Graphs* (SIGs) [2], which provide a visual and holistic panorama of the positive/negative impacts of each security smells and refactorings on each software quality attribute and each microservices' key design principle.

We also illustrate our method by applying it to the *centralized authorization* security smell and its possible refactoring. In particular, we show the SIG displaying their possible impacts on microservices' key design principles and on ISO 25010 security, performance efficiency, and maintainability properties [4], and we discuss how it helps reasoning on whether it is worthy to apply the refactoring or keep the smell in the application.

The rest of this paper is as follows. Section 2 provides some background on SIGs. Section 3 introduces our SIG-based method for trade-off analysis. Section 4 illustrates its application to a known security smell. Finally, Sects. 5 and 6 discuss related work and draw some concluding remarks.

2   Background: SIGs

SIGs allow the systematic modeling of the impact of design decisions (called *operationalizing softgoals*) on quality attributes (called *softgoals*). More precisely, they allow to model the positive or negative impact of different design decisions on the considered quality attributes, hence providing a visual support for an application architect to start a trade-off analysis process [2].

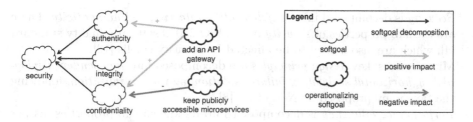

Fig. 1. An example of SIG.

Figure 1 illustrates an example of SIG, displaying the impact of two design decisions (viz., the operationalizing softgoals *keep publicly accessible microservices* or *add an API gateway*) on *security*, with the latter decomposed in three different properties (viz., the softgoals *confidentiality*, *integrity*, and *authenticity*). The positive/negative impact of each decision is depicted as a green/red arrow. Impacts are labeled with +/- to denote that a design decision helps achieving/hurts a quality attribute. Other possible labels are ++/-- to denote that a design decision ensures that a quality attribute is realized/broken, and S+/S- to indicate an expected positive/negative impact, yet to be empirically confirmed.

3   Towards a SIG-Based Trade-offs Analysis

We propose the use of SIGs to support the analysis of trade-offs related to keeping a security smell in a microservice-based application or applying the refactorings known to mitigate its effects. Each SIG is intended to provide a holistic view of the positive/negative impacts (and their rationale) on software quality attributes and microservices' key design principles. Following the recommendations of Oliveira et al. [9], we propose each SIG to display the impact of security smells and refactorings on at most four softgoals. Adding more softgoals will complicate the visualization of the impacts, hence making the trade-off analysis to get too complex to manage.

Given that our ultimate goal is to analyze the impact of microservices' security smells and refactorings, we introduce softgoals for *security* and *microservices' key design principles*. Specifically, we consider *security* as per its definition by the ISO 25010 software quality standard [4], and we take the microservices' key *design principles* defined by Neri et al. [8].

These two softgoals are the main ones that we work with, and should be part of every generated SIG. The other two softgoals depend on the desiderata of an application architect. In this specific work-in-progress paper, to illustrate our method, we also consider *performance efficiency* and *maintainability* from the ISO 25010 software quality standard [4] as two concrete examples.

To enact a more accurate analysis, we decompose the considered softgoals, hence considering all the different aspects of each softgoal separately. In this case, this means to decompose the above-mentioned softgoals as follows:

- *Security* is decomposed into *confidentiality, integrity,* and *authenticity.* These are the sub-properties of *security* in the ISO 25010 software quality standard [4], which are also known to be affected by security smells [12].
- Microservices' key *design principles* are decomposed into *independent deployability, horizontal scalability, failure isolation,* and *decentralization,* following the taxonomy proposed by Neri et al. [8].
- *Performance efficiency* is decomposed into its known sub-properties, as per its definition in the ISO 25010 software quality standard [4], i.e., *resource utilization, time behaviour,* and *capacity.*
- *Maintainability* is decomposed into its known sub-properties, as per its definition in the ISO 25010 software quality standard [4], i.e., *modularity, reusability, analysability, modifiability,* and *testability.*

We exploit SIGs to analyze two different types of design decisions (or *operationalizing softgoals*). These are (i) keeping a security smell or (ii) spending efforts in applying the refactorings allowing to mitigate its effects. This will enable the analysis of the impacts of the security smells and refactorings that we systematically elicited in our previous work [12].

The actual impact of security smells and refactorings is modeled by arcs connecting design decisions to softgoals. Each arc is labelled with "++" or "+", if the design decision makes or helps realizing a softgoal, respectively. An arc is instead labelled with "--" or "-", if it breaks or complicates realizing a softgoals, respectively. We use such labels for the impacts known thanks to our former work done in [8,12]. There are however other impacts of the smells that we expect to occur, even if they are yet to be empirically validated. For these, we use "S-" and "S+", depending on whether the expected impact is negative or positive, respectively. The validation of such expected impacts, as well as of those of other known security smells and refactorings, is in the scope of our future work, as described in Sect. 6.

4   Illustrative Example

Figure 2 illustrates our method applied to the *centralized authorization* security smell, which occurs when a single component is used to centrally authorize external requests sent to a microservice-based application [12]. The *centralized authorization* smell hurts the *authenticity* of the application since the requests exchanged among microservices are trusted without further authorization controls, making them prone to, e.g., *confused-deputy attacks*. This smell also hurts the *decentralization* design principle, since it happens when microservices depend on a central component to manage authorization [8].

We also expect the *centralized authorization* smell to hurt the *time behavior* of the application, since the central authorization component can become a bottleneck if the application considerably grows in the number of microservices. We also expect this smell to hurt the *analysability* of the application, since having a central authorization component makes complex to assess the impact of a change in the authorization mechanism on all microservices. Finally, we expect a positive impact on the *testability* property of the application, since the authorization control should be tested only in one component.

To mitigate the effects of *centralized authorization*, application architects may *use decentralized authorization*, which consists of refactoring the application to enforce fine-grained authorization controls at the microservices-level [12]. The *use decentralized authorization* refactoring helps achieve the *authenticity* security property. This refactoring also helps achieve the *decentralization* design principle, since it suggests decoupling the central authorization component and that each microservice has its own fine-grained controls.

By applying the refactoring, microservices do not depend on a central authorization component. We expect that this helps achieving the *independent deployability* design principle. We also expect that this refactoring has a positive impact on *modularity* and *analysability* since each fine-grained authorization control can be modified independently, minimizing the impact that this has on the rest of the microservice-based application. On the other hand, we expect the considered refactoring to have a negative impact on the *testability* of the application, since the fine-grained authorization controls need to be tested independently, hence scaling in complexity with the number of microservices. We also expect a negative impact on the *resource utilization* property, since this approach requires more information to be transmitted for each request (e.g., always including authorization tokens), therefore causing a higher consumption of network resources.

Figure 2 hence presents a holistic view of the positive/negative impacts of the *centralized authorization* security smell, and its refactoring *use decentralized authorization*. With the above described impacts,[1] we can start then a trade-off analysis. We can indeed reason on whether it is worthy to apply the refactoring, or whether it is more convenient to keep the smell in our microservice-based application. We can start by defining which of these softgoals is more important, which depends on the context and desiderata of the application architecture. This SIG allows us to prioritize the softgoals and select the design decision that best suits the application needs. For example, if *resource utilization* is our priority (e.g., since our application runs on a platform with limited resources, or since increasing resource utilization is too costly), we may decide to keep the smell. Instead, if we have no restrictions on *resource utilization*, and if *testability* has

---

[1] Impacts' rationale can also be included in SIGs as *claims* linked to impact arcs [2]. For readability reasons, we here present it inline, rather than displaying it in Fig. 2.

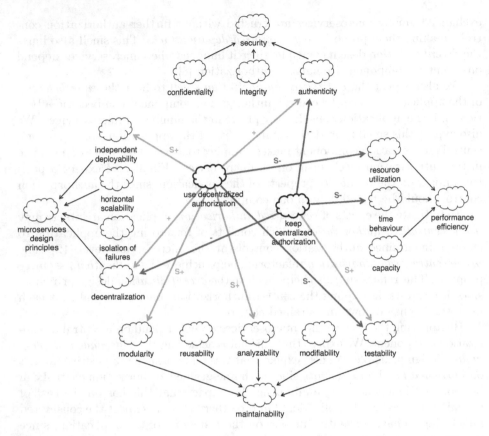

Fig. 2. SIG displaying the impact of keeping the *centralized authorization* smell and its corresponding refactoring on the considered softgoals.

a lower priority than the other softgoals visualized in Fig. 2, then applying the *used decentralized authorization* refactoring seems to be the best option.

5   Related Work

Some previous research has been done to enable trade-off analysis for decision-making process by software architects. Thus, Orellana et al. [10] provided a systematic approach to classify architectural patterns and analyze trade-offs among them using SIGs; This approach differs from ours in the objectives, since they focus on the impact of architectural patterns on systems' quality, but we focus instead on the impact of microservices' security smells and refactorings; i.e., not only on the quality of microservice-based applications, but also on their adherence to microservices' key design principles [8].

Pasquale et al. [11] proposed a requirements-driven approach to automate security trade-off analysis, using a security goal model that allows software engineers to identify and analyze trade-offs among them. In a similar vein, the proposal of Elahi and Yu [3] extends the $i*$ notation by providing a goal-oriented approach to model and analyze security trade-offs of multi-actor systems. Our study differs from these two in their objectives: they focus on security requirements and goals, respectively, but we focus instead on known security smells while also considering microservices' key design principles.

Another related approach was proposed by Márquez et al. [6], the first one that used SIGs with microservices. They proposed to use SIGs to illustrate the impact of microservices design patterns on high availability properties. The resulting SIG can be used to evaluate whether a given design pattern should be included in a microservice-based architecture. However, they addressed only high availability properties, and we focus instead on security smells and their refactorings, examining their impact on multiple quality attributes and microservices' key design principles.

Martini et al. [7] also support reasoning on the trade-off between keeping an identified smell and applying a refactoring, but rather based on technical debt. They indeed measure the negative impact of a smell as the interest paid by keeping the smell, comparing this to the principal cost of applying a refactoring to resolve such smell. They however consider impacts only under the technical debt perspective, in terms of its principal and interest, whereas we propose to trade-off among multiple aspects, like those we discussed in this paper.

Finally, it is worth mentioning the work of Oliveira et al. [9], which presented a systematic method for architectural trade-off analysis based on patterns. This research aimed to help microservice-based application architects to identify and understand the patterns that best suit their specific needs in a project. Our research uses SIGs to provide a holistic view of the impact of microservices' security smells and refactorings on quality attributes and microservices' key design principles.

6   Conclusions

We have introduced a method based on SIGs (Softgoal Interdependency Graphs) to support trade-off analysis related to keeping security smells in microservice-based applications or applying some refactorings. Each SIG aims to provide a holistic view of the positive and negative impacts of a security smell and its possible refactorings on software quality attributes and microservices' key design principles. We have also showcased our method, by applying it to the *centralized authorization* smell, and its impacts on the *security, performance efficiency*, and *maintainability* properties, defined in the ISO 25010 software quality standard [4], as well as on microservices' key design principles [8].

Ongoing research is elaborating SIGs for known microservices' security smells and refactorings, like those described by Ponce et al. [12], as well as validating such SIGs, e.g., through an online survey with practitioners and interviews. This will give expert support to the illustrated impacts and their rationale. We plan to incorporate the validated SIGs into a visual tool to provide holistic support to application architects in deciding whether it is worthy to apply refactorings to mitigate the effects of security smells, or whether it is more convenient to keep them (at least at that specific time). Finally, we will integrate/extend the visualization into a full-fledged environment, enabling to automatically identify security smells in microservice-based applications and to reason on whether to refactor/keep the identified smells.

References

1. Bass, L., Clements, P., Kazman, R.: Software Architecture in Practice, 3rd edn. Addison-Wesley Professional, Boston (2012)
2. Chung, L., Nixon, B.A., Yu, E., Mylopoulos, J.: The NFR framework in action. In: Non-Functional Requirements in Software Engineering, International Series in Software Engineering, vol. 5, pp. 15–45. Springer, Boston, MA (2000). https://doi.org/10.1007/978-1-4615-5269-7_2
3. Elahi, G., Yu, E.: Modeling and analysis of security trade-offs - a goal oriented approach. Data Knowl. Eng. **68**(7), 579–598 (2009). https://doi.org/10.1016/j.datak.2009.02.004
4. ISO: Systems and software engineering – systems and software quality requirements and evaluation (square) – system and software quality models. ISO/IEC FDIS 25010, 2011, pp. 1–34 (2011)
5. Kazman, R., Klein, M., Barbacci, M., Longstaff, T., Lipson, H., Carriere, J.: The architecture tradeoff analysis method. In: Proceedings of Fourth IEEE International Conference on Engineering of Complex Computer Systems (Cat. No.98EX193), pp. 68–78 (1998). https://doi.org/10.1109/ICECCS.1998.706657
6. Márquez, G., Soldani, J., Ponce, F., Astudillo, H.: Frameworks and high-availability in microservices: an industrial survey. In: CIbSE, pp. 57–70 (2020)
7. Martini, A., Fontana, F.A., Biaggi, A., Roveda, R.: Identifying and prioritizing architectural debt through architectural smells: a case study in a large software company. In: Cuesta, C.E., Garlan, D., Pérez, J. (eds.) ECSA 2018. LNCS, vol. 11048, pp. 320–335. Springer, Cham (2018). https://doi.org/10.1007/978-3-030-00761-4_21
8. Neri, D., Soldani, J., Zimmermann, O., Brogi, A.: Design principles, architectural smells and refactorings for microservices: a multivocal review. SICS Softw. Intens. Cyber-Phys. Syst. **35**(1), 3–15 (2020)
9. de Oliveira Rosa, T., Daniel, J.F., Guerra, E.M., Goldman, A.: A method for architectural trade-off analysis based on patterns: evaluating microservices structural attributes. In: EuroPLoP (2020). https://doi.org/10.1145/3424771.3424809
10. Orellana, C., Villegas, M.M., Astudillo, H.: Assessing architectural patterns trade-offs using moment-based pattern taxonomies. In: XLV Latin American Computing Conference (CLEI) (2019). https://doi.org/10.1109/CLEI47609.2019.235086
11. Pasquale, L., Spoletini, P., Salehie, M., Cavallaro, L., Nuseibeh, B.: Automating trade-off analysis of security requirements. Requir. Eng. **21**(4), 481–504 (2015). https://doi.org/10.1007/s00766-015-0229-z

12. Ponce, F., Soldani, J., Astudillo, H., Brogi, A.: Smells and refactorings for microservices security: a multivocal literature review. J. Syst. Softw. **192**, 111393 (2022). https://doi.org/10.1016/j.jss.2022.111393
13. Thönes, J.: Microservices. IEEE Softw. **32**(1), 116–116 (2015). https://doi.org/10.1109/MS.2015.11
14. Zimmermann, O.: Microservices tenets. Comput. Sci. Res. Dev. **32**(3), 301–310 (2017). https://doi.org/10.1007/s00450-016-0337-0

Architecture Modeling, Design and Decision Making

From Informal Architecture Diagrams to Flexible Blended Models

Robbert Jongeling(✉) , Federico Ciccozzi , Antonio Cicchetti ,
and Jan Carlson

Mälardalen University, Västerås, Sweden
{robbert.jongeling,federico.ciccozzi,antonio.cicchetti,
jan.carlson}@mdu.se

Abstract. For the early design and communication of software systems, architects commonly use informal diagrams. Due to their notational freedom and effectiveness for communication, informal diagrams are often preferred over models with a fixed syntax and semantics as defined by a modeling language. However, precisely because of this lack of established semantics, informal diagrams are of limited use in later development stages for analysis tasks such as consistency checking or change impact analysis. In this paper, we present an approach to reconciling informal diagramming and modeling such that architects can benefit from analysis based on the informal diagrams they are already creating. Our approach supports migrating from existing informal architecture diagrams to flexible models, i.e., partially treating diagrams as models while maintaining the freedom of free-form drawing. Moreover, to enhance the ease of interacting with the flexible models, we provide support for their blended textual and graphical editing. We validate our approach in a lab setting and perform an evaluative case study in an industrial setting. We show how the approach allows architects to continue informal diagramming, while also benefiting from flexible models for consistency checking between the intended architecture and the implementation.

Keywords: architecture consistency · software design sketching · blended modeling · flexible modeling

1 Introduction

Software architects make extensive use of informal diagrams for early design and communication [12]. These diagrams can be used to depict, e.g., the intended decomposition of the system into components, the deployment of components across various hardware systems, or the communication between various parts of the system. The use of free-form drawing for these diagrams allows the ad hoc insertion of new semantic elements and provides freedom of sharing ideas without the inhibition of editing tools or stringent adherence to modeling languages. Being free-formed makes these diagrams easy to adopt and, in many cases, preferred to

This research was supported by Software Center https://www.software-center.se.

© The Author(s), under exclusive license to Springer Nature Switzerland AG 2022
I. Gerostathopoulos et al. (Eds.): ECSA 2022, LNCS 13444, pp. 143–158, 2022.
https://doi.org/10.1007/978-3-031-16697-6_10

models created in modeling tools that enforce their conformity to modeling languages. Thus, informal diagrams are vital tools for architects.

In later phases of development, architects may want to use these previously created informal diagrams to reason about the system. For example, it is commonly of interest to check the completeness of the implementation by comparing the consistency between models of the intended architecture and the implementation. Moreover, such consistency is a prerequisite for using the models for further analysis tasks such as change impact analysis. Their lack of committed semantics prevents informal diagrams from being used for these analysis tasks. Therefore, the question arises: *How can we benefit more from informal early architecture diagrams for analyzing systems under development?*

Based on the prevalence of informal diagrams used for communication between stakeholders, as reported in earlier surveys [1,19], modeling experts have argued that informal modeling (often done in drawing tools and contrasted to more formal and less flexible modeling) can be successful if limitations to their structure are postponed as long as possible [2]. In this study, we consider the point of limiting the structure to come at the moment when informal models are starting to be used for analysis tasks such as consistency checking or change impact analysis. The latter use of sketches is not uncommon; in one of the mentioned surveys, half of the respondents mentioned that sketches were useful to later understand the relationships between development artefacts [1].

Analysis tasks can be better supported by considering development artifacts as models of the system. To bridge informal diagramming and modeling, the concept of flexible modeling proposes to extend modeling tools to support more informal tasks [11]. Generally, flexible modeling is about providing the freedom to deviate from the strict graphical syntax of a modeling language. Blended modeling proposes the seamless use of multiple concrete syntaxes for the reading and editing of models [5].

In this paper, we consider a combination of flexible and blended modeling to provide architects with an approach to benefit from their informal diagrams for analysis tasks. Our approach entails the definition of a grammar for a textual model that shall capture specific aspects of the diagram. A set of model transformations then provides a round-trip synchronization between the informal diagrams, the derived textual model, and back, so that the graphical notation can be updated and can continued to be used after changes in the textual model. We validate our approach in a lab setting and perform an evaluative case study at our industrial partner.

2   Motivation and Challenges

In their raw form, informal diagrams lack defined semantics as well as a workable representation and therefore require pre-processing before they can be used for semi-automated analysis tasks such as consistency checking or change impact analysis. Model-based development [18] provides the means to process diagrams in structured and tool-supported ways; by considering them as models of the system, i.e., abstract representations with a defined syntax and semantics. To maintain the freedom of informal diagramming while also providing the additional benefits of modeling, we aim to consider part of the informal diagrams as models and to preserve the remaining parts of the diagrams as well. In the remainder of this section, we discuss four challenges when we want to migrate from informal diagrams to flexible and blended models.

Knowledge Preservation from Existing Diagrams. The first challenge is to preserve the knowledge captured in a potentially large set of existing informal diagrams. Therefore, the challenge is to boost existing informal diagrams with modeling information or to automatically replace them while maintaining their current content. In both cases, manual migration is infeasible due to the scale and number of existing diagrams.

Adding a Textual Syntax. Having a textual syntax in addition to the existing graphical one can be beneficial for various tasks such as version control, creating scripts that interact with the textual models, or simply because a textual representation may be the preferable way to edit the model for some stakeholders. Therefore, we identify the need for blended modeling [5], i.e., the use of a textual and graphical representation of the architecture.

Synchronizing Graphical and Textual Syntax. The textual syntax should not replace graphical representations, but should be a supplementary means of manipulating the models. Moreover, both representations shall be editable, and changes to one of them shall be automatically propagated to the other. Synchronization of textual and graphical notations brings additional challenges in flexible modeling settings, since the layout of diagrams must be maintained during synchronization.

Preserving the Graphical Layout. The layout of informal diagrams may capture the implicit semantics of the design. Therefore, the model should be flexible to include not only semantically relevant modeling information but also implicit information related to the topology of the model, including, e.g., the color, size, location, and rotation of shapes. For example, in a deployment diagram, the placement of boxes relative to each other or the distance between them may convey some meaning to architects about the relative grouping of components. Not all of these implicit semantics are meaningful to capture in a modeling language, nor are they easily formalized. In other modeling formalisms, e.g., UML class diagrams, the exact arrangement of the classes carries no semantics (although it can still be relevant for communication). However, for informal diagrams, these implicit semantics are key, especially since diagrams are used mainly for communication between architects and other stakeholders. Hence, while it may be hard to make these implicit semantics explicit, the layout should be preserved so that the intended meaning of informal diagrams is not lost.

3   Flexible and Blended Modeling of Architectures

In this section, we propose an approach that meets the challenges identified in Sect. 2.

3.1   Approach Overview

Our approach boosts existing informal diagrams by considering parts of them
as models. To do so, we define specific types of graphical elements (shapes)
in the informal architecture diagram as metamodel elements, and thereby all
occurrences of those shapes as model elements. Furthermore, we propose two
unidirectional transformations that (i) create a textual model from an informal
diagram, and (ii) restore a graphical representation based on the textual model,
preserving the layout of the pre-existing informal diagrams. Hence, parts of the
informal diagram that are not defined as model elements are not included in
the textual model, but are restored when transforming the textual model back
to a graphical representation. This approach allows architects to continue with
informal diagramming, also after the definition of the model. An overview of the
transformations and other parts of the approach is shown in Fig. 1. In the following, we include a detailed description of the approach, in which we distinguish
between the blended modeling loop and the preparation steps that define the
textual and graphical formats.

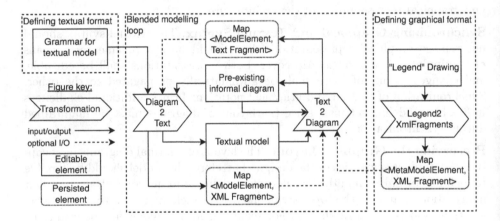

Fig. 1. Schematic overview of our flexible and blended modeling approach.

3.2   Defining Textual and Graphical Formats

The first step of the approach is to define a grammar to which the textual
model of the architecture diagram will conform. To do so, the architects should
identify those aspects of the diagrams they have created that are of interest
for analysis. The grammar should contain concepts for each type of element in
the diagram that will be considered a metamodel element. The textual model is
obtained through the transformation *Diagram2Text*, which in the first iteration
of the blended modeling loop only takes as input the grammar and the informal
diagram.

To define the transformation *Diagram2Text*, it is necessary to define which shapes of the diagram are to be considered as metamodel elements. This information can be directly included in the transformation or fed to the tool by means of a "legend", which is a separate diagram in which the metamodel elements are defined by example. For example, if all yellow rectangles in a diagram are to be considered as instances of the metamodel element "component", then the legend should contain a single yellow rectangle named "component". Then, using the transformation *Legend2XmlFragments*, we create a map of the metamodel element to the XML fragment, in this case from the metamodel element "component". The legend is used to transform newly added elements in the textual representation to a graphical representation, in transformation *Text2Diagram*. Conversely, if no new elements are defined in the textual model, the entire diagram can be reconstructed based on the map of the model element to the XML fragment stored during transformation *Diagram2Text*.

As we will see in Sect. 4, transformations *Diagram2Text* and *Text2Diagram* are currently implemented manually. This is a limitation of the implementation, but not of the approach. In future work, our aim is to automatically generate the transformations inside the blended modeling loop provided a grammar for the textual model and a legend drawing.

3.3 Blended Modeling Loop

The middle part of Fig. 1 labeled "Blended modeling loop" refers to the synchronization between the informal diagram and the derived textual model. We follow a cycle of the loop starting from the box "Pre-existing informal diagram". Given the initial diagram and the grammar, the transformation *Diagram2Text* results in (i) a textual model of the architecture, containing all the model elements identified in the diagram; and (ii) a map of the model elements to XML fragments, containing for each of the identified model elements an XML fragment containing their corresponding graphical representation as obtained from the diagram file.

After changes to the textual model, we can reconstruct the diagram from the textual model by transformation *Text2Diagram*. Each model element in the textual model is expanded to its graphical representation using either (i) the XML fragment stored during the previous transformation *Diagram2Text* or (ii) the XML fragment as a result of transformation *Legend2XMLFragments*. The latter option is used for elements that are newly added or changed in the textual representation and therefore do not occur in the stored map of model elements to XML fragments. Therefore, although both inputs corresponding to these options are marked as optional in Fig. 1, exactly one of them must be used to expand each model element. Thus, *Text2Diagram* makes use of the preserved layout information associated with the model elements during transformation *Diagram2Text*. Furthermore, transformation *Text2Diagram* also restores the remainder of the diagram, i.e., those shapes that were not considered model elements. To do so, it replaces in the original diagram only those shapes that were identified as model elements in the previous step and leaves the remaining shapes unaltered.

To some extent, the layout information of the textual representation is preserved as well; the *Text2Diagram* transformation produces a map that contains an associated text fragment for each model element, which includes all the text after the previously occurring model element and until the model element itself. modeling This input is marked as optional because, during the first time the transformation is executed, no such text fragment information is known, and therefore, is not used.

The approach is thus flexible, as it allows the user to continue to combine modeling and drawing by preserving the existing diagram layout in its entirety, except for the added, modified, or deleted model elements. Moreover, synchronization between textual and graphical representations makes the approach *blended*. Thus, we have obtained flexible and blended models from informal architecture diagrams.

4   Implementation[1] and Validation

In this section, we describe our implementation, validate it by showing how the textual and graphical representations can be automatically synchronized while preserving their layout, and show how architects in our industrial setting benefited from our approach for establishing consistency checks between the architecture model and the implementation.

4.1   Implementation and Validation in Lab Setting

To demonstrate the approach, we implemented it by boosting the functionality of the drawing tool `diagrams.net` with a grammar to capture some aspects of pre-existing informal diagrams in textual models. We now show an example architecture diagram, a corresponding grammar, and transformations for round-tripping between the diagram and the textual model.

Example Architecture Diagram. An example architecture diagram is shown in Fig. 2. The example is an extended version of the architecture diagram encountered in the industrial setting discussed in Sect. 4.2. The diagram shows several layers that represent hardware, drivers, services, and others. The different columns roughly represent groupings of functionality. In addition, the diagram contains the components and their position within the layers and columns. Components are distinguished between in-house developed components (yellow) and third-party components (blue). Dependencies between components are indicated by means of dashed arrows. The example is an anonymized (by removing the names of layers and components) and extended (by adding dependencies) version of a real architecture diagram of the company that could not be shared for intellectual property reasons.

---

[1] The reader is encouraged to have a look at our replication package with our implementation and demo videos, in the following GitHub repository: https://github. com/RobbertJongeling/ECSA-2022-replication-package.

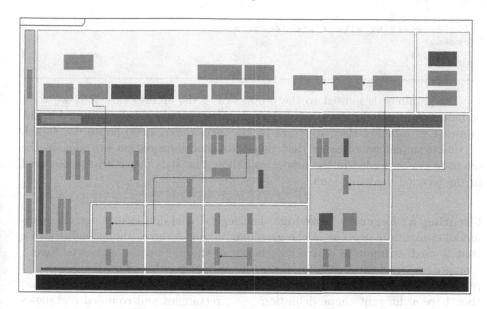

Fig. 2. Example anonymized informal diagram of an instance architecture. (Color figure online)

Defining a Grammar. We aim to capture three aspects of the diagram: layers, components as residing in layers, and dependencies between the components. In this implementation, we create the grammar shown in Listing. 1.1 using TextX [6], which is based on Xtext [21], but does not rely on the Eclipse ecosystem; instead, it allows for grammar specification in Python. The choice of Python is motivated from an industrial perspective to ease the adoption of the approach.

Listing 1.1. Grammar specification for textual model, expressing an architecture in terms of components, dependencies, and layers.

```
Architecture:
    ('components' '{' components+=Component ( "," components+=
        ↪ Component)* '}' )
    ('dependencies' '{' dependencies+=Dependency ( ","
        ↪ dependencies+=Dependency)* '}' )
    ('layers' '{' layers+=Layer ( "," layers+=Layer)* '}' )*
;
Component:
    'component' name=ID
    ('inlayers' '{' layers+=[Layer] ( "," layers+=[Layer])* '}' )*
;
Dependency:
    ('from' fromcomp=[Component])
    ('to' tocomp=[Component])
;
Layer:
    'layer' name=ID
;
```

```
//lines starting with # are comments
Comment:
    /\#.*$/
;
```

The grammar is limited to the properties of the architecture that we want to model. Additional properties of the components could also be included in the model, e.g., whether they are third-party, open-source, or in-house developed. In this example, we consider that this additional information included in the diagram is not needed in the model and show that it is nevertheless preserved in the blended modeling loop.

Creating a "Legend" Drawing. The legend contains shapes for all metamodel elements that occur in the grammar. Figure 3 shows the legend drawing that is used as input to derive the shapes of the metamodel elements "layer", "component", and "dependency". Since the approach is based on the XML representation of the diagram, a requirement when using multiple shapes is that they have a different shape definition (e.g., rectangles and rounded rectangles could have the same "shape" value and would thus be indistinguishable). In the example legend, the element "layer" is defined as a polygon, the component and the third-party component are both rectangles, but with different styles.

Transforming Diagrams to Text and Back. The transformations, like the grammar, are also implemented in Python. To process the diagram, the first step of the transformation *Diagram2Text* obtains a readable XML string from the persisted format. To create the textual model, first all shapes that denote model elements are collected, and then relationships between model elements are identified. During generation of the textual model, it is checked if there is an existing map of model elements to textual fragments that was created during a previous iteration of the blended modeling loop. If so, the textual representation of these model elements is restored; if not, they are newly created based on the

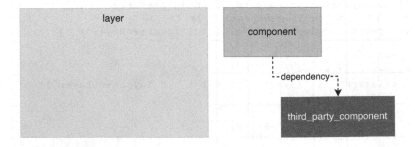

Fig. 3. "Legend" defining the shapes of the metamodel elements *layer*, *component*, and *dependency*.

grammar. When creating the textual model, for each model element, the XML fragment corresponding to its graphical representation is stored.

To recreate the diagram, the transformation *Text2Diagram* replaces all the identified model elements in the existing diagram with those model elements of the textual model. If they already exist, then their graphical representation is taken from the map of model elements to XML fragments. For new components, layers, and dependencies, we rely on the legend to derive the representation of the component. In the current implementation, the legend also determines the position of the new element; hence the new elements are rather crudely placed in the diagram with no regard to the pre-existing layout. This is an implementation detail and not a limitation of the approach.

To validate the transformations, we performed a test for a scenario in which we work with the example diagram. First, we run the transformation *Diagram2Text*. Second, we removed a component, changed a dependency, added a new component, and added a new layer in the textual model. We then executed the transformation *Text2Diagram*. We successfully obtained the new elements and maintained the layout of the unchanged elements. We then moved around elements in the graphical layout and re-run the transformation *Diagram2Text*, we observe in the textual model that the "inlayers" attribute of the moved component has been updated to reflect its current position. A demo video of this procedure is included in the replication package linked at the beginning of this section.

4.2 Evaluative Case Study

In addition to the above validation on a constructed example, we evaluated our approach by implementing it in a concrete industrial setting and using the textual model for consistency checking between an intended architecture and a corresponding implementation.

Industrial Setting. We collaborated with a group of software architects who design and maintain the software architecture for several variants of embedded systems developed in their company. The group has created a reference architecture that is used as a template for deriving the architecture of new products. In practice, architecture descriptions are drawings similar to UML deployment diagrams, but are instead informal diagrams created in Microsoft Visio. When a new product is created, the reference architecture diagram is copied and components are deleted or added as required for that particular product, analogously to *clone-and-own* practices common in the software product line engineering domain.

The created diagrams are similar to the one shown in Fig. 2. However, since the architects are only interested in checking the consistency between included components between the architecture and implementation, we ignore dependencies, the origin of components (third-party or in-house developed) and what layers they belong to.

Need for Consistency Checking. In the studied setting, informal diagrams, such as the one shown in Fig. 2, are used mainly for communication. The ability to edit them freely provides architects with a highly accessible way to make changes. However, now the group has run into the limitations of these diagrams, since the desire has arisen to check the consistency between specific instance architectures and their implementations. Consistency is relevant, since throughout evolution of the system, features and software components may be added, and thereby the instance architecture diagram might go out of date, making it no longer a suitable artifact to use for reasoning about the system.

Envisioned Way of Working. We discussed with architects what way of working could be adopted to facilitate consistency checks between their intended architecture and the corresponding implementation. The following steps were seen as a typical scenario for creating an instance architecture. Step 1 is to duplicate the reference architecture and in the new diagram remove, edit, and add software components to customize an instance architecture. Step 2 is then to create a list (textual representation) of the software components in the instance (this is automated by transformation *Diagram2Text* in our approach). Step 3 is to analyze consistency by checking that the components included in the instance architecture and those included in the implementation are the same. Once defined, the consistency check can be scripted and executed repeatedly throughout the system's evolution.

Consistency Check Implementation. To check the consistency between the architecture diagrams and their implementation, we compare the components included in both. Currently, there are no explicit links between the code and the diagram. In this setting, the architecture and implementation should be considered consistent if they include the same components. Hence, to create a consistency check for this setting, it is required to obtain from the diagram the components it depicts and to obtain from the software implementation a list of the components it contains. Figure 4 shows an overview of the final consistency check implemented.

In Script A (in Fig. 4), a list of components is extracted from the software configuration files, based on several rules that determine whether or not an entry should be considered a component. These rules were defined after discussions with the group of architects and a few iterations to narrow down an exact definition. To extract components from the architecture diagram, we first applied our approach as outlined in Sect. 3 to enhance the informal architecture diagram with modeling information. We define a grammar that expresses the architecture as a set of components (a simplified version of the grammar shown in Listing 1.1) and use our approach to transform the diagram into a textual model conforming to the grammar. In Script B (in Fig. 4), we then extract the names of all the components by obtaining all "component" model elements from the textual model file.

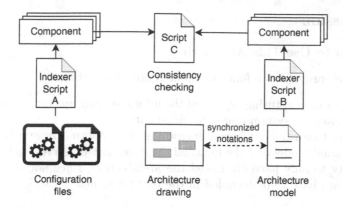

Fig. 4. Consistency checking source code and architecture by first extracting sets of components from configuration files (Script A) and textual model (Script B) as obtained from the informal architecture diagram, and then comparing these sets (Script C).

Script C (in Fig. 4) then compares the sets of components obtained from the configuration files and the textual architecture model. When executing consistency checks in the industrial setting, we identified about 50 components in the architecture and about 40 components in the implementation. According to the architects, this discrepancy is due to an inaccurate model. We found that the model included more boxes marked as components than boxes that should be considered as components. Therefore, in this case, the consistency check provided feedback on the quality of the modeling, rather than on the implementation.

4.3 Experiences from the Studied Industrial Setting

To evaluate our implementation, we have asked the architects of the group to use our tool for a typical task for them: deriving a new instance architecture and modifying it. The architects have copied the existing graphical reference architecture diagram and derived the textual representation using our tool. The textual representation was then modified by removing and adding components. Finally, the architects recreated a graphical representation of the model, where all components had the same layout as before (except for the newly created components, which are placed at a default location in the diagram).

The architects could use our implementation and agree that the functionality meets their requirements as listed in Sect. 2. As we showed, the implementation allows for the creation of automated consistency checks between the architecture and implementation due to (i) capturing the semantics of the informal diagram and (ii) providing an accessible format for the obtained model elements. Finally, we allow the architects to keep using the graphical format they are used to and the topology contained within existing diagrams by means of the synchronization transformations in the blended modeling loop. One of the main benefits the architects experienced was that our approach allowed them to implement consistency checks and thereby showcase the benefits of modeling to their colleagues.

5   Discussion

5.1   When to Use This Approach

Our approach provides the following benefits to architects:

1. a textual model capturing aspects of the informal diagrams that are of interest for analyzing the system under development;
2. the ability to continue informal diagramming, supported by synchronization of the textual model and the informal diagram that preserves its layout; and
3. the ability to only partially model the architecture, since not all aspects of the diagram have to be included in the textual model.

Our approach has value when applied in settings with pre-existing architecture diagrams. In such settings, it may not be straightforward to migrate those diagrams to models with strict semantics. Then, a flexible approach allows the continued use of informal diagrams mixed with some stricter semantics for certain aspects of the diagrams. Moreover, the blended modeling of our approach allows one to maintain the layout of the diagrams, which is useful, e.g., in those cases where the layout conveys implicit semantics.

Our intention is to provide a small degree of modeling in settings in which diagrams are used so that the benefits of modeling can be shown. We showed that the approach can support complex graphical model elements, such as connections and hierarchies. However, supporting intricate informal diagrams that contain many of these complex constructs would require significant effort in the customization of the transformations to appropriately map these (connected) shapes to model elements. Therefore, for more complex graphical needs, it would still be a better option to use an existing modeling language (and the tools that support it) or to develop a DSML in a language workbench. In the evaluative setting, the approach sufficiently captures the model, since we are only interested in capturing the components as model elements.

5.2   Approach Limitations

We identified several limitations of our approach that were acceptable in the studied industrial setting but may restrict its applicability in other settings.

To be able to use the approach, architects should be able to capture in a grammar the concepts from their drawing that are of interest for analysis. This task becomes more challenging with more complex diagrams. Moreover, there might be cases where capturing the semantics of the drawing is made more difficult because the same notation is used to represent different concepts, in which case our approach cannot distinguish them. Nevertheless, when we consider grammar as a formalization of the ideas currently implicit in the architecture, we believe that architects should be able to perform this task.

A related challenge is scaling up the approach to deal with larger and more complex informal diagrams. In our example, the choice of components, layers, and dependencies was made to show that the approach can handle at least three commonly used graphical representations of elements: (i) stand-alone shapes, (ii) containment of shapes in other shapes, and (iii) connectors between shapes. Validating that we can continue to differentiate between different concepts in more complex diagrams remains a task for future work.

The nature of this approach is that the emerging workflow is not very robust to mistakes. For example, using unknown shapes in the diagram will cause them to not be recognized as model elements by the transformations. A way to address this weakness could be to provide custom shape sets as a way to provide a palette for the graphical syntax. In future work, we aim to study these and other means to provide robust ways to combine informal diagramming and modeling.

Our current implementation is based on `diagrams.net`, but our approach is not limited to it. The approach relies on matching model elements with fragments of their graphical representation, which is not limited to the XML-based persistence format of one particular tool. Supporting other drawing tools is a direction for future work.

5.3 Considered Alternative Approaches

Initially, we considered providing architects with a domain-specific modeling language (DSML) that would completely replace their need for informal drawing. To this end, we defined a grammar using Xtext [21] and created a graphical syntax for it using Sirius [8]. The intention was to maintain the graphical syntax that the architects were already using in their drawings, but it turned out to be too challenging to replicate some specific aspects of the existing graphical notation when developing this DSML. More problematically, the resulting tool was considered too heavyweight to be easily adopted in the studied industrial setting, since using the developed DSML requires architects to use an Eclipse instance with some plug-ins. Finally, we rejected the alternative of developing a new DSML following the realization that architects prefer to be able to maintain their current informal modeling practices.

We also looked for alternatives for blended architecture modeling and considered PlantUML. Although it is easy to define the components in its textual notation, positioning them in the graphical notation is not supported by design. Indeed, PlantUML's GraphViz-based generator creates the graphical view of the model, and the user should not want to control the relative positioning of elements too much.

5.4 Other Threats to Validity

External validity is related to the generalizability of the findings [16]. Because of the ubiquity of informal diagrams for architecture and the common desire to use them for analysis tasks, we see a broad applicability of our approach. Still, we need to be careful when claiming that our findings with respect to the usefulness of our approach are general. Future work is required to analyze the suitability of our proposed blended and flexible modeling to other problems in other settings.

6   Related Work

Sketching software architectures has a long history. Tools have been proposed that limit the interpretation of skecthes into existing diagrams, e.g., converting sketches of UML use case diagrams to proper models. Further sketching tools have provided more freedom and other usability features to support sketching for software design [15]. Our approach extends these by providing the possibility to treat the diagram as a model.

Among the existing approaches to textually describe models, there are a large number of text-to-UML tools such as PlantUML [3]. What is typically not supported in these tools is controlling the topology of graphical models, since this is not always relevant for the semantics of the model. However, there are many situations where the layout of the model also conveys semantics [7], such as in our studied setting, where the arrangement of the components has meaning for the architects.

The flexible modeling paradigm [11] can be approached from two directions. Researchers have also begun exploring the support of informal notation in existing modeling tools, e.g., to supplement UML and OCL models [10]. The other direction, studied in this paper, is to consider to what extent we can include formal modeling inside an existing informal diagramming tool. Similar initiatives have been undertaken; for example, it was shown how DSMLs can be created from graphical examples [14] in order to involve domain experts in DSML development. Our approach is able to additionally consider the non-modeling elements of the drawing and maintain its overall layout during a round-trip from graphical to textual notation and back. Additionally, FlexiSketch was developed, which is a tool that allows the user to first create a free-form sketch and then create a metamodel by annotating certain shapes in sketches with metamodel elements [20]. In our approach, we propose to benefit from a pre-existing mature and commonly used drawing tool as the source of informal diagrams and, in addition, provide a textual notation for flexibly created models.

Our solution requires manual specification of the metamodel elements. Another approach has shown the possibility of deriving metamodels by automatically selecting candidate elements and letting the user judge the candidates [4]. A further difference between common flexible modeling approaches and ours is that we do not infer types for later models, but instead boost an existing drawing with modeling concepts. Treating drawings as models has previously been explored, by transforming annotated drawings into an intermediate model representation that can be interacted with using Epsilon model management tools [13,22]. Our approach is more flexible than bottom-up metamodeling [17] or metamodeling by example, since it allows for continued mixing of drawing and modeling, even after the instantiation of the underlying metamodel.

Another proposal for a flexible interpretation of icons for a concrete graphical syntax relies on associating model elements with snippets of vector graphics that represent them [9]. However, the approach does not provide a round trip to a textual notation and does not explicitly consider the layout of the graphical model.

In summary, our approach adds to the existing literature by allowing the migration from informal diagrams in existing drawing tools to flexible textual models that can be used for analysis, while maintaining the freedom of drawing by providing synchronization between the informal diagram and textual model.

7   Conclusion

In this paper, we showed an approach to benefit more from existing informal architecture diagrams by considering them, in part, as models. We describe our implementation and validate it in a lab setting. Additionally, we conducted an evaluative case study in an industrial setting where flexible models are used for consistency checking between the architecture and the implementation, while informal diagrams are continued to be used for communication between architects and other stakeholders. Our approach creates flexible models out of the diagrams; since it requires only their partial consideration as models, other aspects of the diagram can remain in free form. Moreover, our approach creates blended models due to our synchronization mechanism between the diagrams and textual models. The benefit of this approach is that users may continue using the informal graphical notations they were used to, but, in addition, they can benefit from the syntax and semantics brought by modeling. In future work, we plan to study how we can implement flexible and blended modeling in more robust and general ways for use cases where it can be useful.

References

1. Baltes, S., Diehl, S.: Sketches and diagrams in practice. In: Proceedings of the 22nd ACM SIGSOFT International Symposium on Foundations of Software Engineering, pp. 530–541 (2014)
2. Bucchiarone, A., et al.: What is the future of modeling? IEEE Softw. **38**(2), 119–127 (2021)
3. Cabot, J.: Text to UML and other "diagrams as code" tools - Fastest way to create your models, March 2020. https://modeling-languages.com/text-uml-tools-complete-list/
4. Cho, H., Gray, J., Syriani, E.: Creating visual domain-specific modeling languages from end-user demonstration. In: 2012 4th International Workshop on Modeling in Software Engineering (MISE), pp. 22–28. IEEE (2012)
5. Ciccozzi, F., Tichy, M., Vangheluwe, H., Weyns, D.: Blended modelling-what, why and how. In: 2019 ACM/IEEE 22nd MODELS-Companion, pp. 425–430. IEEE (2019)
6. Dejanović, I., Vaderna, R., Milosavljević, G., Vuković, Ž: TextX: a python tool for domain-specific languages implementation. Knowl. Based Syst. **115**, 1–4 (2017)
7. Di Vincenzo, D., Di Rocco, J., Di Ruscio, D., Pierantonio, A.: Enhancing syntax expressiveness in domain-specific modelling. In: 2021 ACM/IEEE MODELS Companion, pp. 586–594. IEEE (2021)
8. Eclipse Foundation: Sirius - the easiest way to get your own modeling tool (2022). https://www.eclipse.org/sirius/

9. Fondement, F.: Graphical concrete syntax rendering with SVG. In: Schieferdecker, I., Hartman, A. (eds.) ECMDA-FA 2008. LNCS, vol. 5095, pp. 200–214. Springer, Heidelberg (2008). https://doi.org/10.1007/978-3-540-69100-6_14
10. Gogolla, M., Clarisó, R., Selic, B., Cabot, J.: Towards facilitating the exploration of informal concepts in formal modeling tools. In: 2021 ACM/IEEE MODELS-C, pp. 244–248. IEEE (2021)
11. Guerra, E., de Lara, J.: On the quest for flexible modelling. In: Proceedings of the 21th ACM/IEEE International Conference on Model Driven Engineering Languages and Systems (MODELS), pp. 23–33 (2018)
12. Hasselbring, W.: Software architecture: past, present, future. In: The Essence of Software Engineering, pp. 169–184. Springer, Cham (2018). https://doi.org/10.1007/978-3-319-73897-0_10
13. Kolovos, D.S., Matragkas, N.D., Rodríguez, H.H., Paige, R.F.: Programmatic muddle management. XMMoDELS 1089, 2–10 (2013)
14. López-Fernández, J.J., Garmendia, A., Guerra, E., de Lara, J.: An example is worth a thousand words: creating graphical modelling environments by example. Softw. Syst. Model. 18(2), 961–993 (2017). https://doi.org/10.1007/s10270-017-0632-7
15. Mangano, N., Baker, A., Dempsey, M., Navarro, E., van der Hoek, A.: Software design sketching with calico. In: Proceedings of the IEEE/ACM International Conference on Automated Software Engineering, pp. 23–32 (2010)
16. Runeson, P., Höst, M.: Guidelines for conducting and reporting case study research in software engineering. Empir. Softw. Eng. 14(2), 131 (2009)
17. Sánchez-Cuadrado, J., de Lara, J., Guerra, E.: Bottom-up meta-modelling: an interactive approach. In: France, R.B., Kazmeier, J., Breu, R., Atkinson, C. (eds.) MODELS 2012. LNCS, vol. 7590, pp. 3–19. Springer, Heidelberg (2012). https://doi.org/10.1007/978-3-642-33666-9_2
18. Schmidt, D.C.: Model-driven engineering. IEEE Comput. 39(2), 25 (2006)
19. Störrle, H.: How are conceptual models used in industrial software development? A descriptive survey. In: Proceedings of the 21st International Conference on Evaluation and Assessment in Software Engineering, pp. 160–169 (2017)
20. Wüest, D., Seyff, N., Glinz, M.: FlexiSketch: a lightweight sketching and meta-modeling approach for end-users. Softw. Syst. Model. 18(2), 1513–1541 (2019)
21. XText: XText - language engineering made easy! (2022). https://www.eclipse.org/Xtext/
22. Zolotas, A., Kolovos, D.S., Matragkas, N.D., Paige, R.F.: Assigning semantics to graphical concrete syntaxes. XM@ MoDELS 1239, pp. 12–21 (2014)

Debiasing Architectural Decision-Making: A Workshop-Based Training Approach

Klara Borowa[✉][iD], Maria Jarek, Gabriela Mystkowska, Weronika Paszko, and Andrzej Zalewski[iD]

Institute of Control and Computation Engineering, Warsaw University of Technology, Warsaw, Poland
klara.borowa@pw.edu.pl

Abstract. Cognitive biases distort the process of rational decision-making, including architectural decision-making. So far, no method has been empirically proven to reduce the impact of cognitive biases on architectural decision-making. We conducted an experiment in which 44 master's degree graduate students took part. Divided into 12 teams, they created two designs – before and after a debiasing workshop. We recorded this process and analysed how the participants discussed their decisions. In most cases (10 out of 12 groups), the teams' reasoning improved after the workshop. Thus, we show that debiasing architectural decision-making is an attainable goal and provide a simple debiasing treatment that could easily be used when training software practitioners.

Keywords: Cognitive bias · Architectural decisions · Debiasing

1 Introduction

Cognitive bias is a term that describes an individual's inability to reason entirely rationally; as such, it prejudices the quality of numerous decisions [18]. Researchers have observed the influence of cognitive biases on day-to-day software development over two decades ago [13]. Since then, it was proven that almost all software development activities are affected by cognitive biases to some extent [9]. Architectural decision-making in particular is not exempt from the influence of cognitive biases [14,18]. However, research on debiasing architectural decision-making is scarce [9], with a clear lack of empirically proven debiasing methods that could be used in practice [10]

In this paper, we endeavour to create an effective debiasing treatment, through expanding on our previous work [1]. The debiasing treatment that we designed consists of an hour-long workshop during which individuals learn about cognitive biases in architectural decision-making (ADM) and take part in three practical exercises. We tested the effectiveness of this debiasing treatment in an experiment, in which 44 master's level graduate students took part. Our study was aimed at answering the following research question:

© The Author(s), under exclusive license to Springer Nature Switzerland AG 2022
I. Gerostathopoulos et al. (Eds.): ECSA 2022, LNCS 13444, pp. 159–166, 2022.
https://doi.org/10.1007/978-3-031-16697-6_11

RQ. Is a training workshop an effective method of reducing the impact of cognitive biases on architectural decision-making?

Through our study, we show that debiasing ADM is an attainable goal, since in most cases (10 groups out of 12) the debiasing treatment was successful. Our workshop provides a debiasing effect and, because of its simplistic design - it can easily be used to train software practitioners to make more rational decisions.

This paper is organised as follows. In Sect. 2 we describe research related to the subject of our study. Section 3 presents the research method, and in particular: the design of the debiasing workshop, our experiment, the study participants and how we analysed the obtained data. Section 4 contains the results of our experiment. In Sect. 5 we discuss our findings. The threats to validity are explained in Sect. 6. Finally, in Sect. 7 we provide a conclusion and describe possible future work.

2   Related Work

Cognitive biases impact how decisions are made by every human being. In particular, they heavily influence intuitive decisions made under uncertainty [17]. This effect occurs due to the dual nature of the human mind, which comprises intuitive and rational decision-making subsystems [8]. Fischoff [5] describes four levels of debiasing (reducing the effect of biases) treatments: (A) warning about the biases, (B) describing typical biases, (C) providing personalised feedback about the biases, (D) an extended programme of debiasing training.

Cognitive Biases Influence on Architectural Decision-Making. Tang [14] described how distorted reasoning may impact software design, by providing a set of examples of biased statements that software designers may use during their work [14]. As software architecture is actually a set of design decisions [7], it may be heavily affected by architects' biases. This makes reducing the impact of biased decision-making an important endeavour in the area of software architecture (see also [18,19]).

Debiasing Architectural Decision-Making. Although there are various guidelines and practices for improving architectural decision-making [15,16], there is a severe lack of empirical research on treatments for undesirable behavioural factors in the realm of ADM [10]. There is a small amount of research on debiasing in Software Engineering. So far, the existing research has rarely proposed debiasing approaches, and empirical validation of the proposed debiasing methods [9] is even less frequent. Notably, Shepperd et al. [12] proposed a successful treatment that improved software effort estimation, through a two- to three-hour-long workshop about cognitive biases. Our team attempted an empirical validation of an anti-bias treatment for ADM [1], but it turned out not to be successful. This may be due to its several weaknesses:

1. We informed the participants about biases through a simple presentation. This treatment is on the lower levels (A and B) of Fischoff's debiasing scale [5]. In comparison, the successful treatment proposed by Shepperd et al. [12] included a workshop and giving personalised feedback (level C debiasing).

2. In order to evaluate whether the treatment provided the desired effect, we compared the performance of two groups of students – one that was shown the presentation, and one that was not. However, this approach does not take into account the teams' individual traits. Those traits may make them more or less susceptible to cognitive biases from the start. It is possible that, when comparing a single team's performance before and after the presentation, the results may have been significantly different.
3. The sample (2 groups consisting of 5 students) was rather small.

This paper summarises our subsequent research that was aimed at developing a successful debiasing treatment by overcoming the above shortcomings.

3   Research Method

The three-hour-long experiment was performed during a meeting on the MS Teams platform. The experiment plan has been made available online [2]. While planning the experiment, we enhanced most steps from our previous approach [1] to both improve the debiasing treatment itself and the validity of the experiment. The basic steps of the experiment included:

1. Preparing the debiasing workshop.
2. Gathering participants.
3. A series of three-hour long meetings during which we conducted the experiment, which consisted of three steps:
   (a) Task 1 – a 1 h-long ADM task.
   (b) The debiasing workshop.
   (c) Task 2 – a 1 h-long ADM task.
4. Analysing the teams' performance during the first and second tasks.

Biases. The debiasing workshop was designed to counter three biases that in previous research turned out to be exceptionally influential on architectural decisions [3,18] and their impact on software engineering overall has already been researched extensively [9]:

1. Anchoring – a biased preference towards initial starting points, ideas, solutions [17].
2. Confirmation bias – when the currently desired conclusion leads the individual to search for confirming evidence, or omitting other information [19].
3. Optimism bias – an inclination towards overly optimistic predictions and judgements [9].

Architectural Decision-Making Task. Each team of participants performed the task twice: before and after the debiasing workshop. The theme (the problem that was to be solved) was different in each task. The task was to design an architecture that could be used as a solution to a given theme, and to record the design using the C4 model notation [4]. The task itself was known to the participants before they took part in the experiment, in order to allow them to prepare and learn more about the C4 model. This was not the case for the themes. All the tasks were supposed to be graded as part of the students' software architecture course. However, the students were given over a week after the experiment to finish and polish their design. During both architectural design tasks, the researchers did not take an active part in the architecting.

Debiasing Workshop Design. The full workshop plan with instruction for workshop organisers have been made available online [2]. The workshop was designed to teach three debiasing techniques:

- The anti-anchoring technique: having proposed an architectural solution, the individual that presents it must explicitly list one disadvantage of the solution.
- The anti-confirmation bias technique: one team member has to monitor the discussion for unjustified statements that dismiss new information and ideas. Such as "We already decided that".
- The anti-optimism bias technique: the team must explicitly mention the risks associated with the design decisions.

These specific techniques were proposed previously as a result of our previous work [1] where we analysed, in detail, how each of the three researched biases usually impacted the teams that took part in the study. However, during that study, the effectiveness of these techniques was not validated. For each of these three techniques, the participants had to actively perform a practical exercise. In this phase of the experiment, the researchers actively facilitated the workshop by encouraging participants to use the debiasing techniques, providing them with examples of the techniques' use, and prompting the participants when they forgot to use the technique that they were supposed to apply.

Sample. The participants were recruited from among master's level graduate students majoring in Computer Science in our Faculty. These graduate students in particular, were taking a Software Architecture course. Although participation could be part of their graded project, it was voluntary. There was an alternative, traditional way, to obtain a grade. At the start of the MS Teams meeting, participants filled a questionnaire that allowed us to obtain basic data about them. Overall, 61% of the participants had prior experience in software development, ranging from 0.3 to 3 years. The questionnaire and its results, containing detailed information about the participants, is available online [2].

Analysis. For the analysis, we used a modified approach of our method from our previous study [1]. In order to analyse the results, we transcribed all recordings of the tasks, during which the participants' created their design. In order to inspect how biases impacted architectural decisions, we applied the hypothesis coding method [11]. This means that we defined a set of codes to be used to mark relevant segments in the transcript in advance, prior to the analysis. The coding scheme and all specific code counts have been made available online [2].

Each transcript was first coded by two researchers separately. Then, all of the codes were negotiated [6] until the coders reached a consensus on each code. Additionally, no transcript was coded by the same researcher that conducted the particular meeting with the participants. Furthermore, we summarised the overall number of codes only twice, after coding 6 and 12 transcripts, to avoid a situation where we would unconsciously chase after a desired number of biased or non-biased arguments in a particular transcript.

Having coded the transcripts, we compared how many biased and non-biased statements/decisions were present before and after the workshop. We defined: (a) a biased decision as one impacted by more biased statements than rational arguments, (b) a non-biased decision as one impacted by more rational arguments than biased statements, (c) neutral decisions as ones impacted by an equal amount of biased and non-biased statements. We also counted the amount of bias influences and the usage of the debiasing techniques during the tasks.

4   Results

Through the analysis process we uncovered the specifics about arguments, decisions, bias occurrences and the use of debiasing techniques in the teams' Task 1 and Task 2 transcripts. All p-values mentioned in this section were calculated using the non-parametric Wilcoxon Signed Rank Test. Through this test, we evaluated whether the changes in specific measured values were statistically different (when the p-value was less than 0.05). All specific numbers for code counts for each team are available online [2].

Arguments. We classified these arguments as either biased (i.e. affected by one or more of the researched biases) or non-biased. Overall, we found 1470 arguments and 487 counterarguments. 54% of the statements before the workshop were biased, compared to 36% after. In general, the percentage of biased arguments decreased after the workshop in the cases of all teams except one.

The increased number of non-biased arguments (p-value = 0.0024) and non-biased counterarguments (p-value = 0.0005), and the decrease of the percentage of biased statements (p-value = 0.002) were significant. However, the changes in the number of biased arguments (p-value = 0.1973) and counterarguments (p-value = 0.8052) can not be considered significant.

Decisions. Overall we found 641 decisions - 266 biased, 281 non-biased and 94 neutral. 52% of decisions before the workshop were biased, compared to 31% after. Only one had a larger percentage of biased decisions after the workshop. In the case of all the other teams, the percentage of biased decisions decreased. The increase in the number of non-biased decisions (p-value = 0.0024) and the decreased percentage of biased decisions (p-value = 0.0020) were significant. However, the change in the number of biased decisions (p-value = 0.0732) can not be considered significant.

Cognitive Biases. Overall, we found 1110 bias occurrences - 558 before and 552 after the workshop. The sum of these counts is different from the number of arguments since: (a) it was possible for various biases to influence one argument, (b) some biased statements were not connected to any architectural decision.

There was no significant change in the overall number of biases between Task 1 and Task 2 (p-value = 0.8647). This means that the debiasing effect (the smaller percentage of biased decisions and arguments) was not achieved by decreasing the number of bias occurrences during the tasks. In fact, the effectiveness of the debiasing treatment comes from increasing the number of non-biased arguments.

Debiasing Techniques. We compared the amounts of technique uses before and after the workshop, since it was possible for participants to spontaneously use a specific technique during Task 1. We identified 133 uses of the proposed techniques - 26 techniques before and 107 after the workshop.

The number of uses of the practices increased significantly during Task 2 (p-value = 0.0005). However, three teams did not increase their use of the anti-bias techniques substantially after the workshop. Despite this, these teams' percentage of biased arguments and decisions decreased during Task 2. Additionally, two teams, despite using a higher number of debiasing techniques during Task 2, had more biased decisions and more biased arguments during Task 2.

Overall, the anti-optimism technique was used most often (15 before and 57 after workshop), while the anti-anchoring technique was used less often (3 before and 30 after workshop), with the anti-confirmation bias technique rarely being used at all (8 before and 20 after workshop). This may be because listing risks came most naturally, while the other two techniques may require much more effort to be used correctly.

5   Discussion

Our results show that the debiasing treatment through the debiasing workshop we designed was successful, both improving the quality of argumentation and design decisions. However, there are some particularities worth discussing in detail, which may help to significantly improve our approach in the future.

Firstly, our approach did not significantly decrease the number of cognitive bias occurrences, biased arguments and biased decisions that impacted our participants (see Sect. 4). Instead, we managed to improve the number of rational arguments and decisions present in the teams' discussions, through which the percentage of biased arguments and decisions decreased. This means that, while it may not be possible to completely get rid of cognitive biases, other ways of rationalising decision-making are possible and could be pursued.

Secondly, the team whose decisions improved the most was the one that had the worst result in Task 1. Furthermore, the team that improved the least was the one with the best result in Task 1. This may mean that, while our treatments successfully improve the performance of initially biased individuals, it may not be as impactful in the case of individuals that were initially less impacted by biases. Since our participants were students with up to three years of professional experience, we do not know yet how different the debiasing effect would be on experienced practitioners (who may be initially less impacted by biases).

Finally, the failure of two teams led us to explore the transcripts in detail. After that, we noticed that their performance dropped at one point, when the participants simply became tired (which they expressed verbally). This is in line with Kahneman's [8] explanation for the existence of two systems - using System 2 is physically exhausting and no human can use it indefinitely. Thus, time for rest may be a crucial factor to bear in mind while attempting debiasing.

6   Threats to Validity

Conclusion Validity: We used non-parametric tests to examine whether the observed changes in the measured values were significant.

Internal Validity: We put significant care into designing the experiment and setting the environment so that no factors other than the workshop influenced the students. The teams did not know the themes for their tasks before the study, and did not have more than 10 min of time to interact with the environment outside during the experiment. Finally, to decrease the chances of the researchers distorting the results during the analysis, we used negotiated coding [6] and calculated the results (code counts) for the transcripts only twice.

Construct Validity: Our method also improves on the one used in our previous study [1] by taking into account not only arguments and biases but also decisions. This factor is crucial since it is possible that, while the overall argumentation may improve, a team can lack regularity when using rational arguments, thus still making numerous biased decisions nonetheless.

External Validity: Our study's weakness is that our participants were all students. While most of them had professional experience, it was limited.

7   Conclusion and Future Work

In this paper we explored whether debiasing through a training workshop is an effective method of reducing the impact of cognitive biases on ADM (RQ). We designed such a workshop and examined its effectiveness (Sect. 3). The results show that the debiasing treatment is effective (Sect. 4), although it does not completely eliminate the impact of the biases (Sect. 5).

Through this work, we show that designing a successful debiasing treatment for cognitive biases in ADM is possible, and propose an effective treatment that can become a foundation for future research. Future research can focus on: testing different debiasing techniques, debiasing that takes into account other cognitive biases, exploring the workshop's effectiveness in debiasing experienced practitioners.

Practitioners can use the presented debiasing workshop for training purposes.

References

1. Borowa, K., Dwornik, R., Zalewski, A.: Is knowledge the key? an experiment on debiasing architectural decision-making - a Pilot study. In: Ardito, L., Jedlitschka, A., Morisio, M., Torchiano, M. (eds.) PROFES 2021. LNCS, vol. 13126, pp. 207–214. Springer, Cham (2021). https://doi.org/10.1007/978-3-030-91452-3_14
2. Borowa, K., Jarek, M., Mystkowska, G., Paszko, W., Zalewski, A.: Additional Material for Debiasing architectural decision-making: a workshop-based training approach, June 2022. https://doi.org/10.5281/zenodo.6751990
3. Borowa, K., Zalewski, A., Kijas, S.: The influence of cognitive biases on architectural technical debt. In: 2021 IEEE 18th International Conference on Software Architecture (ICSA), pp. 115–125. IEEE (2021)
4. Brown, S.: The c4 model for software architecture, June 2018. https://www.infoq.com/articles/C4-architecture-model/
5. Fischhoff, B.: Debiasing. In: Kahneman, D., Slovic, P., Tversky, A. (eds) Judgment Under Uncertainty: Heuristics and Biases. Judgment under Uncertainty: Heuristics and Biases, pp. 422–444. Cambridge University Press, Cambridge (1982)
6. Garrison, D.R., Cleveland-Innes, M., Koole, M., Kappelman, J.: Revisiting methodological issues in transcript analysis: negotiated coding and reliability. Internet High. Educ. 9(1), 1–8 (2006)
7. Jansen, A., Bosch, J.: Software architecture as a set of architectural design decisions. In: 5th Working IEEE/IFIP Conference on Software Architecture (WICSA 2005), pp. 109–120. IEEE (2005)
8. Kahneman, D.: Thinking, Fast and Slow. Macmillan (2011)
9. Mohanani, R., Salman, I., Turhan, B., Rodriguez, P., Ralph, P.: Cognitive biases in software engineering: a systematic mapping study. IEEE Trans. Softw. Eng. 46, 1318–1339(2018)
10. Razavian, M., Paech, B., Tang, A.: Empirical research for software architecture decision making: An analysis. J. Syst. Softw. 149, 360–381 (2019)
11. Saldaña, J.: The Coding Manual For Qualitative Researchers, 3rd edn. pp. 1–440. Sage (2021)
12. Shepperd, M., Mair, C., Jørgensen, M.: An experimental evaluation of a debiasing intervention for professional software developers. In: Proceedings of the 33rd Annual ACM Symposium on Applied Computing (2018)
13. Stacy, W., Macmillan, J.: Cognitive bias in software engineering. Commun. ACM 38(6), 57–63 (1995)
14. Tang, A.: Software designers, are you biased? In: Proceedings of the 6th International Workshop on Sharing and Reusing Architectural Knowledge (2011)
15. Tang, A., Bex, F., Schriek, C., van der Werf, J.M.E.: Improving software design reasoning-a reminder card approach. J. Syst. Softw. 144, 22–40 (2018)
16. Tang, A., Kazman, R.: Decision-making principles for better software design decisions. IEEE Softw. 38(6), 98–102 (2021)
17. Tversky, A., Daniel, K.: Judgment under uncertainty: heuristics and biases. Science 185 (1974)
18. Van Vliet, H., Tang, A.: Decision making in software architecture. J. Syst. Softw. 117, 638–644 (2016)
19. Zalewski, A., Borowa, K., Ratkowski, A.: On cognitive biases in architecture decision making. In: Lopes, A., de Lemos, R. (eds.) ECSA 2017. LNCS, vol. 10475, pp. 123–137. Springer, Cham (2017). https://doi.org/10.1007/978-3-319-65831-5_9

Persistence Factories Architectural Design Pattern

Jorge D. Ortiz Fuentes$^{(\boxtimes)}$ (ID) and Ángel Herranz Nieva (ID)

Universidad Politécnica de Madrid, Madrid, Spain
jorge.ortiz.fuentes@alumnos.upm.es, angel.herranz@upm.es

Abstract. Each screen of the user interface of a mobile or desktop application coordinates one or more use cases. Each one of those use cases may need to access different entities of the persistent data. It is a common practice to inject a provider for each of those entities of the model. Thus, the more use cases the view deals with, the more entity providers need to be injected. If we extend that to all the views of the application, the complexity increases and the impact in maintainability of the application is huge.

In this paper we present an architectural design pattern to address this problem, as well as an analysis of its merits. The main idea behind the architectural pattern is that use cases take care of requesting the required entity providers from a unique element that is the persistence factory. Therefore use cases are created with the required entity provider(s) injected, allowing the other components of the architecture to be completely decoupled from the implementation of the persistence and simplifying the dependency injection process. The included code snippets compare our solution with most used industrial alternatives.

Keywords: Software Architecture · Architectural design pattern · Design pattern · Mobile app · Desktop application · Persistence · Kotlin · Swift

1 Introduction

This article uses *design pattern* (or just *pattern*) to mean a general repeatable solution to a problem or scenario in software engineering, and *architectural design pattern* (or just *architectural pattern*) to refer to a combination of design patterns or other organizational structures that are arranged into a well defined architecture or a piece of it. So, the *strategy pattern* is a behavioral design pattern that enables selecting an algorithm to solve a task at run-time, whilst *Model View Controller* is an architectural pattern that results from combining the strategy, the *observer* and the *composite patterns*. An important and well documented set of design patterns and architectural patterns can be found in [6] and [5].

Most user interface applications, particularly mobile applications, require interaction with persistent data. Well architected ones separate the concerns

© The Author(s), under exclusive license to Springer Nature Switzerland AG 2022
I. Gerostathopoulos et al. (Eds.): ECSA 2022, LNCS 13444, pp. 167–177, 2022.
https://doi.org/10.1007/978-3-031-16697-6_12

using some architectural pattern like Model-View-ViewModel or Model-View-Presenter [4]. In each of this architectural patterns, there is one component that acts as an intermediary between the user interface groups, that we will refer as *views*, and the *model*, that contains both the domain entities and the domain logic. The intermediary component has different names that imply different responsibilities, but for the sake of this discussion, we will refer to them as *MVComps*.

In those well architected applications, the model converses with the data sources and provides the MVComps with the relevant resulting data. The MVComps will in turn take responsibility for presenting that data to the user and provide meaning to the user interactions with the view.

After the publication of the article about the Clean Architecture in 2012, many mobile and desktop applications adopted the ideas explained in it. Although the original writing was extended with a book [9], it doesn't cover the implementation details of its application. So, people have come up with several ways to implement this kind of architecture widely used in industry. The following paragraphs try to describe the fundamental aspects of the most common implementations and name the moving parts used in them.

Inspired by [7], one of the central ideas of that architecture is the implementation of the logic of a *use case* [2] in an object. Those objects often use the *command pattern*, making it trivial to reuse them from any view of the application.

The interaction with the persistence layer is implemented using *entity gateways* [5]. The purpose of an entity gateway is to act as a data source and mediate between the raw persistent data and the domain *entities* (objects defined primarily by its identity [3]) as they are used in the application code. Each entity gateway is usually implemented as a *table data gateway* [5], but other design patterns, like the *repository pattern*, can be used instead.

Use cases that need to create, read, update, or delete one or more entities, use instances of the corresponding entity gateways. Applying the *Dependency Inversion Principle* [8], they use an abstraction of the entity gateway, rather than the actual implementation of it. Thus, the way the persistence is implemented can be replaced at any moment during the development of the application, and more sophisticated results can be achieved by combining different types of persistence or just different sources.

According to the above description, each MVComp needs all the use cases that can be executed from its view. At the same time, each use case needs to be provided with the relevant entity gateways. The dependency graph becomes quite complex with only a few views and use cases, and a nightmare for a full fledged commercial application.

A use case factory may be used to simplify the injection of multiple use cases, but that only solves part of the problem. We still need to provide the required entity gateways and keep track of the relationships. The more entities involved, the harder it gets. In this article, we introduce the *persistence factories*, an architectural pattern that aims to reduce this complexity by: (1) simplifying the dependency injection process, (2) decoupling the code from the implementation details of persistence layer, and (3) handling the persistence in a consistent way, independently of the relationships involved or other details that may only apply to some persistence mechanisms, e.g. authentication.

2 The Problem

To illustrate how our design pattern proposal manages the complexity of assembling several use cases, data sources and MVComps, we present a non-trivial *to-do* example. For readers that have stumbled upon *Getting Things Done* (GTD) [1], the guiding example is a simplified version of GTD. For the rest, you can take the example as an enriched version of a basic *to-do list* application. The data model is presented in Fig. 1 as a UML class diagram.

Most modern applications tend to be rich in functionality and compete among them by the implemented features, so it is very common to have more than one use case in the same view. In our example, it is very likely that you will have a view with the details of a *task*. The view depicted in Fig. 2 can be used both for creating or editing a task. In that view, you can use the following use cases, where the number references the red circles in the user interface:

0. Access a *task* by its id (required to display the contents of the currently selected task).
1. Access a list of *contexts* in order to tag the *task* with a *context*.
2. Access a list of *projects* in order to assign the *task* to a *project*.
3. Create a new context, should the one that you need not have been defined yet.
4. Create a new project, should the one that you need not have been defined yet.
5. Create or update the current task as described in the view.

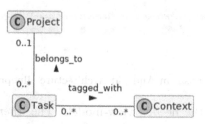

- *Task* instances represent tasks to be done by the user.
- *Project* instances represent user projects, that have a collection of tasks.
- *Context* instances represent *tags* that let the user decide how, when, or where the task is to be done (e.g. Home, Office, Calls, etc.).

Fig. 1. GTD simplified data model

Fig. 2. UI with different use cases

To implement those use cases, you will need to provide each use case with the required data sources as shown in the following excerpt that constructs a `TaskEditViewModel`:

```
TaskEditViewModel(GetTaskUseCase(tasksRepo),ListContextsUseCase(contextsRepo),
              ListProjectsUseCase(projectsRepo),CreateContextUseCase(contextsRepo),
              CreateProjectUseCase(projectsRepo),CreateTaskUseCase(tasksRepo))
```

Six use cases are injected in the view model, each one with its corresponding data source, that implements the entity gateway abstraction. Other use cases may require access to more than one entity of the model. The complexity of the dependency injection will grow enormously with the number of use cases and required repositories. With this approach maintainability is compromised. Let's explore the industry proposal and then let's see how our proposal solves it.

3 Industry Solutions

The following code is an actual excerpt from the Android Architecture Blueprints, a showcase shared by Google (https://github.com/android/architecture-samples) that implements a factory of view-models:

```
    class ViewModelFactory constructor(private val tasksRepo: TasksRepository)
        : ViewModelProvider.NewInstanceFactory() {
        override fun <T : ViewModel> create(modelClass: Class<T>) =
            with(modelClass) {
5           when {
                isAssignableFrom(StatisticsViewModel::class.java) ->
                    StatisticsViewModel(GetTasksUseCase(tasksRepo))
                isAssignableFrom(TaskDetailViewModel::class.java) ->
                    TaskDetailViewModel(
10                  GetTaskUseCase(tasksRepo), DeleteTaskUseCase(tasksRepository),
                    CompleteTaskUseCase(tasksRepo), ActivateTaskUseCase(tasksRepo)
                    )
                // Cases for other view models
                else -> throw IllegalArgumentException("Wrong VIM: ${modelClass.name}")
15          }
            } as T
        }
    }
```

Listing 1. View Model Factory proposal in Android Architecture Blueprints

The views use the factory to get the needed view-models. The *when* block, lines 5–15, provides an instance of each view-model type for the requested class. Each view-model gets an instance of each of the use cases that it might use. And each of them gets a reference to one entity gateway.

For models in which more entities are involved, all the connections have to be explicitly set by the factory. When the app evolves, these injections become more of a burden and adding a single use case implies changes in other parts of the application; a symptom of coupled code.

The example shows that having the use cases defined in their own classes, instead of hard-coding the logic where needed in the MVComps, improves reuse. They can be used in each of the MVComps where they are needed. For example, `GetTasksUseCase` is used in both the `StatisticsViewModel` and the

`TasksDetailViewModel`. However, the *ad hoc* injection used for each of the MVComps is still tedious and error prone. The injection of those use cases can be simplified using a factory that is passed onto the MVComps. They will use it to get instances of the desired use cases and execute them, using their output as needed. We will refer to that factory as the *use case factory* and the following code shows its implementation:

```
class UseCaseFactory {
    fun getTaskUseCase(id: UUID, completion: (Task) -> Unit): UseCase =
        GetTaskUseCase(id=id, completion=completion)
    fun listContextsUseCase(completion: (List<Contexts>) -> Unit): UseCase =
        ListContextsUseCase(completion=completion)
    // Other use cases
}
```

The use case factory returns instances of the command abstraction: objects have a method `execute()` that runs the use case logic. The method takes no parameters and returns no results. Instead, use cases get their parameters and what to do with the results via their constructors.

Finally, a callback function in the MVComp, e.g. `userAction`, will be called on a UI event:

```
class SomeMVComponent(ucf: UseCaseFactory) {
    var property: Type1
    fun userAction() {
        val useCase = ucf.relevantUseCase(param) { result -> property = result }
        useCase.execute()
    }
}
```

The function gets the relevant use case from the factory, passing parameters and saying what to do with the results of the execution of the use case. The last step is to execute the use case.

The full design might seem unnecessarily complex at first glance, but it has important advantages:

- The MVComp is fully decoupled from the domain logic implemented in the use cases.
- The MVComp can access *any* of the use cases through the use case factory. Injecting a single object, all the logic is available to that view. It also means that adding a use case to a MVComp (or removing it) doesn't change the injection of the domain logic at all.
- The MVComp is easier to test: a test double of the use case factory replaces the logic.
- Replacing the implementation of a use case in the use case factory, allows using the new version throughout the entire application, i.e. the dependency injection graph doesn't change.
- Finally, all the use cases get access to their required implementation of the persistence through the use case factory, making them easy to test.

Unfortunately, this popular approach presents some important drawbacks:

- Each new use case requires adding a method to the use case factory.
- When the use case number grows large, a single use case factory may become hard to manage.
- It doesn't deal with the complexity of models that use more than one entity and in which those entities have relationships. Other requirements for accessing the persistence, like authentication, are also ignored in this approach. That responsibility is not part of the use case factory itself, but there is no modular solution that deals with this in a systematic, extensible and repeatable way.

In the next section we present the architectural pattern that tackle this last drawback.

4   The Persistence Factories Architectural Pattern

Intent. A persistence factory is an object whose purpose is to hide the implementation details of the actual persistence layer from the rest of the application. It simplifies the interaction with the persistence by using a generic interface that is common to all the entities thanks to the power of generics. The application of the pattern takes out the burden from the MVComp of connecting each use case with the right entity gateway as well as keeping track of the relationships between the different entities or other parameters like authentication or pagination settings.

Motivation. Although there are clear benefits of using use case factories, there are two limitations that are more relevant for applications with more than one entity and a non trivial number of views and use cases:

- When use cases use different entities, the use case factory has to get access to each of the entity gateways and keep track of any relationships. This responsability doesn't belong in the use case factory and should be done elsewhere.
- Some implementations of the persistence might have additional requirements to be used, e.g. authentication in the case of a REST API. Keeping track of that in each of the entity gateways is hard, because it might require duplication of the credentials and would have problems to invalidate them, among other things. But it also doesn't belong in the use case factory, because it is unrelated to the implementation of the domain logic. It is instead related to the persistence and may be unnecessary for some implementations of the persistence, e.g. authentication for a local database.

These problems can be solved by using a persistence factory. The use case factory only needs a reference to the persistence factory, that is used by the use cases to get the required entity gateways. On the other hand, the additional requirements, like the authentication credentials, are preserved and handled by the factory itself. Different implementations of the persistent factory will use the parameters required for the type of persistence they support.

Participants.

MVComps 1–n defines the component responsible for getting user input, running the use cases, and telling the view how to update its contents when required.

Use Case Factory defines an object with a method for each of the available use cases. It keeps a reference to the persistence factory to be able to obtain entity gateways on demand.

Use Case defines the generic interface for all of the use cases, i.e. the command pattern.

Use Case 1–m defines each of the use cases that implement the command pattern and can be created by the use case factory.

Entity Gateway Factory defines an object with a method for each of the available entity gateways. It keeps the parameters for the type of persistence used, like authentication credentials.

Entity Gateway defines a generic interface for every entity gateway object, typically a CRUD.

Entity Gateways 1–o defines each of the entity gateways for each of the entities of the model.

Structure. The following informal class diagram shows the structure of the architectural pattern.

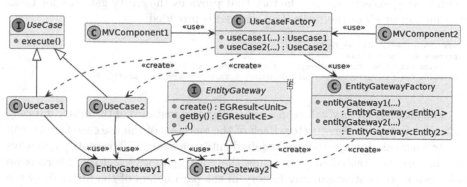

Implementation. We start by defining the interface used by the entity gateways and that can be used by all of objects returned by the persistence factory. Although there are other options, a common approach is to implement CRUD operations: a method to create an instance in the persistence, a method to update an existing entity, a method to delete it, and two more methods to read them, one or a list of them. It should use generics and a type parameter in order to apply to all of the entities. The result of each method is encapsulated in the sum type EGResult that represents the result of the operation in case of success or an error otherwise. For example, in

```
interface EntityGateway<Entity : Identifiable> {
    fun create(entity: Entity): EGResult<Unit>
    fun getBy(id: UUID): EGResult<Entity>
    // ...
}
```

the method `create` can be used to create the entity described in the type parameter and will output a a successful result containing no information (`Unit`) or an error. Then, we should define a class for each of the entities that have to be used in the model. Those classes will implement that entity gateway interface and will conform the set of entity gateways returned by the persistence factory. The following class shows the in-memory projects entity gateway:

```
class ProjectsInMemRepo(val data: InMemoryData) : EntityGateway<Project> {
  override fun create(entity: Project): EGResult<Unit> { /* ... */}
  override fun getBy(id: UUID): EGResult<Project> {
    val project = data.projects.firstOrNull { project -> project.id == id }
    return if (project != null) { EGResult.Success(project) }
        else { EGResult.Failure("Not found") }
  }
  override fun fetchAll() = EGResult.Success(data.projects)
  // ...
}
```

The code snippet shows an implementation in which the projects are stored in a structure that is hold in memory. This way of storing the data is not usually useful for a production app, but it is perfect for a proof of concept and the first iterations. The persistence factories will be simplified replacing all those entity gateways by the ones that use the desired persistence.

The entity gateway factory will have one method for each of the entity gateways. The methods may take parameters to handle relationships. For example, the following excerpt shows a factory that provides the entity gateway for tasks in a project or all of the tasks if no `projId` is provided:

```
class InMemoryEntityGatewayFactory {
  private val imd = InMemoryData()
  override fun projectEntityGateway() = ProjectsInMemRepo(imd)
  override fun taskEntityGateway(projId: UUID?) = TaskInMemRepo(imd, projId)
}
```

The use case factory will keep a reference to an instance of the entity gateway factory, injected via constructor. Each of the methods of the use case factory will create a use case by injecting the required entity gateways. Those entity gateways will in turn be created in-place using the entity gateway factory. There is no reference to the entity gateway factory in the parameters of the methods of the use case factory. Hence, the MVComps, that hold and use the use case factory, don't need to know anything about the persistence and its implementation:

```
class UseCaseFactory(val egf: InMemoryEntityGatewayFactory) {
  fun createProject(request: ProjectRequest, handler: Handler<Unit>): UseCase =
    CreateProjectUseCase(egf.projectEntityGateway(), request, handler)
  fun createTask(request: TaskRequest, handler: Handler<Unit>): UseCase =
    CreateTaskUseCase(egf.tasksEntityGateway(request.projId), request, handler)
  // ...
}
```

This provides a total decoupling of the MVComps from the persistence. Each MVComp creates and consumes instances of use cases on demand using the use case factory. The following excerpt shows a view-model for the list of projects. The init function gets executed when the `ProjectsListViewModel` is instantiated, gets the use case to retrieve the list of projects and stores them in the property that is observable. The view, that should observe changes in that property, gets notified and updates what it displays.

```
class ProjectsListViewModel(val useCaseFactory: UseCaseFactory) : ViewModel() {
  private val projects = MutableLiveData<List<Project>>(listOf())
  init {
    val useCase = useCaseFactory.listProjects {
      when (it) {
        is DomainResult.Success -> { projects.value = it }
        else -> { /* Show error */ }
      }
    }
    useCase.execute()
  } // ...
}
```

As a result of using persistence factories the dependency injection process is much simpler than the one shown previously in Listing 1. Replacing the persistence factory on the creation of the use case factory results in a different persistence implementation being used in the MVComps.

```
class ViewModelFactory(val useCaseFactory: UseCaseFactory)
  : ViewModelProvider.NewInstanceFactory() {
  override fun <T : ViewModel> create(modelClass: Class<T>) =
    with(modelClass) {
      when {
        isAssignableFrom(ProjectsListViewModel::class.java) ->
          ProjectsListViewModel(useCaseFactory = useCaseFactory)
        isAssignableFrom(ProjectEditViewModel::class.java) ->
          ProjectEditViewModel(useCaseFactory = useCaseFactory)
        // Cases for other view models
        else -> throw IllegalArgumentException("Wrong VM: ${modelClass.name}")
      }
    } as T
}
```

Listing 2. View Model Factory simplified with persistence factories

The injection of the persistence factory into the use case factory is done in the `Application` subclass or in a singleton module of your favorite dependency injection framework:

```
class GtdApp: Application() {var ucf = UseCaseFactory(InMemoryEntityGatewayFactory())}
```

Applicability. Persistence factories are relevant and useful for applications that use more than one entity and for which their domain logic can be organized around use cases and a use case factory. They can be used with in-memory persistence, REST APIs or even property local key-value stores. They also help encapsulating the implementation details required to interact with those persistence mechanisms. They are a good method for decoupling the code from the usage of some persistence libraries that tend to spread their presence throughout all the code. Thus, they become an excellent defense mechanism to get a more resilient code, containing the impact of the dependency on a persistence library that needs to be replaced for one reason or another.

They simplify the creation of more complex persistence mechanisms, combining local and remote databases to achieve advanced features like backend sync or multi-backend uploading.

They allow unit testing the use case logic independently of the implementation details of the persistence. Using test doubles for persistence implementations is trivial with this approach and can be successfully used for integration tests, making the verification faster and less fragile.

5   Conclusions

This work introduces *the persistence factories* architectural pattern. Its presentation is achieved through a moderately complex example in a real-world application. Some relevant implementation details are addressed in order to fully understand its application.

Existing industry approaches solve the injection and re-use of several uses cases, but suffer from increased complexity when uses cases need to work with several entities and its persistence. In this common situation, our approach simplifies the resulting design.

It makes the dependency injection much simpler. A comparison of Listing 1 and Listing 2 shows that using our approach, a single parameter is enough to have all the use cases available to each of the MVComps and persistence is not specified at this level. The use case factory knows about the persistence factory and its methods to provide each of the entity gateways. MVComps and the use case factory are decoupled from the persistence and its implementation details.

Changes to the persistence layer (from local to remote, adopting or replacing a third party library, adding authentication or encryption...) are concealed into the persistence factory and don't affect the rest of the application, reducing impact and effort required for those.

Persistence factories simplify working uniformly with different types of persistence that may raise different errors, thanks to the result types and the errors defined at this level. The improvements in the dependency injection process and the decoupling of the code can be leveraged for an enhanced testability. Also, the pattern facilitates iterations on implementation of the persistence, starting with a persistence factory that uses an in-memory storage and evolve into any other.

References

1. Allen, D.: Getting Things Done. The Art of Stress-Free Productivity, Penguin, January 2003
2. Cockburn, A.: Writing Effective Use Cases. Addison-Wesley Longman Publishing Co., Inc. (2000)
3. Evans, E.: Domain-Driven Design. Addison-Wesley (2004)
4. Fowler, M.: GUI Architectures, July 2006. https://martinfowler.com/eaaDev/uiArchs.html

5. Fowler, M., Rice, D., Foemmel, M., Hieatt, E., Mee, R., Stafford, R.: Patterns of Enterprise Application Architecture. Addison-Wesley Professional (2002)
6. Gamma, E., Helm, R., Johnson, R., Vlissides, J.: Design Patterns: Elements of Reusable Object-Oriented Software. Addison-Wesley Longman Publishing Co., Inc. (1995)
7. Jacobson, I.: OO Software Engineering: A Use Case Driven Approach. Addison-Wesley (1992)
8. Martin, R.C.: OO design quality metrics. In: Proceedings of Workshop on Pragmatic and Theoretical Directions in Object-Oriented Software Metrics (1994)
9. Martin, R.C.: Clean Architecture: A Craftsman's Guide to Software Structure and Design, 1st edn. Prentice Hall Press (2017)

Feature-Based Investigation of Simulation Structure and Behaviour

Sandro Koch[(✉)], Eric Hamann, Robert Heinrich, and Ralf Reussner

KASTEL – Institute of Information Security and Dependability,
Karlsruhe Institute of Technology (KIT), Karlsruhe, Germany
{sandro.koch,eric.hamann,robert.heinrich,ralf.reussner}@kit.edu

Abstract. Reusing a simulation or parts of a simulation is difficult as often simulations are tightly coupled to a specific domain or even to the system analysed by the simulation. In this paper, we introduce a specification approach that allows simulation developers to model the structure and behaviour of a simulation with a domain-specific modelling language. The specification is used to compare a simulation or parts of a simulation to identify features that can be reused. The results show that our approach can find similar features based on their architectural structure and behaviour. Our approach enables developers to identify and then reuse simulation features.

Keywords: simulation reuse · feature compare · simulation specification · domain-specific modelling language

1 Introduction

Due to the increasing complexity of system properties, simulations are becoming more complex. The rise in complexity of a simulation requires that previously implemented simulation features are reused in subsequent simulation projects to save time and resources. The specialisation of simulations for a particular domain or system impedes reusability for other domains or systems. The decomposition of a simulation into distinct features allows the developer to manage and reuse features individually. A *simulation feature* is an abstraction of a property to be analysed. A *simulation component* comprises the implementation of a simulation feature (i.e., packages, classes, and simulation algorithms). To identify simulation features that could be reused, the developer can compare the architectural structure (i.e., classes, interfaces) of the corresponding simulation component to an architecture specification (e.g., component diagram) on a syntactic level. An identical structure, however, is not sufficient to determine a reusable simulation feature [7]. The developer also has to consider the behaviour of a simulation component; ergo, they must determine whether the discovered simulation component is a semantic match (i.e., has the desired behaviour) when compared to

This work was supported by the Federal Ministry of Education and Research (BMBF) under the funding number 01IS18067D, and the KASTEL institutional funding.

© The Author(s), under exclusive license to Springer Nature Switzerland AG 2022
I. Gerostathopoulos et al. (Eds.): ECSA 2022, LNCS 13444, pp. 178–185, 2022.
https://doi.org/10.1007/978-3-031-16697-6_13

another simulation component. Manually analysing a simulation component is time-consuming and error-prone.

In this paper, we focus on *Discrete-Event Simulation* (DES). DES is a type of discrete simulation where states only change at instantaneous points in time. We provide an approach to support the decomposition of DES by specifying simulation components in structure and behaviour. We employ a modelling approach with metamodels to specify simulation components. To identify pre-existing simulation components, we compare the specifications of simulation components regarding the structure and behaviour. The identification of simulation components is divided into two stages: First, we compare simulation components based on their structure; we convert the specifications into graph notation and do a graph-isomorphism analysis to identify similar structures. Second, we compare simulation components based on their behaviour by converting the specification to *Satisfiability Modulo Theories* (SMT) notation and then utilising an SMT-Solver to identify similar behaviour.

The paper is structured as follows: We introduce the problem statement in Sect. 2. Our specification language, the structure comparison, and the behaviour comparison are presented in Sect. 3. In Sect. 4, we evaluate (i) our specification metamodel by investigating its applicability using a case-study-driven approach and (ii) the accuracy of our comparison approach by comparing different specifications of simulation components. The paper concludes with a discussion of related work in Sect. 5, a summary and a description of future work in Sect. 6.

2   Problem Statement

The specification of a simulation feature can be derived from its requirements. The implemented simulation component must meet these requirements. Whether a component can be reused is determined by whether it meets the given specification, i.e., whether its structure and behaviour fit the desired criteria. We identified three problems when simulation components need to be compared to find and reuse already existing components instead of developing these components from scratch. *P1*: Depending on the complexity of a simulation component, comparing its structure at the code-level is time-consuming. Thus, we require a specification-based approach to describe the structure of a simulation component. Developers can use the specification approach to identify a similar structure of simulation components across different simulations. *P2*: The structure of a simulation enables that a component can be technically integrated (i.e., matching interfaces); however, the exact behaviour of the simulation can differ. To gain more insight, information about the component is required; thus, we require that the specification approach also supports the specification of a simulation's behaviour. Comparing simulation components requires comparing the components at the code-level. Code contains details that are not relevant to identifying a matching component. *P3*: Due to the irrelevant details at the code-level, it is costly to compare and identify simulation components. This problem results in unused components that developers could reuse, resulting in redeveloped components. Thus, we require the approach to identify an identical component specification in a set of component specifications. Also, we require that the approach can identify a component with an identical structure and behaviour, although entities, attributes, and events are named differently.

3   Specification Language and Feature Identification

This section presents our contributions to address the problems in Sect. 2.

3.1   Specification Metamodel

Our contribution to address the specification part of problems **P1** and **P2** is the definition of a *Domain-Specific Modelling Language* (DSML) to describe the structure and behaviour of a simulation component. To process the models specified in the DSML, we define a metamodel as underlying abstract syntax of the language. The generalisation we make is always referring to entities and attributes on the type-level, i.e., referring to static objects instead of specific instances. We also exclude the specification of simulation outputs because the simulation result does not impact simulation behaviour. In the definition of the metamodel, we separated elements concerned with the structure of a simulation from those concerned with its behaviour. We define the *structure* of a simulation as the set of basic building blocks: events, entities and attributes. While there are different definitions of the term *behaviour*, we define the behaviour of a simulation as the effects of events on the state of the simulation world, i.e., the changes to attributes triggered through events. A *Simulation* contains a set of *Entities* and *Events*, and each entity contains a set of typed *Attributes*. Additionally, we model a *writes* relationship between events and attributes to describe which attributes affect an event (i.e., delay and when it is fired).

Two additional concepts are necessary to specify the behaviour of a simulation. A simulation changes the simulation world during its runtime. To describe those changes, the metamodel must allow a specification of changed attributes as part of the simulator specification. Attribute changes can be linked to events during which they occur since in DES, such changes can only happen at events. This is always the case in DES because an event is defined as any point in time that marks a change in the simulation world. The state of the simulation world is affected by the order and time that events are scheduled and events may cause other events to be scheduled with a certain delay. The *Schedules* and *WritesAttribute* classes represent the aforementioned two additional concepts.

3.2   Structure Comparison

To address problems **P1** and **P3**, identifying simulation components based on their structure, we compare the structure of two components based on their specification. We use a graph-based representation of these specifications with annotated nodes and edges. Entities, events and attributes are represented as nodes while schedules- and writes-relationships as well as parent-child relationships between entities and attributes are represented as edges. The graph contains the entire specification of schedules- and writes-relationships. However, the presence of the behavioural specification does not affect the structural comparison as the schedules- and writes-relationships are annotated to the edges of the *reads* and *writes* dependencies of the *events*. We consider two simulation specifications structurally similar if their graph representations are isomorphic, i.e., if there is a bijection between the structural elements (i.e., entities, attributes, and events) of both simulations. Regarding entities and attributes, a graph isomorphism ensures the simulation worlds of both simulation components can store the same information.

3.3   Behaviour Comparison with SMT

To address the problems **P2** and **P3**, identifying simulation components based on their behaviour, we compare their behaviour specification. While a description of the structure of simulation components with the structural metamodel holds enough information to employ a graph-based structural comparison, the use of expressions in the behavioural metamodel makes this approach not viable for behaviour comparison. The expressions in the specification can be entirely expressed as first-order logic formulas, and they can be used as part of SMT instances. We will use representations of those expressions as SMT formulas to build SMT instances whose satisfiability/validity is coupled to the behavioural similarity of two events.

Representing Behaviour in SMT: To compare schedules- and writes-relationships to determine the behaviour of a simulation componnent, we need to capture the effect of these concepts on the simulation world as SMT formulas. Schedules-relationships indirectly affect attributes in the simulation world by specifying scheduled events that can affect attributes or schedule other events. We consider two schedules-relationships to have the same behaviour if they always schedule the same event with the same delay (cf. Listing 1.1). All SMT formulas in SMT-LIB syntax shown here include variable declarations for all attributes accessed in those formulas. We consider two writes-relationships to have the same behaviour if they affect the attribute in the same way. For n writes-relationships from event A to attribute C with condition-expressions $C_{1..n}$ and write-functions $F_{1..n}$ Listing 1.3 shows the combined SMT formula to describe the effect A has on C.

```
// condition:
(declare-fun waitingPassengers () Int)
(assert (> waitingPassengers 0))
// delay:
(declare-fun delay () Double)
(assert (= delay 15))
```

Listing 1.1. Delay specification

```
// all read-attributes
(declare-fun ...)

(assert (not (= C_A C_B)))
(assert (not (= D_A D_B)))
```

Listing 1.2. General schedule comparison

Comparing Schedules-Relationships: Without loss of generality, we assume that for every pair of events, E_1 and E_2, there is at most one schedules-relationship from E_1 to E_2. The following concepts can be extended to multiple schedules-relationships by finding a bijection between the schedules-relationship from E_1 to E_2 in both simulator specifications. This is possible because the effect of each schedules-relationship on the simulation world is self-contained and independent of other schedules-relationships, a property not present with writes-relationships. With this assumption and a given mapping of events, we can compare the (unique) schedules-relationship from event A to event E in simulator S_1 with the schedules-relationship from event B to event F in simulator S_2, where A and B, as well as E and F, need to be a structural match.

```
(declare-fun old () Int)
(declare-fun value () Int)

// additional inputs
(declare-fun ...)

(assert (=> (C_1) (= value F_1)))
...
(assert (=> (C_n) (= value F_n)))

(assert (=> (not (or C_1 .. C_n))
   (= value old)))
```

Listing 1.3. General write specification

```
// simulator S_1
event A {
   reads Z.waitingPassengers
   writes Z.waitingPassengers = 0
      when waitingPassengers != 0
}
// simulator S_2
event B {
   reads Z.waitingPassengers
   writes Z.waitingPassengers = 0
}
```

Listing 1.4. Writes-relationships with identical behaviour

With the same logic, we can compare the conditions of the schedules-relationships. Let C_A and C_B be the condition-expressions of the schedules-relationships from events A and B, respectively, and D_A and D_B the delay-expressions. Then the behaviour of the schedules-relationships is identical if the SMT formula shown in Listing 1.2 is not satisfiable. If the formula is satisfiable, there is an assignment of input variables for which the condition- or delay-expressions evaluate to different values. With the SMT-LIB command (`get-model`) a solver can output such an assignment of input variables. This enables our approach to identify whether two events have the same behaviour and generate an assignment of attribute values to demonstrate that they do not.

Comparing Writes-Relationships: For schedules-relationships, we assumed that there is at most one schedules-relationship between one event and another. For write-relationships, we cannot make a similar assumption that there is at most one write-relationship in event A that writes to attribute C because the effect of A on C is the result of the combination of all write-relationships from A to C. Therefore, write-relationships (to a single attribute) cannot be compared separately. First, we present an example with a single write-relationship to an attribute and then extend the concept to a general formula. Listing 1.4 shows two events writing to a (matched) attribute *waitingPassengers*. Although the conditions alone are not equivalent, it shows that the effect on the attribute is the same for both events.

4   Evaluation

In this section, we present the evaluation of our approach to specify and compare simulation components.

4.1   Evaluation Goals and Design

The evaluation of the specification DSML and comparing approach follows the Goal Question Metric (GQM) approach [1]. The first goal **G1** is to evaluate whether our DSML for the specification of simulations, which covers structural and behavioural information, is able to specify components of real-world simulations. The second goal **G2** is to evaluate, whether our approach can identify similar components based on their structure. Our last goal **G3** is to check, whether our approach can identify similar components based on their behaviour.

The questions to be answered are: **Q1** – Can our DSML model the structure of a real-world simulation? **Q2** – Can our DSML model the behaviour of a real-world simulation? Even if each component could be modelled with our DSML, it is only a vehicle to enable us to compare the components of the case study. Therefore, we need to answer the following question: **Q3** – Can our approach identify simulation components when compared to other components identical in structure and behaviour?

M1 Applicability: To answer the questions **Q1** and **Q2**, we use the following metric. For the case study, we randomly selected ten simulation features and we modelled the implementation of the features (i.e., components) using our metamodel. Then, we identify the number components that could be modelled. By investigating the number of components that could be modelled, we can infer the applicability of our DSML to the case study.

M2 Accuracy: To answer question **Q3**, we use the following metric, and a scenario-based evaluation. We use the components derived for **M1** to find matching components. First, we compare the structure using the graph-isomorphism approach. Then, if a structural match is identified, we compare the behaviour using our SMT-based approach. We determine the accuracy by calculating the metric F_1 score, which is a harmonic mean of precision and recall. Identifying t_p, t_n, and f_n are scenario-specific; thus, we explain how we identify them when we introduce the scenarios. Given the number of true positives, false positives, and false negatives, precision and recall are calculated as $precision = \frac{t_p}{t_p + f_p}$ and $recall = \frac{t_p}{t_p + f_n}$. F_1 score is calculated as the harmonic mean of precision and recall: $f_1 = 2 \frac{precision \times recall}{precision + recall}$.

Case Study: We selected a publicly available case study as we want to model the specification of the internal structure and the behaviour as precisely as possible. The simulation framework Camunda is a workflow and simulation engine based on the Business Process Modelling Notation 2 (BPMN2). Due to the size of the Camunda BPM Platform (over 500,000 lines of code), we could not model the simulation as a whole; therefore, we focused on ten features of the simulation.

Scenarios: We developed two scenarios where we test whether our approach can find a simulation component when compared to other components. In addition to the specification of the ten simulation components (Ft_1 to Ft_{10}). To verify that our structure comparison does not take the names of the entities, attributes, and events into account, we obfuscated them (O_1 to O_{10}). *The first scenario, S_1* compares the components Ft_1 to Ft_{10} with each other to find the correct match. If the correct component is identified, we count it as t_p, if a wrong component is identified, we count it as f_p, and if the component cannot be identified, we count it as f_n. *The second scenario S_2* compares each component Ft_1 to Ft_{10} with each obfuscated component O_1 to O_{10} to find the correct match. If the correct component is identified, we count it as t_p, if a wrong component is identified, we count it as f_p, and if the component cannot be identified, we count it as f_n.

4.2   Evaluation Results and Discussion

Applicability. The ten components (Ft_1 to Ft_{10}) contain a total amount of 19 entities. We were able to model all 19 entities with our DSML. Besides the entities, the components also contain 26 events in total. Almost every component contains an event called *execute* as an initial event. The behaviour of this event is different for each component; thus, we had to model each individually. We were able to model each of the 26 events. We designed the DSML to model simulations regarding their structure and behaviour. The results show that we can at least model the selected components of the case study.

Accuracy. Regardless of identical components (S_1) or obfuscated components (S_2), the results for scenarios S_1 and S_2 show, that all 20 components could be found. No component was missing or misinterpreted. These results lead to a score of precision, recall, and F_1 of 1.0. In total, 20 components were identified by our approach. The overall results for our evaluation are 1.00 for precision, 1.00 for recall and 1.00 for F_1. The results for comparing simulation components are promising. In a set of individual components, we can identify components that match regarding structure and behaviour. These preliminary results are encouraging, but we have to model more case studies before we can determine whether our approach can be applied to different types of DES.

5   Related Work

In this section, we list related approaches and research concerned with decomposing simulations, reuse in simulation, and the description and comparison of discrete event simulations. In software engineering, the decomposition and composition of software is a well-researched field, but none of these approaches considers the semantics of analyses or simulations. In contrast to our work, the extracted modules do not necessarily represent a semantically cohesive module (i.e., feature). The FOCUS approach gives mathematical semantics for structure and behaviour of software systems [6], it also supports the representation of quality properties and domain-specific properties [4]. However, these approaches are too broad and too ambiguous for non-domain experts to model DES. Heinrich et al. [3] propose a reference architecture for DSMLs used for quality analysis. However, their architecture focuses only on the input models of the quality analysis. Approaches like first order predicate logic [8] investigate logical implications for various forms of logic. Clarke et al. [2] investigate the satisfaction of temporal logic formulas by automata, and Richters et al. [5] check the consistency of object structures regarding data structures (e.g., class structure). In contrast, our approach allows the straightforward transformation of declarative expressions into SMT-instances and their comparison with an SMT-solver.

6 Conclusion

In this paper, we present a domain-specific modelling language for decomposing discrete event simulations by specifying the architectural structure and the behaviour of simulation features. We evaluated our approach by specifying simulation features of an open-source simulation. The findings show that our approach can identify similar structure and behaviour in simulation components. In this work, however, we have only tested the applicability of our approach to one case study. We plan to model more simulations to investigate our approach's applicability further.

References

1. Basili, V., Caldiera, G., Rombach, D.: The goal question metric approach. In: Encyclopedia of Software Engineering, pp. 528–532 (1994)
2. Clarke, E.M., Emerson, E.A., Sistla, A.P.: Automatic verification of finite-state concurrent systems using temporal logic specifications. ACM Trans. Program. Lang. Syst. **8**, 244–263 (1983)
3. Heinrich, R., Strittmatter, M., Reussner, R.: A layered reference architecture for metamodels to tailor quality modeling and analysis. IEEE Trans. Softw. Eng. **47**, 26 (2019)
4. Maoz, S., et al.: OCL framework to verify extra-functional properties in component and connector models. In: 3rd International Workshop on Executable Modeling, Austin, p. 7. CEUR, RWTH Aachen (2017)
5. Richters, M., Gogolla, M.: Validating UML models and OCL constraints. In: Evans, A., Kent, S., Selic, B. (eds.) UML 2000. LNCS, vol. 1939, pp. 265–277. Springer, Heidelberg (2000). https://doi.org/10.1007/3-540-40011-7_19
6. Ringert, J.O., Rumpe, B.: A little synopsis on streams, stream processing functions, and state-based stream processing. Int. J. Softw. Inform. **5**, 29–53 (2011)
7. Talcott, C., et al.: Composition of languages, models, and analyses. In: Heinrich, R., Durán, F., Talcott, C., Zschaler, S. (eds.) Composing Model-Based Analysis Tools, pp. 45–70. Springer, Cham (2021). https://doi.org/10.1007/978-3-030-81915-6_4
8. Tomassi, P.: An introduction to first order predicate logic. In: Logic, pp. 189–264. Routledge (1999)

Architecture Reconstruction and Recovery

ARCHI4MOM: Using Tracing Information to Extract the Architecture of Microservice-Based Systems from Message-Oriented Middleware

Snigdha Singh[✉], Dominik Werle[iD], and Anne Koziolek[iD]

KASTEL – Institute of Information Security and Dependability,
Karlsruhe Institute of Technology, Karlsruhe, Germany
{snigdha.singh,dominik.werle,koziolek}@kit.edu
https://mcse.kastel.kit.edu

Abstract. Microservice architectures that use Message-oriented Middleware (MOM) have recently seen considerable evolution regarding extensibility, re-usability and maintainability. Of particular interest are systems that are distributed and deployed with mixed-technologies. On the one hand, such MOM-based microservice systems improve flexibility through their messaging middleware. On the other hand, configuration for the above systems has to quickly adapt to required changes because of the continuous development process. Architecture reconstruction methods from dynamic data can keep architecture documentation and models in synchrony with the implemented architecture for such systems. However, the existing dynamic analysis methods for architecture reconstruction do not support the extraction for MOM-based microservice systems. The main challenge here is to understand and capture the asynchronous sender-receiver communication via the messaging middleware and to reconstruct the architecture model from it. In our work, we provide the ARCHI4MOM approach to automate the architecture extraction process. We instrument the sender-receiver and messaging services, collect run time data, analyse the trace data and construct the model from it. Architects can use the extracted architecture model for system refactoring and analysis of MOM-based systems. Thus, it reduces the cost and time required for manual architecture extraction process. We evaluate the accuracy of the approach by comparing the extracted model components to a manually crafted baseline model for a case study system.

Keywords: MOM-based system · Reverse Engineering · Architecture Extraction · Performance Prediction · Dynamic Analysis

1 Introduction and Motivation

Today's software systems are extensively using Message-oriented Middleware (MOM) to communicate in distributed microservice environments [9]. MOM

© The Author(s), under exclusive license to Springer Nature Switzerland AG 2022
I. Gerostathopoulos et al. (Eds.): ECSA 2022, LNCS 13444, pp. 189–204, 2022.
https://doi.org/10.1007/978-3-031-16697-6_14

enables message-based communication between the components in order to achieve loosely-coupled and asynchronous communication. This provides benefits in terms of service maintainability and extendability, since microservices can be tested and deployed separately. MOM provides an intermediate layer between the message sender and receiver to decouple them from each other. In order to meet various requirements, there exists technologies like RabbitMQ[1], Kafka[2] to enable MOM-based communication. Such technologies use MQTT[3] or AMQP[4] protocols for message exchange between the messaging middleware.

During the continuous software development process, the architecture of MOM changes when the system changes. When a new requirement demands the addition of new components, the system's developers have to understand how it will change the architecture of the system, for example, by requiring changes in the configuration of the MOM or the introduction of additional communication channels. This continuous development, evolution, and software maintenance creates the problem of architecture erosion in the existing software when the knowledge of the system's architecture is not adapted after changes to the system [14].

The loss of architecture knowledge makes it difficult for the system architect of software systems to understand and refactor the system. At the same time, the refactoring process is time-consuming and costly. One solution to this general problem of erosion is the approach of architecture reconstruction through reverse engineering (RE) of an existing software system. Despite the importance of architecture knowledge recovery for MOM-based systems, only few studies exist on RE for architecture recovery in MOM-based microservice systems [1,13].

To build the component-based architecture model, we have to identify the components and their communication behaviour. Static analysis approaches for RE make it possible to extract the models from the existing source code [11]. Such techniques sometimes fail to provide all the required information about the components. Hence, it is good to collect data during run time to gather the information not covered via static analysis.

In case of synchronous HTTP communication, there is a direct communication (i.e., messages are sent directly to a specific receiver) where all the microservices have to be available during their message exchange. In such communication, the sender microservice has information about the receiver microservice because HTTP follows the send and acknowledgement principle. In case of MOM-based microservice system, microservices (components) communicate via messaging middleware asynchronously. Unlike HTTP communication, sender and receiver components do not know each other. Often, this information is hard to collect from the available architecture documents.

The first problem is to identify the sender and the receiver components. The second challenge is to understand and capture these components and model the

---

[1] HTTPs://www.rabbitmq.com/.

[2] HTTPs://www.confluent.io/Kafka-summit-lon19/Kafka-vs-integration-middle ware/.

[3] https://mqtt.org/.

[4] https://www.amqp.org/.

system's architecture. However, the state-of-the art approaches do not support the architecture reconstruction of the asynchronous MOM-based communication which is typically found in modern microservice systems [6,17].

To handle the above problem, we propose the method ARCHI4MOM, which supports the architecture extraction of modern MOM-based microservice systems. With our work, we present an approach for the automatic extraction of architectural models from MOM-based microservice applications based on tracing information. We introduce an implementation of these concepts on the basis of a flexible and extensible architecture. An overview of the steps of the approach is shown in Fig. 1.

We leverage existing frameworks and library standards for OpenTracing, which is a method for the distributed tracing of data preparation and processing [5]. For our work, we re-use parts of the existing builder pattern architecture of Performance Model Extractor (PMX) [8,17] allowing the extraction of architecture models that are instances of the Palladio Component Model (PCM) [2]. To evaluate the approach, we use a community example system, flowing retail[5], which implements a system where microservices communicate with each other via MOM. We analyse the extracted model elements and compare them with a manually created model to evaluate the accuracy of our approach.

The rest of the paper is organized as follows: Sect. 2, gives the foundations, Sect. 3, describes the complete architecture design of ARCHI4MOM, Sect. 4, presents the technical details of the architecture recovery approach along with the implementation methods. In Sect. 5, we evaluate our approach with the case study scenario. Section 6, classifies our work with respect to the state-of-the art literature. Section 7, provides the concluding remark with possible future ideas.

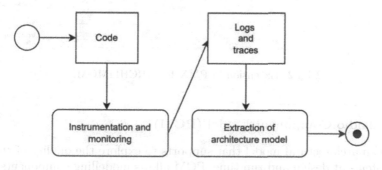

Fig. 1. Overview of the Approach.

2   Foundation

First, we introduce different concepts and techniques our approach uses and highlight the specific challenges of MOM-based systems for architecture reconstruction.

---

[5] HTTPs://github.com/berndruecker/flowing-retail.

2.1 PMX

In the proposed ARCHI4MOM approach, we extract architecture models for MOM-based microservice applications from tracing data by extending the PMX approach. PMX is used to collect and analyse [17] tracing data and extract a PCM architecture model out of it.

We discuss existing PMX challenges and our motivation to extend it further [15]. First, the current implementation of PMX only considers synchronous communication between microservices. It does not support the architecture extraction of MOM-based microservices, where an asynchronous sender-receiver communication happens. Second, PMX depends on the monitoring tool Kieker for tracing data collection. Kieker does not comply with current standards in the field of distributed tracing, and therefore PMX cannot analyse data collected from modern MOM-based systems. Third, PMX extracts PCM models that do not contain concepts for modelling messaging communication via middleware. To meet the above limitations, we extend parts of PMX as shown in Fig. 2 and make it compatible for MOM-based systems. We discuss the extension in details in Sect. 3.1.

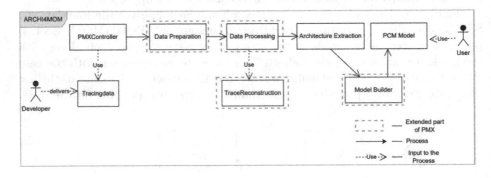

Fig. 2. Extension of PMX for ARCHI4MOM.

2.2 Palladio Component Model (PCM)

PCM is an architectural model that supports to explore the quality of the software systems at design and run time. PCM allows modelling components of the system, and these models of components are reusable. It consists of different views of the system, the *Repository model, System model, Resource Environment model, Allocation model* and *Usage model*. In our architecture extraction approach, we extract the *Repository model* and the *System model* from the trace information. The *Repository model*, contains data types, components, and interfaces. Each component provides at least one *ProvidedInterface* and an arbitrary number of *RequiredInterfaces*. The *ProvidedInterfaces* define the services provided by the component, the *RequiredInterfaces* define the services required to operate. This happens with *ProvidedRole* and *RequiredRole*.

PMX uses PCM modelling language for generation of architecture model. These PCM model elements do not model asynchronous message-based communication. Therefore, the existing PMX fails to support the architecture extraction of MOM-based microservice systems. We integrate new PCM modelling elements into ARCHI4MOM to enable the extraction for the MOM-based systems.

2.3 Message-Oriented Middleware (MOM)

To understand model extraction, it is required to recognize different possible communication types in MOM-based systems and represent it in the model. We focus the message exchange mechanism via "topics" which facilitates publish-subscribe method. The messages are published to the "topics" and then the subscribers receive all the messages published to the topics they subscribed to. Figure4 shows the example application that shows how the "topics" connect to a MOM middleware. The sender microservice (component A) sends messages to Topic T and the topic forwards the message to the receiver microservice (component B) subscribed to the MOM. The existing architecture extraction methods including PMX do not consider the extraction of sender-receiver communication via the messaging middleware as explained here.

2.4 Flowing Retail Case Study System

We use Flowing-Retail (FL) as our case-study system, which simulates a production process where goods are retrieved, fetched and shipped after being ordered and paid by the customer. In this application, the microservices communicate through an asynchronous messaging method. For our purpose, we use the variant of the system that is based on Kafka messaging middleware with the Spring messaging framework. The system consists of six microservices: *Checkout, Order, Payment, Inventory, Shipping, Monitor* and one "topic" *flowing-retail* to communicate between these microservices. The internal communications between the microservices, take place via message channel. For external communication, with other microservices and third party libraries, FL uses an external Kafka messaging broker to store and forward external messages to all subscribed services. We only focus on the communication between microservices using the Kafka message broker and ignore the internal asynchronous communication at the moment.

3   ARCHI4MOM Structure

ARCHI4MOM is mainly guided by the following research question: How to generate the architecture model for MOM-based microservice systems from traced information, which is collected dynamically by instrumenting the source code of a software system? ARCHI4MOM provides a generic framework for describing asynchronous communication and implementations for specific frameworks. These frameworks are implemented by concrete classes who handle the details of the chosen standard or language. We show the parts we extend in existing

PMX in order to support the architecture extraction in ARCHI4MOM. This overcomes the challenges of existing PMX described earlier. In the following, we describe the different parts of the approach shown in Fig. 2.


```
{
    "data": [
        {
            "traceID": "532de50458050082",
            "spans": [
                ....,
                {
                    "traceID": "532de50458050082",
                    "spanID": "015891c441167ca9",
                    "flags": 1,
                    "operationName": "receive:input",
                    "references": [
                        {
                            "refType": "FOLLOWS_FROM",
                            "traceID": "532de50458050082",
                            "spanID": "c00c953c439352cf"
                        }
```

```
    "data": [
        {
            "traceID": "f34f282ae9b7a6df",
            "spans": [
                ....,
                {
                    "traceID": "f34f282ae9b7a6df",
                    "spanID": "d47b4a01e709635a",
                    "flags": 1,
                    "operationName": "findOwner",
                    "references": [
                        {
                            "refType": "CHILD_OF",
                            "traceID": "f34f282ae9b7a6df",
                            "spanID": "f34f282ae9b7a6df"
                        }
```


Fig. 3. Comparison of Traces Structure between Asynchronous ARCHI4MOM old Synchronous PMX.

3.1 PMXController

PMXController is the first entry point for the extraction process, which enables the extraction process to start independently and allows the easy integration of the process to the continuous development pipeline.

3.2 Data Preparation

Before starting the extraction, a preparation of its input is necessary. In this step, we instrument the source code with the Jaeger[6] tracing tool and collect tracing data. We use the OpenTracing API which supports Kafka-based messaging systems. The use of the OpenTracing standards solve the first limitation of existing PMX and extend the usability to support modern MOM-based systems. This dependency enables the auto-instrumentation of systems with Spring and Kafka. We add the dependency to all microservices to generate the trace in each service. The trace data consists of several spans composed of tags, logs and other information. The asynchronous trace data introduces a set of new information for MOM-based asynchronous microservices from OpenTracing which is not present earlier. We transform the *Trace*, *Span* collected from OpenTracing, to the internal trace structure of ARCHI4MOM, which are called *ExecutionTrace*, *MessagingExecution.* Like wise, other important mappings are represented in Table 1. We map the information to recognizes the messaging spans from normal spans. We later use it in the *traceReconstructionService*. The next step after instrumentation is the collection of tracing data. We collect them in the form of JavaScript Object Notation (JSON) files. This becomes the input to Data Processing phase.

[6] https://www.jaegertracing.io/.

Table 1. Mapping of new OpenTracing data to ARCHI4MOM structure.

OpenTracing	ARCHI4MOM
Span	MessagingExecution
Trace	ExecutionTrace
Operation	MessagingOperation
TraceID+SessionID	TraceInformation
AsynchronousCall	AsynchronousCallMessage
AsynchronousCallReply	AsynchronousReplyMessage

3.3   Data Processing

In the Data Processing phase, we analyse the structure of the traces. In synchronous methods, the sender and receiver are present in one span, which makes it easier to track the behaviour. In asynchronous communication, the information is not present in the same span because they communicate through the middleware. Therefore, the execution of methods in different components needs to match based on the tagged information. We require finding this information from the trace span and collect them for data analysis. This is the novelty in our approach.

With the span reference relationships, we extract the communication pattern. We determine the nature of the current span for synchronous or asynchronous communication. For our work, we focus on the tags and logs since this provides relevant information about the communication. For example, in case of synchronous communication it is CHILD-OF and in case of asynchronous communication it is FOLLOWS-FROM. Figure 3 shows the difference in the communication traces collected from old PMX with synchronous Spring-based application in comparison with the asynchronous MOM-based application in case of FL. We notice that the structure of the trace widely varies in both types of communication. This result is because of changing the communication type from synchronous to asynchronous.

After the trace reconstruction, we find all the spans of send operation do not have information about the *topics*, they send to or receive from. Often, this information is missing in collected spans. From the traces, we manually search for the topic name. Then, we iterate over all the sending spans with a *FOLLOWS-FROM* or *message-bus* relation tag and add the *topic* name to all the receiving spans from a given sending span, that have no topic set in their tags or logs. Thereby, we identify the message type that has been sent to the receiver. For example, the *message-bus* tag is used for identification of topic names in case of Spring-Kafka messaging middleware. Asynchronous MOM-based applications have more operation-related data which we identify in this step and integrate in architecture extraction step, for example identification of the *topic name, components* and corresponding *interfaces*. In ARCHI4MOM, all these new information about asynchronous communication is integrated into PMX, which handles the existing issues. We use this information later to generate *DataInterfaces*.

3.4   Architecture Extraction

In order to extract the complete PCM architecture model that supports the messaging behaviour of MOM-based systems, we require new model elements. For this reason, we combine recent additions to the PCM which support asynchronous communication. It introduces[7] additional model elements for representing asynchronous communication and also provides a simulation for this type of communication. We integrate new model elements to existing PMX and enable the PCM to represent messaging middleware and sender-receiver relation. These new components are:

- *DataChannel* responsible for data transfer providing a *DataSinkRole* and requiring a *DataSourceRole*.
- *DataInterface* determines the type of data transfer and has exactly one signature.
- *DataSinkRole* is a *ProvidedRole* and describes which data is received by the *DataChannel*.
- *DataSourceRole* is a *RequiredRole* and describes which data is send to the *DataChannel*.

3.5   Model Builder

In the Model Builder phase, we use the extracted data to create a model instance. There is no logic available in PMX to construct the model for asynchronous communication. We introduce the logic to generate the new PCM model elements to support model building for messaging communication.

We illustrate the extended implementation logic, we adapt to build the PCM model, with an example. Assuming microservice C communicates with a *DataChannel* D through two different *DataSinkRole*, we require two *DataInterfaces* DI1, DI2 and two *DataSinkRoles* R1 and R2 with the respective *DataInterfaces* D1-R1 and DI2-R2 to architect the communication. With two different roles, C can process the messages received from D differently, depending on *DataInterface*. We transform the knowledge into model generation.

FL case study component *Monitor* microservice always receives messages. So it has several *DataSinkRoles* depending on the *DataInterfaces*. This relation is represented in the architecture construction logic. For a sending operation, the corresponding component has a *DataSourceRole* and for a receiving operation, the component has a *DataSinkRole*. The number of sink roles of *DataChannel* depends on the number of different types of messages it receives, and hence on the number of *DataInterfaces*. Sender microservice components send the messages via *DataSourceRole* to the *DataChannel* and receiver microservice consumes the message via *DataSinkRole* from the *DataChannel*.

---

[7] HTTPs://github.com/PalladioSimulator/Palladio-Addons-Indirections/tree/master/bundles/org.palladiosimulator.indirections/model.

As a result, in the case of the *DataChannel*, we have two possibilities to represent the sending roles. Both are illustrated in Fig. 5. In the first case, we see a single source role for each *DataInterfaces* in the *DataChannel*, where the message is sent several times from the *DataChannel* and received by all the components in the *DataChannel*. In the second, we see several source roles for a single *DataInterface* in a *DataChannel*. In our work we choose the second alternative, because in FL case study every message is sent simultaneously to at least two other microservice components, which is easily captured by the second possibility.

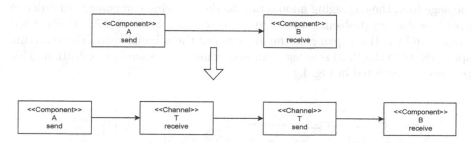

Fig. 4. Message Communication with Topic T.

4   Implementation of ARCHI4MOM

In this section, we discuss the implementation of our approach with reference to the FL case study. Our description is structured according to Sect. 3. We adjust the OpenTracing structure, by adding logic for new tags and logs pairs, discussed in Sect. 3.3. ARCHI4MOM adds new logs which not only supports and recognizes messaging spans but also adjusts them before and after the trace reconstruction.

In the case of FL system, all the microservices are subscribed to the "topic" *flowing-retail*. When a microservice sends a message, all other microservice components except *Checkout* receive it. However, not all microservices process it further. All microservices communicate through Kafka messaging, which makes it difficult to figure out the behaviour of the communication. The communication between the sender and receive is hard to capture since they do not talk directly.

We face the problem in identifying the data type and hence the *DataInterface* to transform it into model elements from the trace information. In order to tackle this, we consider the microservice that processes a given message further is a *DataInterface* and put it in the architecture model. Thereby, we extract 6 *DataInterfaces* in FL case study. Considering the messaging communication from sender to Kafka middleware and Kafka middleware to receiver, we model the Kafka middleware as a*DataChannel*.

When a component sends a message to the other component, the message goes through a messaging middleware. It looks like two sending operations: first, sending from the component to the messaging middleware and then from the message broker to the receiving component. For example, we have an operation O, where a component A sends a message M to a component B through topic T, we will then have two operations O1 and O2. O1 is then a sending operation from A to T and O2 from T to B. But, in our observation, each message sending operation is represented by two spans, a sending span and a receiving span. In each sending span, we extract three spans, the first span is the sending of a message from a component to a message broker, the second is the receiving of that message by the messaging middleware and the third is the sending of the message from the messaging middleware to the receiving component. In order to avoid consistency problems, we assign the new tags *FOLLOW-FROM* discussed earlier, and the third span gets the identifier of the original span. The receiving spans refers to the third sending span and connects the sending operation. This process is illustrated in Fig. 4.

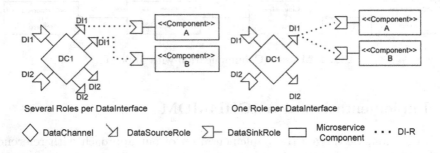

Fig. 5. Roles per DataInterfaces.

We process the spans and transform them in the ARCHI4MOM internal structure. For example, the microservice *Order-Camunda* from the case study FL sends a message to another microservice. The first span is the sending operation from the *Order-Camunda* service followed by the receiving operation from the "topic" *flowing-retail*. We use this analysis to extract the control flow of the architecture model extraction.

The next step is the creation of an architecture model. In our case, *DataChannels* and *DataInterfaces* are created as a part of PCM repository model to represent the MOM-based communication. In PCM, every component obtains a corresponding interface to communicate with each other. As already discussed, we model source and sink roles, which are characterized by a *DataInterface* to represent the data type. We can realize the above implementation in the extracted architecture of FL case study described in evaluation section.

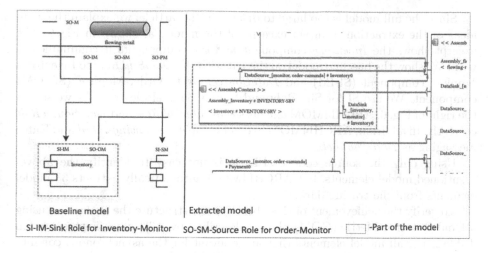

Fig. 6. Excerpts of Extracted and Manual Model.

5 Evaluation

In order to evaluate the extracted model, we compare it to a baseline (manual) model. We use the available reference architecture description of FL[8] and create the PCM baseline model from it. In order to ensure the ground truth, we validated the manual model by 3 developers. The manual PCM model considers new model elements described in Sect. 3.4, in order to support modelling of asynchronous message-based communication. The manual model contains 6 microservice components, 1 topic, 17 *DataSourceRoles*, 17 *DataSinkRoles* model elements [4].

We collect the traces after 20 iterations. We collect the traces for Order creation, Payment and successful Delivery. The longest trace we collect have 116 traces with all the services. We use Jaeger UI in order to view and collect the traces. We ensure to include all 6 services of FL in our evaluation. We search and locate the model elements in the extracted architecture model. The actual extracted model contains 18 *DataSourceRoles*, 14 *DataSinkRoles*, 6 *DataInterfaces* and 1 *DataChannel*. We observe, ARCHI4MOM identifies 1 more *DataSource* which we cannot identify from the architecture description. Also, there are 3 less *DataSinkRoles* compared to manual model. This is because, in the System model, 4 *DataSourceRoles* use only 1 *DataSinkRole*. We can observe the difference between the extracted model elements and manual model elemnts in the last row of the Table 3. The first number 18 represents the extracted model element and second number 17 represents the corresponding manual model elements in 18/17 notation. We share all the relevant diagrams and source code[9].

---

[8] https://github.com/berndruecker/flowing-retail/tree/master/kafka/java.
[9] https://doi.org/10.5281/zenodo.6778977.

Since the full model is too large to discuss in this article, we explain the main ideas of the extraction using an excerpt of the model, as shown in Fig. 6. The excerpt shows the *Inventory* component and the components it communicates with. We show the baseline model on the left with the *DataSinkRole* to Inventory-Monitor component (SI-IM) and *DataSourceRole* to Order-Monitor (SO-OM) component. We use SI for SinkRole and SO for SourceRole here. As we see on the right of Fig. 6, ARCHI4MOM extracts the *DataSinkRole* and *DataSourceRole* correctly. In addition, ARCHI4MOM extracts "topic" as *flowing-retail* and Kafka messaging as *DataChannel*.

Using only the source code of FL, it is not easy to identify the above-mentioned model elements, but ARCHI4MOM automatically extracts 38 model elements from the tracing data.

To verify the achievement of this objective, we structure the evaluation using a Goal Question Metric (GQM) plan as described by [16], which is presented in Table 2. For all model elements that are relevant for the asynchronous communication, we observe the model elements created by the extraction approach and in the baseline by the expert. Both sets are compared using Precision, Recall and F1 score. Overall, the results of the evaluation show that the extraction of MOM-based microservices based on dynamic tracing data is possible for systems communicating asynchronously to achieve $(100\%) Precision$, $(95.65\%) Recall$ and $(97.8\%) F1\text{-}score$ and is shown in Table 3.

5.1   Threats to Validity

In this section, we address threats to validity for case-study-based research in software engineering.

Internal Validity. Addresses whether all implementation possibilities of asynchronous communication have been considered. In our case study, we analysed publish-subscribe based communication with Kafka and extracted the architecture for the same. We evaluated the results with the baseline model. One factor that is hard to eliminate is the expertise of the person modelling the case study architecture. We consider this factor by creating a baseline that is as accurate as possible to avoid unfairness in our evaluation approach.

External Validity. Addresses whether the findings of the case study can be generalized to other cases of interest. We can not say, at this point, if the approach can be successfully applied to the industrial set up with more than 100 microservices. We aim to increase the external validity by focusing on a case description that comes from the research community. Furthermore, we consider the case study system which is used by most researcher and uses popular middleware for MOM like Kafka and RabbitMQ.

Table 2. The GQM-Plan for Evaluation.

Goal	Purpose	Achieve
	Issue	Complete extraction
	Object	Architecture extraction of MOM-based microservices
	Viewpoint	Software architects
Questions	Q	Are all *DataSourceRole*, *DataSinkRole*, *DataInterfaces* are extracted?
Metrics	M1	Precision
	M2	Recall
	M3	F1-score

6   Related Work

In our observation, we categorize the state-of-the-art literature for architecture extraction of MOM-based systems into three main categories. First, based on the type of input used by several approaches. If the input used by the approaches are the artefacts, documents, and source code of the system, we categorize it as static analysis for architecture extraction. Otherwise, if the approach use inputs such as logs, spans, traces collected dynamically from the system for architecture extraction, we categorize it as dynamic analysis. There exists some approaches which combine both the approaches for more accurate architecture extraction, and we categorize it as hybrid approach. Second classification is based on what kind of microservice systems are taken into consideration for the architecture extraction. For example, whether the microservice systems communicating synchronously with each other or they communicate asynchronously via messaging middleware. Third, whether the outcome of the approaches focuses on architecture extraction, behavioural extraction or performance model extraction. Based on the discussed categorization of the state-of-the-art literature, we place our work in the category of dynamic analysis for architecture extraction for the microservice systems which communicate explicitly via messaging middleware. Therefore, we narrow down our discussion focusing to the related work relevant to our work.

Table 3. Extracted model elements for Flowing-retail.

	Microservices	DataSourceRole	DataSinkRole	DataInterface
	Checkout	1	1	1
	Order-Camunda	8	5	1
	Payment	2	1	1
	Inventory	1	1	1
	Shipping	1	1	1
	Monitor	5	5	1
Total	6\6	18\17	14\17	6\6

Granchelli et al. [7] present an approach (MicroART) which takes system's service descriptor as input for static analysis and container communication logs for dynamic analysis to generates the model for messaging systems. The main limitation of MicroART approach is manual refinement of the generated model. It needs a software architect to manually resolve the sender-to-message broker and message broker-to-receiver interactions into sender-receiver interactions before the final architecture is generated, which makes the recovery process slow and prone to error. In our approach, we automatically extract the relation for message-based systems and transform it into an architecture model.

Alshuqayran et al. [1] propose the MiSAR approach for architecture recovery of microservices systems with hybrid approach. This approach provides manual mapping rules to identify the microservices as an infrastructure component and hence not as a component for modelling the basic messaging behaviour. The approach lacks to capture the asynchronous dependencies between sender-receiver communication via messaging middleware, which is the main focus in our approach.

Kleehaus et al. present Microlyze [10], which analyses the system statically and dynamically to extract the architecture semiautomatically. The Microlyze discovers the microservices using the service discovery Eureka, and then it finds the communication between the microservices using distributed tracing technology Zipkin. However, the discovery process ignores the detection of microservices and the communication among each other and with the messaging middleware. Therefore, the architecture is not suitable for MOM-based microservice systems.

Brosig et al. [3] propose a method to automatically extract the architecture and performance models of distributed microservices. Their approach uses runtime monitoring data in order to extract system's architecture and performance model parameters. Their work is based only on Enterprise Java Beans, Servlets, Java Server Pages, therefore fails to support microservice communication via messaging middleware.

Mayer and Weinreich [12] aim to recover the architecture of REST-based microservice systems. The approach combines a hybrid approach to automatically extract relevant information from the system and recover the architecture from the information. The metamodel of this approach only supports REST-based systems, but not asynchronous MOM-based microservice systems.

7   Conclusion and Future Work

In our work, we capture the asynchronous communication related information between MOM components and other components in MOM-based microservice systems and transfer them into an architecture model. We mainly focus on the sender-receiver message exchange via state-of-the art messaging middleware. ARCHI4MOM approach introduces an automated and flexible architecture extraction method to support modern mixed-technology systems. In order to precisely fit the extracted architecture models to MOM-based systems, we build upon the data model of OpenTracing standards and libraries. In addition, our data preparation phase provides an extension point to import data from different tracing standards other than OpenTracing. This adds necessary flexibility for the model preparation and generation phase.

In the future work, we plan to test our approach with other middleware systems communicating with more topics. Currently, we extract the repository and part of system model and hence plan to extract the usage model for complete performance model extraction. We evaluated our approach with an academic-oriented case study, but in reality there could exist systems which use the asynchronous as well as synchronous communication between its components. Considering this, we think that it is important in the future to merge our implementation with the extraction's approach for synchronous communication to be able to model such mixed-technology microservice systems. Although we have successfully applied our approach to MOM-based microservice application and extracted the architecture, we want to further extend our approach with the above-mentioned variations to make it more general and useful for the user.

Acknowledgement. This work was supported by the German Research Foundation (DFG) Research Training Group GRK 2153: Energy Status Data - Informatics Methods for its Collection, Analysis and Exploitation and by KASTEL Security Research Labs. We thank Fatma Chebbi for implementing and evaluating the approach as a part of her Bachelor's thesis [4].

References

1. Alshuqayran, N., Ali, N., Evans, R.: A systematic mapping study in microservice architecture. In: 2016 IEEE 9th International Conference on Service-oriented Computing and Applications (SOCA), pp. 44–51. IEEE (2016)
2. Becker, S., Koziolek, H., Reussner, R.: The palladio component model for model-driven performance prediction. J. Syst. Softw. **82**(1), 3–22 (2009)
3. Brosig, F., Huber, N., Kounev, S.: Automated extraction of architecture-level performance models of distributed component-based systems. In: 2011 26th IEEE/ACM International Conference on Automated Software Engineering (ASE 2011), pp. 183–192. IEEE (2011)
4. Chebbi, F.: Architecture extraction for message-based systems from dynamic analysis. Bachelor's thesis, Department of Informatics, Karlsruhe Institute of Technology (KIT) (2021)
5. Cinque, M., Della Corte, R., Pecchia, A.: Advancing monitoring in microservices systems. In: 2019 IEEE International Symposium on Software Reliability Engineering Workshops (ISSREW), pp. 122–123. IEEE (2019)
6. Di Francesco, P., Malavolta, I., Lago, P.: Research on architecting microservices: trends, focus, and potential for industrial adoption. In: 2017 IEEE International Conference on Software Architecture (ICSA), pp. 21–30. IEEE (2017)
7. Granchelli, G., Cardarelli, M., Di Francesco, P., Malavolta, I., Iovino, L., Di Salle, A.: Microart: a software architecture recovery tool for maintaining microservice-based systems. In: 2017 IEEE International Conference on Software Architecture Workshops (ICSAW), pp. 298–302. IEEE (2017)
8. Heinrich, R.: Architectural runtime models for integrating runtime observations and component-based models. J. Syst. Softw. **169**, 110722 (2020)

9. Hohpe, G., Woolf, B.: Enterprise Integration Patterns: Designing, Building, and Deploying Messaging Solutions. Addison-Wesley Professional, Boston (2004)
10. Kleehaus, M., Uludağ, Ö., Schäfer, P., Matthes, F.: MICROLYZE: a framework for recovering the software architecture in microservice-based environments. In: Mendling, J., Mouratidis, H. (eds.) CAiSE 2018. LNBIP, vol. 317, pp. 148–162. Springer, Cham (2018). https://doi.org/10.1007/978-3-319-92901-9_14
11. Krogmann, K.: Reconstruction of Software Component Architectures and Behaviour Models Using Static and Dynamic Analysis, vol. 4. KIT Scientific Publishing, Amsterdam (2012)
12. Mayer, B., Weinreich, R.: An approach to extract the architecture of microservice-based software systems. In: 2018 IEEE Symposium on Service-oriented System Engineering (SOSE), pp. 21–30. IEEE (2018)
13. Singh, S., Kirschner, Y.R., Koziolek, A.: Towards extraction of message-based communication in mixed-technology architectures for performance model. In: Companion of the ACM/SPEC International Conference on Performance Engineering, pp. 133–138 (2021)
14. Terra, R., Valente, M.T., Czarnecki, K., Bigonha, R.S.: Recommending refactorings to reverse software architecture erosion. In: 2012 16th European Conference on Software Maintenance and Reengineering, pp. 335–340. IEEE (2012)
15. Treyer, P.: Extraction of Performance Models from Microservice Applications based on Tracing Information. Master's thesis, Department of Informatics, Karlsruhe Institute of Technology (KIT) (2020)
16. Van Solingen, R., Basili, V., Caldiera, G., Rombach, H.D.: Goal question metric (GQM) approach. Encyclopedia of software engineering (2002)
17. Walter, J., Stier, C., Koziolek, H., Kounev, S.: An expandable extraction framework for architectural performance models. In: Proceedings of the 8th ACM/SPEC on International Conference on Performance Engineering Companion, pp. 165–170 (2017)

AutoArx: Digital Twins of Living Architectures

Sven Jordan[1]([✉]), Lukas Linsbauer[2], and Ina Schaefer[3]

[1] Volkswagen AG, Wolfsburg, Germany
sven.jordan@volkswagen.de
[2] Technische Universität Braunschweig, Braunschweig, Germany
[3] Karlsruhe Institute of Technology, Karlsruhe, Germany

Abstract. Software systems become increasingly interconnected and complex, leading to a heterogeneous system landscape. This entails that architecture information and architecture documentation become more important. Currently, architecture documentation is a mostly manual task, which is costly, tedious and error prone. Even if initial documentation of a system's architecture is available, it needs to be kept up-to-date as the system evolves, as otherwise its quality will decay to a point where it does not reflect the actual system and is not useful anymore. Therefore, automated support for maintaining and evolving architecture information and documentation of complex systems is highly beneficial to architects and other stakeholders. To achieve this, architecture information must be automatically recovered from heterogeneous data sources at different points in time and consolidated and integrated to provide an up-to-date representation of the system. Subsequently, the recovered architecture information must be automatically updated whenever data sources change over time. In this work, we present an early concept of a co-evolving digital architecture twin to model the system architecture via an architecture information model that combines and relates architecture information recovered from different sources at different points in time. We propose a framework for automated recovery, integration, and co-evolution of architecture information to create and maintain a digital architecture twin that is continuously and automatically updated as the system evolves. We present the general concepts and framework and discuss use cases to motivate benefits.

Keywords: Digital Twin · Software Architecture Recovery · Co-evolution

1 Introduction

Software systems become increasingly interconnected and complex, leading to heterogeneous system landscapes. At the same time, systems evolve frequently to adapt to different environments, advances in technology, or changing customer requirements. During maintenance and evolution of systems, it is important to have high quality and up-to-date documentation (e.g., architecture models)

© The Author(s), under exclusive license to Springer Nature Switzerland AG 2022
I. Gerostathopoulos et al. (Eds.): ECSA 2022, LNCS 13444, pp. 205–212, 2022.
https://doi.org/10.1007/978-3-031-16697-6_15

available [2], as it is a key driver for a software architect to understand a system, comprehend dependencies and decide on future enhancements.

However, as a system evolves, so must its documentation, as otherwise it does not reflect the actual system anymore and its quality and usefulness decrease [1]. The initial creation and continuous maintenance of documentation is linked with high effort, as it is a primarily manual task that is tedious and error prone. Furthermore, different stakeholders require different views on a system at different levels of abstraction or granularity [5]. Explicitly documenting all these different views does not scale, as it adds to the effort of keeping the documentation consistent with the system by also keeping its different views consistent with each other [10,14].

To counter the problem of orphaned or low-quality documentation, software architecture recovery methods [15] are used that recover different kinds of architectural information from various data sources [2]. They can reduce the manual effort for creating and maintaining documentation [12]. While, currently, these approaches operate in isolation, we argue that there is a lot of potential in the combination and integration of architecture recovery approaches. The consolidation of recovered architecture information is not an easy endeavor, as recovery results can complement or contradict each other, they must be related to each other and commonalities and redundancies must be dealt with. Furthermore, architecture recovery methods [5,15] produce a snapshot of the system, leading to the quick decay of the recovered architecture information. This implies that the architecture recovery methods need to be applied continuously.

To address these challenges, we propose a *Digital Architecture Twin (DArT)* based on digital twin concepts [4]. For the creation and maintenance of a DArT, we present the *AutoArx (Automated Architecture) Framework*. It provides the means to populate the underlying architecture information model by automatically recovering and integrating architecture information from diverse data sources by utilizing different recovery approaches. Whenever a data source (e.g., source code or requirements specifications) changes, these changes are recovered and integrated so that the DArT reflects the current state of the system, continuously co-evolving with it. We also aim to provide a query language to dynamically and efficiently retrieve architecture information of the desired type, abstraction, granularity, view and version that is tailored to the specific needs of different stakeholders. This enables numerous use cases such as guided architecture design via architecture recommendation systems or continuous compliance checking to prevent architecture drift.

2   Application Scenarios

In this section, we discuss three selected application scenarios of the DArT.

Tailored, Holistic and Up-to-Date Documentation. Different stakeholders are interested in different aspects of a system. The DArT can be used to create tailored documentation on demand, providing desired views (e.g., static structure or dynamic behavior) of selected parts of a system at desired levels of abstraction.

As the DArT continuously recovers architecture information from various sources (e.g., existing documentation as well as information recovered from source code) it can create up-to-date and holistic documentation.

Automated and Continuous Compliance Checking. The DArT can be used to monitor whether the actual system has diverged from the planned design, referred to as software architecture erosion, decay, or drift [19]. As the DArT contains both, the explicitly documented system architecture as well as the actual system architecture recovered from its most recent implementation artifacts, the two can be compared to perform an as-planned and as-is comparison in order to detect and counteract erosion at an early stage.

Design Recommendation and Guidance. The discovery of architectural styles or patterns in a system is essential for the identification and reuse of beneficial styles and patterns, the identification and exclusion of anti-patterns, or the discovery of design decisions [17] that lead to the current architecture of a system. This enables guided architecture recommendation that can propose architectural designs when planning the evolution of a system. Re-using design and making consistent choices leads to a more homogeneous system and enables better estimation of effort. When extending the concept of a DArT to entire system landscapes, it can also support users by proposing suitable architectural designs that align well with existing patterns and design choices of comparable systems with similar requirements.

3   Background and Related Work

In this section, we distinguish architecture information and documentation and explain architecture recovery methods.

3.1   Architecture Information and Documentation

Architecture information describes various architectural aspects of a system, such as interfaces between components, applied styles and patterns, design decisions, or requirements. It can be recovered from the various artifacts of a system (e.g., source code in a version control system or existing architecture documentation) using *architecture information recovery methods*. Other sources of architecture information could be build, integration or deployment scripts as well as issue tracking systems or project documentation.

Architecture documentation is the representation of architecture information in a human readable form by means of an appropriate notation (e.g., UML diagrams). It allows to share architecture information between stakeholders and also enables the necessary communication and analysis of a system. Architecture information is often documented from different perspectives, categorized into views (e.g., structural, behavioral or deployment), and on different levels of abstraction (e.g., classes, packages or components).

3.2   Architecture Information Recovery Methods

Architecture recovery is the process of extracting architecture information from a system's implementation (e.g., source code or build scripts) or from architectural artifacts (e.g., textual documentation). Current architecture recovery approaches range from manual process guidelines to automatic methods. Methods like ACDC [18], Bunch [16] or RELAX [13] recover structural information about a system.

For illustration we introduce as an example a simple calculator system. It consists of four classes: Main as entry point; UI for the user interface; Calculator for the actual calculations; and BufferedImageCustom for a logo. ACDC [18] is a pattern-driven clustering method, which recovers structural information in the form of comprehensible clusters based on dependencies and global variables. Figure 1a shows the simplified results of ACDC when applied to the calculator example, which is structurally clustered as one subsystem (*SimpleJavaCalculator.ss*). Related to the subsystem are the class dependencies which can be either external classes (e.g., java.lang.Object) or application specific classes (e.g., UI). RELAX [13] uses two main steps for architecture recovery. First, it employs a Naive Bayes classifier, in which every document (i.e., Java source file) is classified into eight pre-defined categories like security or database, categorizing the functionality. Second, it clusters the classified documents based on the classification results and dependencies. Figure 1b shows the simplified results of RELAX when applied to the calculator example. The clustered system (SimpleJavaCalculator) is at the center, connected to it are classified classes. The UI class is classified as gui, the Calculator class as text, the Main class as networking, and the BufferedImageCustom class could not be classified (no_match).

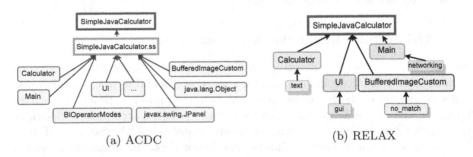

(a) ACDC   (b) RELAX

Fig. 1. ACDC and RELAX results for the calculator example

Other approaches also recover and combine architecture information. The SAVE-Tool [3] evaluates software architecture and source code of a system and shows the convergence, divergence and absence between them focusing on source code. The ARCADE-Workbench [11] is a process-oriented approach that extracts version-based architecture information by employing various appropriate architecture recovery methods, but requires manual work to combine the results.

4 AutoArx Framework

We propose the *AutoArx Framework* to automatically create and co-evolve a *Digital Architecture Twin (DArT)*. We employ proven *architecture information recovery* methods leveraging different data sources and combine their results in an *architecture information model* to obtain an overarching representation of a system's architecture. The framework is shown in Fig. 2. In the following, we describe each component.

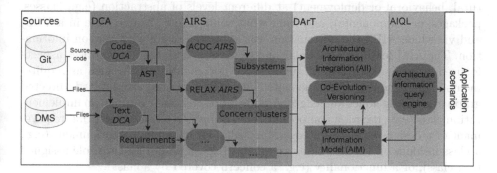

Fig. 2. AutoArx Framework Overview

4.1 Data Collection Agents (DCAs)

Architecture is reflected in many different artifacts (e.g., source code in version control systems or textual documentation in document management systems) that can be leveraged by architecture recovery methods [6]. *Data Collection Agents (DCAs)* are responsible for observing and collecting structured data (e.g., an abstract syntax tree or a list of requirements) from identified sources. DCAs become active whenever a respective data source changes in any way (e.g., a new version is added in a version control system). For example, the Code DCA parses source code in a Git repository and produces an abstract syntax tree (AST).

4.2 Architecture Information Recovery Services (AIRS)

Architecture Information Recovery Services (AIRSs) use the collected data and apply architecture recovery methods. For example, the ACDC AIRS expects as input an AST, applying a pattern-driven clustering approach resulting in subsystems representing structural information of the system (see Fig. 1a). An AIRS becomes active whenever any DCA offers new data of a type that can be processed by the AIRS. For example, the ACDC AIRS is triggered whenever the Code DCA provides a new AST. As the DArT shall be continuously updated, AIRS must be automated and provide results with reasonable latency.

4.3   Digital Architecture Twin (DArT)

The *Digital Architecture Twin (DArT)* is at the core of *AutoArx*. It comprises a component for the consolidation and integration of architecture information recovered by different AIRSs at the same point in time as well as from the same AIRS at different points in time into the *Architecture Information Model (AIM)*.

Architecture Information Model (AIM). The *Architecture Information Model (AIM)* combines different kinds of architectural information (e.g., structural, behavioral or deployment) at different levels of abstraction (e.g., classes, packages, or components), and from what sources (e.g., source code in a VCS) and via which AIRS the information was extracted along with version information. The AIM features a modular and extensible design and comprises aspects focused on primary drivers of architecture documentation [9], such as requirements, design choices, or components. The AIM is treated as a labeled, directed graph comprising nodes and edges. A node represents, for example, an implementation class (e.g., `Main`), a component (e.g., *SimpleJavaCalculator.ss*), a requirement or a design pattern. An edge represents, for example, a containment (e.g., a class inside a package), a role assignment (e.g., a design pattern role assigned to a class), or a functionality (e.g., a concern covered by a class).

Architecture Information Integration (AII). The *Architecture Information Integration (AII)* integrates information recovered by different AIRS into the AIM. It uses newly recovered architecture information and compares it with architecture information already present in the AIM. It can be considered as a function $AII(m_1, m_2) = m_3$ that receives as input the current AIM of the DArT m_1 and an AIM produced by any of the AIRS m_2 and computes the integrated AIM m_3. The AII is performed based on rules and similarity values (structure and name similarity). If the same architecture information (e.g., components) is integrated multiple times, it increases the confidence in the recovered architecture information. If conflicting architecture information is integrated, it is added as additional information, avoiding to lose the architecture information from the AIRS. Supplementary information is added to the AIM and increases the confidence of the existing results. Based on rules, we take different integration actions (e.g., merging clusters or adding new structural layers). Interpretation of the AIM and its contents is a human task at present. For example, if two architecture recovery methods have a different focus but operate on the same input, we argue that the approaches might recover information at different levels of granularity or accompanying information. For our calculator example, this would mean that ACDC recovers subsystems based on classes, whereas RELAX recovers the concern of the compilation units of the system. As classes are assigned to compilation units, we integrate ACDC and RELAX by identifying compilation units, their classes and linking the recovered concerns to parts of the recovered subsystems.

Co-evolution and Versioning. An important aspect of the DArT is its co-evolution with the actual system. For this, a continuous exchange between the DArT and the actual system is necessary. The proposed AutoArx framework is able to keep the information in the DArT up-to-date by reacting to changes in the system artifacts. Whenever the software system changes and adapts to new requirements (e.g., by adding or removing components), so does the DArT. To maintain a version history of the information in the DArT we employ an internal version number, which is increased every time information is integrated into the AIM. Information recovered by different AIRS based on the same changed data source are processed together and yield the same version.

4.4   Architecture Information Query Language (AIQL)

The information in the DArT is made accessible via a *query engine* and corresponding *Architecture Information Query Language*. It allows to query architecture information stored in the AIM. For example, a query could retrieve technical components and the respective requirements for the software system, structural information about interactions of two components, or changes in used architectural styles and patterns between two versions of the system.

5   Evaluation Plan

For evaluating the integration of architecture information into the AIM we adapt metrics for evaluating certain aspects of modeling languages [7]. These metrics have proven to be adaptable and applicable in a wider area and allow us to assess aspects such as coverage or granularity of integrated information. We plan to evaluate the usability and functionality of our AIQL based on a framework for query language evaluation [8]. To evaluate the DArT and the AutoArx framework as a whole, we are applying it to various publicly available open source systems. Finally, we are planning to conduct a user study together with our industry partner to assess applicability and usefulness in practice.

6   Conclusion

In this paper, we introduce the idea of co-evolving digital architecture twins that consolidate heterogeneous architecture information sources into a unified architecture information model that is a holistic and up-to-date representation of a system's architecture. In addition to the most recent information, every element in the architecture information model is versioned so that past states can be retrieved and compared. We propose a framework and its components for automatically creating and co-evolving the architecture twin with the actual system. To make the information in the architecture twin accessible, we envision an architecture information query language to query for specific information, granularity, and point in time. Based on the query language the architecture twin can be leveraged in many different application scenarios.

References

1. Behnamghader, P., Le, D.M., Garcia, J., Link, D., Shahbazian, A., Medvidovic, N.: A large-scale study of architectural evolution in open-source software systems. Empir. Softw. Eng. **22**(3), 1146–1193 (2016). https://doi.org/10.1007/s10664-016-9466-0
2. van Deursen, A., Hofmeister, C., Koschke, R., Moonen, L., Riva, C.: Symphony: view-driven software architecture reconstruction. In: WICSA, pp. 122–134. IEEE Computer Society (2004)
3. Duszynski, S., Knodel, J., Lindvall, M.: SAVE: software architecture visualization and evaluation. In: CSMR, pp. 323–324. IEEE Computer Society (2009)
4. Eramo, R., Bordeleau, F., Combemale, B., van den Brand, M., Wimmer, M., Wortmann, A.: Conceptualizing digital twins. IEEE Softw. **39**(2), 39–46 (2022)
5. Falessi, D., Babar, M.A., Cantone, G., Kruchten, P.: Applying empirical software engineering to software architecture: challenges and lessons learned. Empir. Softw. Eng. **15**(3), 250–276 (2010)
6. Garcia, J., Popescu, D., Mattmann, C., Medvidovic, N., Cai, Y.: Enhancing architectural recovery using concerns. In: ASE. IEEE Computer Society (2011)
7. Guizzardi, G., Ferreira Pires, L., van Sinderen, M.: An ontology-based approach for evaluating the *domain appropriateness* and *comprehensibility appropriateness* of modeling languages. In: Briand, L., Williams, C. (eds.) MODELS 2005. LNCS, vol. 3713, pp. 691–705. Springer, Heidelberg (2005). https://doi.org/10.1007/11557432_51
8. Jarke, M., Vassiliou, Y.: A framework for choosing a database query language. ACM Comput. Surv. **17**(3), 313–340 (1985)
9. Knoll, M.: Handbuch der software-architektur. Wirtschaftsinformatik **48**(6), 454 (2006)
10. Kruchten, P.: The 4+1 view model of architecture. IEEE Softw. **12**(6), 42–50 (1995)
11. Laser, M.S., Medvidovic, N., Le, D.M., Garcia, J.: ARCADE: an extensible workbench for architecture recovery, change, and decay evaluation. In: ESEC/SIGSOFT FSE, pp. 1546–1550. ACM (2020)
12. Le, D.M., Behnamghader, P., Garcia, J., Link, D., Shahbazian, A., Medvidovic, N.: An empirical study of architectural change in open-source software systems. In: MSR, pp. 235–245. IEEE Computer Society (2015)
13. Link, D., Behnamghader, P., Moazeni, R., Boehm, B.W.: Recover and RELAX: concern-oriented software architecture recovery for systems development and maintenance. In: ICSSP, pp. 64–73. IEEE/ACM (2019)
14. Link, D., Behnamghader, P., Moazeni, R., Boehm, B.W.: The value of software architecture recovery for maintenance. In: ISEC, pp. 17:1–17:10. ACM (2019)
15. Lutellier, T., et al.: Comparing software architecture recovery techniques using accurate dependencies. In: ICSE (2), pp. 69–78. IEEE Computer Society (2015)
16. Mancoridis, S., Mitchell, B.S., Chen, Y., Gansner, E.R.: Bunch: a clustering tool for the recovery and maintenance of software system structures. In: ICSM, p. 50. IEEE Computer Society (1999)
17. Shahbazian, A., Lee, Y.K., Le, D.M., Brun, Y., Medvidovic, N.: Recovering architectural design decisions. In: ICSA, pp. 95–104. IEEE Computer Society (2018)
18. Tzerpos, V., Holt, R.C.: ACDC: an algorithm for comprehension-driven clustering. In: WCRE, pp. 258–267. IEEE Computer Society (2000)
19. Whiting, E., Andrews, S.: Drift and erosion in software architecture: summary and prevention strategies. In: ICISDM, pp. 132–138. ACM (2020)

Author Index

Printed in the United States
by Baker & Taylor Publisher Services

Printed in the United States
by Baker & Taylor Publisher Services